Sexual Chemistry

Dr Ellen Grant graduated MB ChB with
commendation at St Andrews University and
gained a DObstRCOG. She worked at
University College Hospital and the
headquarters of the Family Planning Association
in London in the 1960s studying the effects of
a wide range of oral contraceptive pills. The
results of these studies and later research into
migraine carried out at the Princess Margaret
Migraine Clinic at Charing Cross Hospital in the
1970s were published in the *British Medical
Journal* and the *Lancet*. Dr Grant is a medical
adviser to Foresight and has served on the
Council of the Dyslexia Institute. She is
married to neurosurgeon Norman Grant and
they have a son and two daughters.

Also by Ellen Grant

The Bitter Pill

Dr ELLEN GRANT

Sexual Chemistry

Understanding Your Hormones,
The Pill and HRT

CEDAR

A Mandarin Paperback
SEXUAL CHEMISTRY

First published in Great Britain 1994
as a Cedar Original
by Mandarin Paperbacks
an imprint of Reed Consumer Books Ltd
Michelin House, 81 Fulham Road, London SW3 6RB
and Auckland, Melbourne, Singapore and Toronto

Reprinted 1994 (twice)

Copyright © Ellen Grant 1994
The author has asserted her moral rights

A CIP catalogue record for this title
is available from the British Library
ISBN 0 7493 1363 3

Printed and bound in Great Britain
by Cox & Wyman Ltd, Reading, Berks

Contents

Acknowledgements

I should like to thank my husband Norman, Stewart, Rhona and Katharine, and my mother Margaret Tarvit for their unfailing help and support and my late father Stewart Tarvit for inspiration. Ken Pugh of Reed Consumer Books organised this publication and my editor, Sarah Hannigan, provided fresh insights and lots of patience.

My friends and colleagues include Nim Barnes of Foresight; Dr Elisabeth Lodge-Rees; Dr Gina Schoental; Dr Kitty Little; Mr Ian Burn, Medical Director of King Edward VII Hospital, Midhurst, and Chairman of the World Federation of Surgical Oncology Societies; Dr Frank Clifford Rose, ex-President of the World Federation of Neurologists; Dr John MacLaren Howard; Dr Stephen Davies; Adrian Hunisett; Melita Dean and the staff of Biolab Medical Unit; Dr Neil Ward of Surrey University; Professor Derek Bryce Smith of Reading University; Dr John Pryse-Davies and Dr Isobel Gal who worked at Queen Charlotte's Hospital; Dr John Mansfield, President of the Society for Environmental Medicine; Dr Harry Chasty of the Dyslexia Institute; Dr Bevé Hornsby of the Hornsby Centre; Professor Ifor Capel of North East London University; Dr David Horrobin; Professor Victor Wynn and Dr Ian Godsland of the Wynn Institute; Dr Graham Shepherd; statistician Jane Galbraith and Professor Klim MacPherson. Many thanks to them all for their help.

Foreword

by Dr John McLaren Howard DSc.FACN

The many people who really enjoy medical science presented in a readable format will just love this book. Readers will find it easy to move from one major point to another without losing interest. That is because of the use of real patient examples and statements of the major findings of many research workers.

In my opinion, this book will light a flame that no pill, potion or medical dogma will be able to put out.

More and more people are saying that they do not want to take drugs or hormones. Many have more than enough intelligence to understand the implications of this book. *Sexual Chemistry* gives the general public the opportunity it wants to read the truth.

Hormones Through the Ages

More and more people are being given hormones. Over the past fifty years exposure to sex hormones has increased dramatically. Besides being used to change the course of natural reproductive cycles as contraceptive pills, hormones are also prescribed to women as treatment for an ever enlarging range of medical and gynaecological conditions.

More surprisingly, female hormones are also being given to men when their mothers take fertility treatments, drugs to prevent miscarriage or to dry up lactation, or as contraceptives during breast feeding. They are prescribed to the more feminine homosexual partner and to older men to treat prostatic cancer.

Among the apparently large number of different hormones which are safe? There are only three basic sex hormones and any effective dose has wide-spread actions.[1] The three sex hormones have separate functions:

- oestrogen develops females;
- testosterone develops males;
- progesterone maintains pregnancy.

These three hormones are crucial for sexual relationships and reproduction. All three are steroids closely related to the notorious anabolic steroids which tempt athletes and their coaches. In fact the male hormone, testosterone, is used as a body building steroid and the female hormones, especially progesterone, also act in this way.

Both our own and prescribed hormones are extremely powerful and even at low concentrations can interfere with our genes. Both the hereditary-carrying double-strand DNA in the nucleus of our cells and the single-strand messenger RNA, which instructs our cell's metabolic factories, are easily damaged. There is a question that needs to be asked. Is the human race capable of surviving the onslaught of these very powerful prescribed hormones on its genetic inheritance?

A distinguished scientist, Dr Gina Schoental, has predicted that men will only start to worry about the damage caused by the contraceptive pill and prescribed hormones when they find out how they are being affected. In 1992, men were given the clearest of warnings.[2,3] Danish reproduction researchers checked back to 1938. Since then the quality of semen has declined so rapidly in pill-taking countries that the average man's sperm count has fallen by 50 per cent. The volume of the ejaculate has decreased. Testicular cancer has increased two to four times, while the number of baby boys born with undescended testes and external genital abnormalities have been increasing each year to affect one in fifty. In Finland, which has only recently started to give the pill to teenagers, the men still have excellent sperm production.[4]

What happened in 1938? Elizabeth Carlsen and her colleagues suggest that the changes may have come about by increased exposure to oestrogens as some doctors, including Schoental, have been proposing for several decades. Is it a coincidence that 1938 was the year when the first synthetic oestrogen was made in Britain? *Diethylstilboestrol (or DES) was soon being given to every other new mother who wanted to cut down her milk supply or stop breast feeding. It was even given, in huge doses, to bring on labour. More dangerously, as it has turned out, oestrogen was given to women in early pregnancy in an attempt to prevent recurrent miscarriages* but the usefulness of DES was being questioned as early as 1953 because the abortion rate actually increased.[5,6] Among the children surviving this hormone overdose, girl babies exposed during the early weeks of their development are more likely to have genital abnormalities and later develop genital and breast cancers. Boys born with undescended testes or with penile anomalies are more likely at a later date to have low sperm counts and to develop testicular cancer. Hypospadias is the commonest penile abnormality. In this condition the urinary tube, the urethra, fails to reach the end of the penis and instead opens out on its under surface. Hormone exposure increases the chances of mental illness in both sexes in later life.[7] Progesterones are still being prescribed in early pregnancy as part of test-tube baby programmes in spite of their effect on developing children. Even Dr John Rock, co-developer of the contraceptive pill along with Gregory Pincus, has published that both natural and synthetic progesterone can cause multiple abnormalities and, like oestrogen, if taken during pregnancy can increase the number of miscarriages.[8]

While the contraceptive pill was first used in Mexico, Puerto Rico and the USA in the 1950s, doctors in Britain have taken the lead in prescribing these hormones (oestrogens and progestogens) for contraception to very young women years before doctors in any other country. In 1971 less than one in ten single women in the UK had taken oral contraceptives. By 1981 most women under the age of twenty-five had been prescribed hormones for contraception before conceiving their first baby.

British and American doctors led the world in prescribing oestrogens in pregnancy and as hormone replacement therapy (HRT) to prolong women's active sex lives after the menopause. Oestrogens are given to make up the deficiencies caused by early removal of womb and ovaries, in an attempt to prevent depression, flushing and thinning of bones. The sharp increase in breast cancer has lead to the anti-oestrogen tamoxifen being given to healthy women even though it is a close relative of DES.

What has happened to these American and British women and their children? What has been learned? The facts are alarming. Breast and cervical screening programmes struggle to keep pace with the increases in cancer which were accurately predicted from animal studies. Breast cancer has doubled in the UK and nearly trebled in the USA. Early cervical cancer was almost unheard of in young women, but now, one in six women in their thirties asking me for preconception care, has already had a positive smear. So many women developed endometrial cancer due to taking HRT that progestogens are now added to the oestrogens, turning HRT into the pill. One in three women in HRT surveys has already had her womb removed, often years before the normal age for the menopause, and many have also had their ovaries removed. One in five children now have special needs.

Barbara Seaman in her book *Women and the Crisis in Sex Hormones* and Germaine Greer in *The Change* have both said that most women know nothing about the hormones they have been taking.[9,10] They don't know the names or doses or exact dates and times when they took them, and they certainly don't know how the hormones act. I find this to be very true of my patients. Women frequently say that they have had no side effects and yet when questioned, it becomes clear that their headaches, breast lumps, cystitis, positive cervical smears, mental upsets or whatever, often started or were diagnosed during the time they were taking these steroids.

Doctors, confused by their own lack of basic understanding and even more by the puzzling data from large-scale studies, tell their patients that their complaints are not due to their pills or hormones. Perhaps the doctors are unaware of the connections. Many patients are worried by the lack of clear guidance from their professional medical advisers. Women who know that hormones don't suit them often turn instead to alternative medicine. The increase in complementary medicine, with its range of qualified and unqualified practitioners using acupuncture, homeopathy, aromatherapy, herbalism and so on, has barely kept pace with the numbers of patients, predominantly women, who are looking for better health.

The cost of health care in the UK has risen year by year and governments seem to be pouring money into a bottomless pit. Has the basic thinking gone wrong? I think it has, and that is why I want to put the record straight – find the truth behind the myths – and explore the consequences for the 'sex hormone generations'.

The mysteries of why hormones can be used for such various and conflicting reasons are intriguing. How can the same hormones be given to:

12–15-year-olds

As the morning after pill	For painful periods or acne

16–50-year-olds

To prevent contraception as the pill	For period problems
To start bleeding	To stop bleeding
To stop ovulation	To treat infertility (IVF or GIFT)
To prevent miscarriages	To induce labour
For premenstrual symptoms (PMS and PMT)	To stop lactation
	To suppress allergies and symptoms from hidden infections and candida

40–80-year-olds

As hormone replacement therapy (HRT)	In deficiency diseases
Atrophic vaginitis	Osteoporosis
Painful intercourse	Arthritis
Stress incontinence	Thin wrinkled skin
	Allergic reactions like flushing

7

And to suppress hormone-dependent cancers, although surgical or medical castration is their main treatment?

What is the effect of age? Why is the response to hormones of a baby in the womb, at birth or as a growing child different from that of a sexually mature adult? Why are the effects on old women different from those in young women?

Luckily, in recent years, highly accurate biochemical analysis, such as is available at Biolab in London, has greatly helped our understanding of what is going on in this area. The most basic essentials for healthy cells can be measured to one part per billion, using space age technological methods. Essential minerals, vitamins, amino acids and fatty acids can be measured and deficiencies shown on a computer print-out. Reasons for deficiencies can also be diagnosed and treated. A new era is dawning.

HOW DO SEX HORMONES WORK?

Hormones are chemical messengers, made in the brain and special glands: they are carried in the blood stream to activate distant cells. The human body has ten thousand billion cells, but the main targets for sex hormones are the reproductive tissues – the womb, breasts, ovaries and testes – and also the brain and pituitary gland. These are the tissues most likely to develop cysts or tumours when hormones causing unnatural stimulation or suppression are prescribed.

At the target cells, receptors are waiting for each individual type of hormone. The sex steroids attach to these special receptors and together they activate the cell and its nucleus. Sex hormone receptors are most plentiful during the reproductive years and scarce in children and older people.

Hormone means 'urging on' in Greek. Hormones incite cells to act out the instructions in our genes, carried by DNA in the nucleus of our cells, so that the cells start to grow, divide into two and make secretions. Oestrogen stimulates cells lining the womb to grow rapidly and divide, becoming a higgledy-piggledy, untidy pile of large dividing cells. Progesterone, which simply means a steroid that prepares for pregnancy, halts this frantic activity and instead urges the cells to make more and more starch and protein until they reach bursting point. The secretion in the womb is then ready to feed an embryo and then a baby. The secretion in the mother's breasts, with the help of a brain hormone called prolactin, becomes milk for the baby when he or she is born. Together, the hormones stimulate a rapid overgrowth and dilation of blood vessels.

All our cells divide and renew themselves throughout our lives. Before a cell divides, the DNA strands thicken and double in size. In between cell divisions the nucleus accumulates nutrients, especially amino acids and zinc. The nucleus enlarges and divides with each half receiving a replica of the cell's inherited DNA. In an adult, cells divide after they have doubled their nuclear material which happens after *weeks or even months but, in an embryo, the cells divide every ten to fifteen minutes*. An embryo must have an abundant supply of blood – bringing nutrients. A developing baby is very vulnerable to lack of nutrients or interference with its system of blood vessels. Oestrogen stimulates the rapid growth and division of cells both in the baby and in the womb. Progesterone makes the womb lining secrete food for the developing egg and suppresses any immunological rejection of the baby which contains its father's foreign proteins. Both hormones combine to induce the maximum enlargement of the placenta – a system of blood vessels on which the baby's growth and development depends. Taking extra hormones increases the need for essential nutrients in both men and women.

Communicating Hormones

Adjoining cells communicate by flows of electricity or diffusion of gaseous nitric oxide (NO). For more distant messages, hormones are released into the surrounding fluid or blood and carried to receptors on the cells of target organs. These communicators are either made up of chains of amino acids, small proteins or, in the case of the sex hormones, four-ring steroids.

Besides controlling sexual development and function, hormones also help to control growth and muscle building, and they regulate the digestive system, blood sugar levels, blood pressure and fluid balance. Hormones hold the key to subjective feelings and changes in blood chemistry associated with stress.

A close interlinking of these different functions has been seen by studying animals. For example, when some animals become frightened, a long chain of amino acids in their brain divides into three separate hormones. One hormone changes the colour of the animal's skin so that it can try to hide, another is the stress hormone preparing it for fight or flight, while a third part becomes an endorphin or morphia-like painkiller. This close connection between skin pigment and stress is important for us too. Black skin cancers (melanomas) are caused, not only by sunbathing, but also by the increased use of oral contraceptive hormones and HRT and the changes in a woman's stress chemistry which these prescribed hormones automatically induce.

Brain Hormones

Special brain hormones, neurotransmitters, made from amino acids in the hypothalamus at the base of our brain, help to regulate our biological clock. In tune with our other senses, such as sight, smell and intellect, they either encourage or block the release of pituitary hormones. The pea-like pituitary gland is closely attached to the hypothalamus by a stalk of nerves and blood vessels and hangs beneath the brain inside its own small bony cavity. The pituitary hormones directly stimulate the production of sex hormones: oestrogens and progesterone in women's ovaries or testosterone in men's testicles, the basis of sexual chemistry.

The production and actions of these brain, pituitary and sex hormones can be blocked if we are short of essential trace elements. One of these, zinc, is especially important. Our bodies are not able to store zinc and we need to take in and absorb enough each day. Recently the exact chemical structure of an oestrogen receptor has been worked out.[11] Hormone receptors are proteins which are made from long chains of amino acids folded round zinc atoms to acquire three-dimensional stability. Fingers of amino acids which protrude from the protein hormone receptors curl round and activate our DNA. They are known as 'zinc fingers' because the zinc atoms form a rigid knuckle at the base of the finger. Amino acids are unable to fold properly to make hormone-receptor proteins in the absence of zinc.

The discovery that adequate zinc status is fundamental to good health is very important. Many women, and nowadays even some men, are being prescribed hormones as replacement therapy when they are really short of zinc. It is not without good reason that fresh oysters have long been prized. Oysters are nature's aphrodisiac because they are exceptionally high in zinc which, unlike testosterone prescriptions, can increase both sperm quality and personal testosterone levels. In zinc-deficient states, sperm manufacture, ovulation and sex hormone production can be impaired, affecting sexual desire and fertility. Taking extra hormones can increase these faults. The many effects of zinc deficiency on health have been extensively researched.

Enzymes and Co-Enzymes

The speed and control of the body's chemical reactions are greatly aided by special protein molecules called enzymes. A growing baby, in particular, needs well functioning enzyme systems.

Enzymes have co-enzymes, minerals and vitamins, which become used up during reactions. Zinc is also a co-enzyme along with other minerals such as chromium, manganese, selenium, iron, cobalt and copper which are present in our body in very small amounts and are known as trace minerals, or trace elements. Shortages of these essential minerals and vitamins are very common and cause many illnesses and degenerative diseases by blocking important enzymes.[12]

Zinc Deficiency

Shortage of zinc is the commonest of all the essential nutrient deficiencies. Zinc deficiency affects nearly all my patients who have taken hormones, sometimes even including those who are already taking supplements if their absorption is also impaired.

Cell zinc deficiency is best diagnosed from samples of sweat and white blood cells.[13] Zinc is the most important of the essential nutrients with very severe deficiency being fatal. *Zinc is crucial for the growth and division of cells, for brain development and function and indeed for the normal functioning of every single cell.*

Zinc deficiency was discovered to be the cause of the delayed growth and poorly developed sex organs of a group of Iranian dwarfs in the 1950s. Children with poor growth are often severely zinc deficient. In other children, zinc deficiency contributes to dyslexia, learning problems, upper respiratory infections, hyperactivity and food allergies. We have some evidence that there has been a fall in children's sweat zinc levels in the last decade. The fathers and mothers of the dyslexic children we tested also had low zinc levels. Falling zinc concentrations, plus an increase in often symptomless genital infections, along with early hormone exposure are the main reasons for the decline in sperm counts.

Why is zinc so important? There are many zinc-dependent enzymes, critically involved in the transfer of evolution's messages and instructions from our genes. Both cell and blood zinc levels are lowered by oestrogen, progestogens and testosterone. Men tend to have lower sweat zinc levels than boys and need extra zinc to make millions of sperm each day. Zinc is depleted by a regular intake of alcohol and tobacco.

Magnesium Deficiency

Although magnesium is present in our cells in fairly large amounts, most patients have lowish concentrations of magnesium in their sweat and red cells. Adequate concentrations of magnesium are needed for hundreds of enzyme systems including energy transfer.

Lack of magnesium causes interference with cell membrane transport leading to accumulation of sodium and therefore swelling of the cells and loss of calcium. This causes thinning of the bones or osteoporosis, while lack of potassium inside the cells causes weakness and tiredness. Nerves, blood vessels and muscle cell function soon become impaired when there is a shortage of magnesium.

A simple arm muscle contraction test shows the changes. Two small metal heat sensors are taped onto an arm. They detect minute changes in temperature as the arm muscles contract. When magnesium is deficient, the print-out shows a delayed irregular jerky response rather than a crisp, smooth, quick reaction.[14] The muscles readily become painful, cramped and are damaged by exercise. *Magnesium deficiency is a main cause of backache, neckache and joint problems, which afflict both the athletic and the sedentary. Along with zinc deficiency, it is a major cause of osteoporosis.*

Magnesium is known as nature's calmer. Lack of it causes anxiety, insomnia and heart irregularities such as palpitations. Only very slowly is the medical profession coming to realise the importance of magnesium in preventing vascular disease.[15] Recently there was great media interest in publications showing that intravenous magnesium significantly reduced the number of deaths from acute heart attacks although this was originally described in the 1950s.[16]

Magnesium levels inside our cells are lowered by the sex hormones, especially by progesterone, which contributes to premenstrual symptoms and the side effects of the mostly progesterone-like oral contraceptives. Oddly enough, in spite of the evidence that prescribed oestrogens and HRT temporarily delay the onset of osteoporosis, they also deplete cells of magnesium.

Messages in the Genes

Inside the cell nucleus there are extremely long and very thin threads made of the nucleic acid DNA (Deoxyribonucleic acid) arranged like spiralling ladders, the famous double helix. While sugars and starches, fats and proteins are mostly used by the cell for energy and structure, nucleic acids (DNA and RNA) are used for storing and expressing genetic information. The development of the billions of human cells comes from the DNA in a single fertilised egg. The DNA is able to reproduce itself precisely by pulling the rungs of the ladders apart each time a cell divides. The information stored in the DNA about how to make brain, muscle, bone and all the other specialised tissues is passed on to the newly formed cells.

The ladder threads of DNA are called chromosomes and were first discovered in the cells of fruit flies. Humans have 46 chromosomes having inherited 23 chromosomes from each parent. Females have two X chromosomes and males have one X chromosome and one Y chromosome.

Genes, located on precise places on the chromosomes, are the active parts of the gigantic DNA molecule and by dividing and instructing the cell's activities, they determine, for example, our hair and eye colour and all the many characteristics we inherit from our ancestors.

Limiting the Damage
Although our DNA is incredibly long, four simple groups of chemicals known as bases are repeated throughout in a variety of sequences. The arrangement of these four bases carries all we have inherited since life began but we only use a minute part of this vast store of information. DNA can remain unchanged for generation after generation because the bases are not easily altered by chemicals, enzymes or radiation. The bases are protected by an outside layer of phosphate groups and sugars. Although it is difficult to change the exact chemical composition of each DNA base, it can happen, for example, by excessive hormone stimulation. Provided plenty of zinc is available the damage can be repaired. Zinc sufficiency is especially important in early pregnancy otherwise the baby may have congenital abnormalities.

If any damage to DNA is not repaired, a permanent mutation is introduced. This can result in any number of deleterious effects, including loss of control over the growth and proliferation of the mutated cell, which may lead to cancer, as well as congenital disease. Radiation exposure in fathers has been linked with leukaemia in their future children, and oestrogens given to pregnant women can cause vaginal cancer in their daughters and testicular cancer in their sons.

Critical Times for Both Parents

Evidence from studying children born to Dutch women during a famine in the Second World War shows that a developing egg is most vulnerable if the mother is starving during the two weeks immediately before conception. This is when the egg is leaving its protective cyst in the ovary and travelling to meet the incoming sperm in the Fallopian tube before embedding in the lining of the womb. *Children conceived when the mother was starving were one hundred times more likely to have congenital abnormalities.* When the height of the famine was during pregnancy the children were less likely to be born abnormal, although we know severe zinc deficiency in early pregnancy increases the chance of early miscarriages. Men make sperm continuously and each sperm takes three to four months to develop in the testes from a resting cell to a fully active motile sperm. Men have a longer critical time than women for avoiding genetic damage to their children.

Men should be able to produce large numbers of sperm which swim in a highly nutritious fluid secreted by the testes and the prostate gland. A surprisingly high percentage of sperm in any ejaculate is immature or abnormal or unable to swim – not motile. The numbers of active, mobile, healthy sperm depend on the man having a good intake of zinc, magnesium and essential fatty acids. The sperm counts can match zinc levels with a low sperm count improving when zinc levels rise.

DNA in both the developing sperm and egg is also very susceptible to damage from some chemicals. For example, nitrous acid, formed in the cell from nitrosamines, nitrites and nitrates, can change bases in the DNA. Nitrosamines are formed when semen is mixed with bacteria, as in genital infection or anal intercourse (which has helped spread HIV). Nitrites are used as food preservatives and nitrates as soil fertilisers. Nitric oxide stimulates nerves, dilates blood vessels and creates a penile erection. The simple gas is also used by large white blood cells to kill invading bacteria. Nitroso compounds powerfully suppress immunity, as do progesterone and testosterone.

Progesterone maintains pregnancy by suppressing antibody and immune system cell production even in the small amounts present at the end of a menstrual cycle. This means that a woman with an infected cervix (neck of the womb) is especially susceptible to HIV infection and even more so if she is pregnant. Some antibiotics, especially the tetracyclines, are particularly likely to affect DNA and cause congenital abnormalities.

Ovulation

If zinc levels are adequate, the brain hormones tell the front part of the pituitary gland to make two hormones. A man makes both hormones continuously. In a woman the hormones are released in two separate surges. In the first half of her cycle the first hormone stimulates an egg to develop, and then, at mid-cycle, the second hormone stimulates the egg's release from the ovary.

A woman is born with a lifetime's supply of eggs in her two ovaries enclosed in protective cysts. When the first pituitary hormone is released by brain hormone stimulation at puberty the reproductive clock starts and ticks away for as long as forty years if it is left unmolested and fully nurtured. Each month a follicle starts to develop and make oestrogens. The first pituitary hormone is simply named follicle stimulating hormone (FSH). Infertile women may be given very large amounts of FSH and the result is often twins, triplets or quads because several cysts have developed at once. At ovulation, when the egg bursts out of the cyst, the follicle turns yellow as it secretes progesterone and is called the 'corpus luteum'. The second pituitary hormone is therefore named the yellowing hormone or luteinising hormone (LH).

In men, FSH encourages the testes to develop and it supervises a continuous production line of sperm. LH promotes a steadily ongoing secretion of the male hormone testosterone which causes sexual desire and stimulates a man to have sexual relationships and sexual intercourse with a woman.

Implantation

When a woman ovulates each month, the egg is flushed into the pelvic cavity near the fringed opening of the Fallopian tube. The egg is propelled along the tube until it meets sperm swimming towards it. One sperm usually penetrates one egg which starts to divide into a mass of cells and then embeds or implants in the womb wall a few days later. Magnesium deficiency can prevent implantation and some women are unable to start a pregnancy until any deficiency has been corrected.

Pregnancy

Levels of oestrogen and progesterone rise and further egg production is stopped. The hormone levels go on rising during pregnancy and because of their high profile in the body the brain stops secreting its egg stimulating hormones. The contraceptive pill hormones mimic this effect and continually dupe the brain into thinking that pregnancy has occurred.

Prolactin from the pituitary and oestrogen and progesterone from the corpus luteum continue to be secreted at high levels. The foetal tissues (chorion), connecting the embryo to the lining of the womb, make their own special stimulating hormone. These hormones need enough zinc and magnesium.

The foetal hormone stimulates the mother's ovaries, or gonads, and is therefore called human chorionic gonadotrophin (hCG). Detecting this foetal hormone in a mother's urine is a sure sign that she is pregnant and the basis of hormone pregnancy tests. After three months the foetal connecting tissues have grown into a fully developed vascular placenta, rich in zinc and magnesium. The placenta takes over the manufacture of the increasingly large amounts of oestrogen and progesterone needed for good baby growth and development.

Avoiding Miscarriage

Normally, the mother does not reject the implanting egg which contains foreign proteins from the father. The reason is that progesterone, even in the relatively lowish amounts secreted at the end of the last menstrual cycle, powerfully suppresses both cellular immunity and antibody production. Progesterone maintains pregnancy. If progesterone levels fall, the womb contracts and a miscarriage is the result. Then ovulation restarts.

If the mother is short of zinc and magnesium she may have an early miscarriage or early labour with a small-for-dates premature baby or, conversely, a long and difficult labour. Blood and sweat levels of both zinc and magnesium tend to fall during pregnancy. Many women need careful monitoring and extra nutritional supplements to avoid recurrent miscarriages which are very common in ex-pill takers. Such women tend to have extremely low zinc levels and seem unable to maintain normal zinc status without supplements often because of contraceptive-pill-induced absorption problems.

Birth and Lactation

Usually, signals from the baby induce labour nine months from the first day of the last menstrual period. Progesterone levels begin to fall as the placenta converts more progesterone into oestrogen. The womb muscle becomes sensitive to increasing amounts of another brain hormone called oxytocin which brings on the labour contractions. Labour pains increase until the baby is born. The levels of oestrogen and progesterone then fall. In response to the baby suckling on the nipple the brain maintains high levels of the milk producing hormone, prolactin. Breast milk gives the baby a zinc-rich, nutritious diet which contains maternal antibodies protecting against infection until the baby's immune system matures provided the mother herself is well nourished.

Because progesterone levels are very high during pregnancy, the suppression of the mother's own immune system means she is more susceptible to infections including viruses like HIV and fungal infections like thrush. Cancers, especially breast cancer, can grow rapidly during pregnancy. After pregnancy, while lactating, oestrogen dominance gives her own antibody production a boost and this benefit is passed on to her baby in the milk. A new mother needs extra zinc and enough essential fatty acids in her diet. An animal can restore its levels after giving birth by eating the placenta. If human mothers are severely zinc deficient they are unable to make enough oestrogen and can become depressed, suffering from postnatal depression. This condition should be preventable by checking essential nutrient levels before, during and after pregnancy.

SEX HORMONES – NATURAL AND SYNTHETIC

Cholesterol has been given a very bad press. Diets high in cholesterol and animal fats can cause heart attacks, but cholesterol is essential for life. Cholesterol helps to make and regulate the fatty core of the insulating double membranes which partition and surround each cell and nucleus in our body.

While most of our cells can make cholesterol, extra is needed in the liver, adrenal glands, ovaries, testes and placenta, to make bile acids, vitamin D and steroid hormones. Cholesterol is the parent compound of the sex hormones and all the other closely related steroid hormones.

The sex hormones are made up basically of seventeen carbon atoms arranged in four rings to which extra sidearms may be added. Both testosterone and progesterone have an extra carbon side-arm which is missing in oestrogens. Dr Carl Djerassi, the chemist who synthesised the

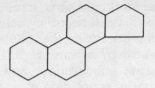

Oestrogen-type
steroid hormone

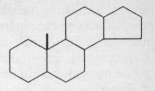

Progesterone- or
testosterone-type
steroid hormone

progestogen norethindrone in Syntex Laboratories in Mexico in the early 1950s, says this extra carbon atom is the most important carbon in bisexual history. While nature can quickly remove the extra carbon side-arm to convert male hormones into female hormones, it took him years of trying to do the same thing. Eventually he managed to make a synthetic oestrogen, ethinyl oestradiol.

At about the same time in the early 1950s, Dr Frank Cotton at Searle Laboratories made norethynodrel, the progestogen used in Enavid, the first oral contraceptive. The structures of some of these synthetic progestogens are more like oestrogen and some are more like testosterone. The result is that, while they are mainly used for their progesterone-like actions, they can also have additional female or male hormone effects. For example one progestogen may cause breast enlargement and another may cause acne and growth of facial hair. The ability to mass produce synthetic hormones was hailed as an important progress. If plant sterols or animal hormones are taken by mouth, they are mostly destroyed in the gut. By contrast, these new hormones could be given in very small doses as pills with immensely powerful effects.

Cholesterol and steroid hormones have the same basic structure of seventeen carbon atoms fused into four rings which makes a key to fit into the target cell's receptors. Different attachments to the rings give each hormone its own identity, function and very exact locking mechanism.

Cell receptors are highly specific for each type of steroid hormone, but the number of receptors and their willingness to accept that particular key is influenced by other hormones. For example, oestrogen primes the cells lining the womb to accept and be activated by progesterone.

Progesterone is the most primitive sex hormone and it is present in early life forms such as fungi. Some fungi, especially mycotoxins, have very strong oestrogenic actions when eaten.

In animals and humans, metabolic pathways convert cholesterol firstly into progesterone, then into testosterone and then into oestrogen. Progesterone is also the parent steroid for the hormones of the cortex (outside part) of the adrenal glands. The adrenal steroids like cortisol and corticosteroids control the body's muscle building and fluid balance, block the body's inflammatory response to infections and upgrade the body's response to stress.

$$\begin{array}{l} \text{cholesterol} \\ \downarrow \\ \text{progesterone} \rightarrow \text{adrenal steroids} \\ \downarrow \\ \text{testosterone} \\ \downarrow \\ \text{oestrogen} \end{array}$$

All members of these closely linked pathways have powerful and different biological activities. Enzymes and their co-enzymes are needed and used up by the continuous steroid production line. If certain pathways are excessively stimulated, or blocked, or if the enzymes become deficient, serious metabolic imbalances of the endocrine orchestra can, and do, happen.

External Sex Hormones

The body's own internal hormones are called endogenous, while those from outside, eaten in food or prescribed as medication, are called exogenous hormones. What is the difference? Most oestrogens, whether natural and endogenous, or synthetic and exogenous like ethinyloestradiol or stilboestrol (DES), still act exactly like oestrogens, have the same actions and attach themselves to oestrogen receptors.

Exogenous hormones, even if natural like those extracted from pigs' ovaries, pregnant mares' urine or post-menopausal women's urine, may have different and unexpected effects on the recipient's own immune system. Immunology is a relatively new science and many allergic reactions are dismissed as psychological. But oestrogens and progesterone have a profound and opposite effect on immunity. In general, oestrogen stimulates and progesterone and testosterone suppress immune pathways.

Hormones, both natural or laboratory-made synthetics, like those in most commonly used oral contraceptives, can produce a wide range of overlapping actions in animals and humans. The protein hormone receptors for oestrogen, thyroid or adrenal stress hormones are very similar and giving one may stimulate the effects of the others. Actions may be:

1 Like progesterone – progestogenic
2 Progestogen blocking
3 Like oestrogen – oestrogenic
4 Oestrogen blocking
5 Androgenic – like testosterone
6 Androgen blocking
7 Adrenal steroid hormone-like action – muscle building, fluid retention, raising blood pressure, stopping reactions to infection and causing biochemical stress.

All exogenous hormones tend to cause biochemical stress

by raising cortisol levels. Muscle-building anabolic steroids have been banned for use by athletes but sex steroid hormones have never been more widely prescribed. Today's men, women and children are subject to all kinds of entirely preventable illnesses because of the unnecessary use of steroid hormones. It is no secret in the medical world that oestrogens promote cancer in women and testosterone promotes cancer in men.

For the past hundred years, castration has been the mainstay of treatment for advanced cancer of the breast, womb, ovary and prostate. More recently, hormone blocking drugs have been used to the same ends and are even being given to healthy women.

The profligate use of exogenous hormones before and during pregnancy and during lactation hits the developing child when his or her sex, personality, intelligence and future health are being determined. We need to look carefully at the consequences.

KEY POINTS

- The three steroid sex hormones, oestrogen, progesterone and testosterone are prescribed more than ever before.
- Taking sex steroids interferes with basic cell chemistry affecting reproductive and general health.
- Sex steroids are still given during pregnancy although known to cause congenital abnormalities and to increase miscarriages.
- Wide-ranging effects damage future generations.
- Alarming fall in sperm counts and increases in sex-hormone-dependent cancers.

Chapter Two

Hormone Balance

Sexual Development

Olympic athletes are given sex tests using cells scraped from the inside of the mouth. Why isn't a person's sex obvious without this scrutiny? A mother usually knows whether she has a son or a daughter. External sex differences can even be detected in scans carried out as early as the twelfth week of pregnancy. Parents choose whether or not they want to know the sex of their baby before birth but the vital question for their child's development is whether nutritional deficiencies have been put right before conception and during pregnancy.

Our sex is decided from the earliest second of our life. The fertilised egg is already male or female. Every cell in a man carries an X and a Y chromosome and every female cell has two X chromosomes. This means that all the mother's eggs have an X chromosome. If the father's sperm also carries an X chromosome, the baby will be a girl. On the other hand, there is a fifty-fifty chance that his sperm will carry a Y chromosome and the baby will be a boy. Sperm can be separated into male or female types and used to predetermine a baby's sex, useful if a genetic disease is carried by one of the sexes exclusively.

As early as five to six weeks from conception a baby boy needs a surge of testosterone – four times higher than the usual infant level. This surge of testosterone must be taken up by the sensitive testosterone receptors to switch on the special male developments in the brain and both internal and external genitals. This normal development can be thwarted if key nutrients are in short supply or if hormones are taken by the mother. *A genetic male XY baby cannot grow into a normal man unless he has enough testosterone at critical times when his brain is developing. If his mother is zinc deficient his brain and sex organs may not develop properly due to lack of hormones and their receptors.*

Early in life a baby has the anatomy to become either a man or a woman. There are two canals which can either connect the ovaries to the vagina via the Fallopian tubes and uterus, or else connect the testes to the male urinary system. Like the ovaries, the male testes develop in the abdominal cavity. Normally, under the influence of testosterone, both testicles have descended into the scrotum by the time a boy is born. Tubes connect the testes to the urethra below the neck of the bladder. The prostate gland surrounds the urethra and secretes a nutritious fluid to help carry the sperm down the urethra inside the penis, into the vagina, through the womb and into the female's Fallopian tubes. The skin in both sexes is affected by the sex hormones forming the external genitalia. The urethra lengthens inside the penis of a man where it is surrounded by spongy tissue which floods with blood causing it to harden in an erection. Ejaculation of the semen containing millions of sperm happens during sexual intercourse and orgasm.

In men the same tube, the urethra, passes both urine and semen and genital infections can back-track quickly into the bladder and prostate and pus-cells appear in the urine. If an infection spreads further back and reaches the testicles dramatic falls in sperm count and even infertility can be the result. In women, the urinary system – kidneys, ureters, bladder and urethra – remain separate from their genital tissues, but, as the urethra opens near the entrance to the vagina, infections can be transmitted from the neck of the womb, the cervix, to the bladder or kidneys.

While the two distinct types of genital systems are developing, inappropriate hormone stimulation can cause permanent changes. If a mother is given oestrogens in early pregnancy, her XY genetically male baby can be born with female-type genitalia – the male is feminised. If the mother is given testosterone or a progestogen, which is very similar to testosterone, her XX genetically female baby can be masculinised displaying dubious genitalia and a small penis at birth. There exists a wide range of fairly rare syndromes varying from missing or extra chromosomes to enzyme defects in hormone production and to lack of hormone receptor sensitivity. When exogenous prescribed hormones, mycotoxins, or meat hormones are added to this hotch-potch, anything can happen. The baby boy or girl is also more likely to develop cancer of the testes or ovaries up to forty years after early inappropriate hormone stimulation. Some risk multiple endocrine cancers.

Brain Sex

A common change in brain development, often unnoticed until sexual maturity, is homosexuality. Recent surveys find that two per cent of men are bisexual with half of these being exclusively homosexual.[1] There is confusion as to whether or not their numbers are increasing as is the general impression. The number of patients attending the Charing Cross Hospital transsexual clinic has doubled during the 1980s. Unfortunately the fifty-year-old Kinsey data, giving a ten per cent homosexuality rate, has been questioned as a fraudulent overestimate obtained from unrepresentative samples by questioning prisoners, sex offenders and male prostitutes.[2] Since extra testosterone is needed for normal male development and normal male brain orientation, there are more males affected than females. Some male and female homosexuals object to the scientific evidence that their sexual orientation has resulted from imbalanced hormone influences during critical phases of their development. When lecturing at a feminist meeting in Oxford on the history of exogenous hormone use, three rather angry lesbians questioned me afterwards. They were annoyed to have their beliefs disturbed, preferring to think that their sexual preferences were their choice and not something that had been determined before they were even born. Some women having been badly treated by men, turn instead to the company of women, but the influence of hormones on sexual development is irrefutable. Much depends on the organisation of the control mechanisms. Recently male homosexuality in pairs of brothers has been linked with the inheritance of a particular genetic configuration on the X chromosome which they received from their mothers.[3]

Many experiments on animals, such as rats and monkeys, show how sexual behaviour can be altered. In rats the critical time for brain sex determination is after they are born. If a newly born male rat is castrated before its brain has become masculinised, it will behave like a female. If the male rat is castrated later on, after it has been bathed in male hormones, its behaviour will stay masculine. Once the critical time is past, the feminised rat cannot regain its original masculine identity by being given extra testosterone. Monkey brains, like human brains, change during early pregnancy. Hormones given at different times produce different behaviour in the offspring.

Testosterone is anabolic and men tend to have bigger muscles, bones and brains than women of the same height. But there is controversy about whether there are other differences in brain anatomy. Obviously, parts of the brain function differently with the different release of brain hormones. Equally obviously, men and women think in different ways. In general, women are more intuitive, sociable, talkative and interested in a wide range of issues. Men tend to be more interested in machines and mathematics and like to gain very detailed technical knowledge of a subject. *Brain Sex* by Anne Moir and David Jessel reviews these psychological differences and the evidence for anatomical differences.[4] They claim that a male brain is more developed in its right half, while females have better connections than men between the two halves of the brain. The authors suggest that the better connections are the secret of women's intuition – their ability to take in, analyse and form a judgement on all sorts of minute information often not noticed by men. Men are more able to keep judgements and emotion separate and less able to voice their emotions. Men have better abstract mathematical and spatial abilities and are more likely to be composers and technicians. While there are many more male than female scientists, how many men have been given the credit for Nobel prize winning discoveries when a woman colleague had intuitively and painstakingly gathered together what really mattered and first made the vital breakthrough? For example, there is now interest in Lise Meitner's original nuclear fission discoveries and in Rosalind Franklin's first DNA photographs.

In 1991 Cheryl McCormick and Sandra Witelson at McMaster University in Ontario, found that the cognitive abilities of homosexual men were intermediate between those of heterosexual men and women. Homosexual men scored lower than heterosexual men in tests of spatial ability but higher in tests of verbal fluency.[5] The study was mentioned in the *British Medical Journal* as further evidence that homosexuality is determined before birth by exposure to atypical concentrations of sex hormones.

The authors of *Brain Sex* quote the work of Dr Gunter Dorner, who describes three stages of sexual development. First, the hormones order the appearance of the male or female reproductive system. Then the hypothalamus is organised differently in each sex, ready to cope with the different FSH and LH secretions. In the third stage, 'gender-role centres' develop as part of the way the brain is wired up, controlling our future psychological reactions

29

to hormone stimulation. Dorner's theory could explain why not all homosexuals appear effeminate and not all feminine-looking men are homosexuals.

Apart from the fact that women tend to have smaller brains than men, neurosurgeons are not aware of other physical differences when looking at the brains of men or women. Differences in brain sex must therefore be fairly subtle.

Dyslexia

At least one in ten children has dyslexia – specific learning difficulties. Dyslexia is more common in some families than in others. As the unravelling of the gigantic human genome continues to give new insights, a particular region of the number One chromosome has been implicated this time in the inheritance of the tendency to develop dyslexia.[6] But zinc is crucial for normal brain development and function and, as baby boys need extra zinc during their development to make extra testosterone, boys are more likely to suffer from dyslexia than girls. Three times more boys are affected. The largest amounts of zinc in the brain are found in the hippocampus, important for short-term memory, and in the eyes. Dyslexics have particular problems with short-term memory and some have difficulty focusing both eyes for reading. Virtually all the dyslexic children we have tested using a sweat test are short of zinc.[7] This may be difficult to correct with supplements. In animals, resistance to supplementation can happen if the animal has been short of zinc during the critical time of brain development early in pregnancy.

Many dyslexics are cross lateral. Instead of having a dominant right eye, right hand and right foot, there is a confusion. Aiming a gun may be difficult: instead of using the right eye and right hand, a dyslexic boy may want to use his right eye and left hand. He may write with his left hand but play table tennis with his right hand. There is a lack of dominance.

A simple test for laterality is to dot as quickly as possible in opposite corners of a rectangle for one minute – first with one hand and then with the other. The hand which can make the most dots in the time is the dominant hand. If both hands make an equal number of dots the brain has equal laterality – with no dominant side.

The brains of a few dyslexic adults have been examined and disorganised cells with fewer connections have been found.[8] There may be abnormalities in the retino-cortical pathway connecting the eyes and the brain.[9] Children who are hyperactive with behaviour problems, like dyslexic children, are more likely to be boys, have allergies and be zinc deficient.[10,11] Brain anatomy, brain function and brain organisation are very dependent on adequate zinc levels, but because growing boys need more zinc than girls, boys are more vulnerable to damage when there is a shortage. If a girl's brain is damaged due to lack of zinc during development her problems may be less obvious until puberty. A girl is less likely to be dyslexic or hyperactive or complain about her problems at school, but she is likely to have difficult periods instead. If the zinc deficiency persists she may have painful irregular periods and start having mood changes as her hormone levels fluctuate.

Dyslexic children and adults cannot do what other people can manage automatically. They often have trouble reading, writing, spelling, counting, concentrating and organising. Their problems make it difficult or impossible to acquire and use simple skills. They are often thought to be of low intelligence or bone idle.

Mary

Mary was seven years old. She was cycling round and round the garden in delight. She had been tested and told that she was dyslexic and was so relieved that she was not just stupid. For a girl of exceptional intelligence, this was an important milestone. She could now have extra classes and her parents could try to find a school which could cope with a girl who could be top in some subjects but bottom in others. Mary never made a fuss and tended to say that things were all right. When she was thirteen years old, Mary's school report was excellent. She was interested in everything, talented at sport and had high marks in all her subjects except English. She passed in ten 'O' level subjects, including English language after several attempts. She wanted to become a scientist but needed science 'A' levels and these were too difficult for her.

A hair test showed high zinc and high copper levels and high toxic metals. What did this mean? A few years later her sweat minerals were also measured. The high hair zinc really meant zinc deficiency. The hair had stopped growing and all the minerals were artificially high in the hair but the zinc was low in the sweat. The copper was still very high. Since then Mary's mineral tests have varied from normal to severely zinc deficient, even while taking supplements. Copper levels have varied between high, normal and too low, perhaps due to changing hormone levels affecting normal control mechanisms or due to gut candida following repeated courses of antibiotics, adding to her difficulties. Now she keeps well if she sticks to a low allergy diet and takes nutritional supplements. Dyslexic children need biochemical monitoring or their future health can be impaired, and any deficiencies need to be treated.

A study described at the 1992 British Dyslexia Association conference revealed that even the youngest dyslexic children can be tense and frustrated. They start life with a high level of tension. The anxiety scores in boys are highest until puberty, when, with helpful education, their anxieties tend to subside. With girls the opposite is the case. Their anxiety scores rise throughout their teens.[12] I was asked if there was a biochemical reason for this, in view of our discovery of the prevalence of zinc deficiency. I think there is. A most important chemical change happens to girls at puberty. The increase in oestrogen raises their serum and sweat copper levels. The Biolab range for boys, girls and men is the same, but when girls become women their copper levels are much higher. Copper is higher still if they become pregnant or take the contraceptive pill. The paper we published in the *British Medical Journal* in 1988 showed that dyslexic boys and girls were not only zinc deficient but that they also tended to have higher copper and higher toxic metals like lead and cadmium compared with matched controls.[7]

Low zinc and high copper cause mental turmoil and, in extreme cases, schizophrenia.

The most worrying part of our dyslexia paper was published separately. Dr John Howard had tested 150 'healthy' boys and girls ten years earlier in the late 1970s. Both boys and girls had exactly the same ranges for sweat zinc, averaging 710 parts per billion.[13] But during the next ten years there was a fall in the 'healthy' control children's zinc levels to 520 while the dyslexic children's levels were only 320. These differences between the groups were highly significant.

The mothers had difficulty finding any really healthy schoolfriends. Two of the first ten children we enrolled as controls were boys with undescended testicles. The descent of the testicles from the abdominal cavity should take place before birth if the mother has enough zinc. The incidence of undescended testes has doubled in the last twenty years. Two of the mothers became friendly because they met at a fertility clinic. Both were given hormones in early pregnancy. One mother had a dyslexic son, while the other had a son with an undescended testicle who volunteered as a 'healthy' control.

Other evidence, such as falling school test results both in the USA and the UK suggest that there is indeed a true fall in children's academic performance.[14,15] Increases in childhood asthma in the UK and Australia suggest there is also an increase in allergic illness.[16,17] Both of these may be a result of poor zinc status.

This is a very serious situation which needs urgent action. Since our *British Medical Journal* publication little that is helpful has happened. Children are given day-long psychological tests, extra special remedial lessons, coloured spectacles, even occasional brain scans but, incredibly, their disordered biochemistry is seldom treated first or at all.

I think the reasons for these deteriorations are obvious. In 1971 only 9 per cent of single women in England and Wales had taken the pill, but by 1981, 90 per cent of women had been prescribed oral contraceptives before their first pregnancy.[18,19] We know that pill-induced zinc deficiency can last for years, affecting future fertility and future children.

Extra Hormones During Pregnancy

As normal brain development is controlled by critical fluctuations in hormone balance during early pregnancy, it is clearly dangerous to interfere and give hormones at this time. But in spite of the thousands of scientific publications on the subject, more women than ever before in the history of the human race are given hormones not just immediately before pregnancy but in the crucial weeks following conception when the baby's brain is developing. When I checked with a well-known test-tube baby (IVF) unit exactly when they could tell which sex a baby was on an ultrasound scan, the radiologist said, 'It should be at twelve weeks of pregnancy but very often you can't tell until the baby is born. With baby girls especially, the external genitalia are often swollen so the scan could be misleading.' I asked if they gave hormones during pregnancy. She replied, 'We usually give progesterone until twelve weeks.' What is going to happen to these girls? They look normal soon after they are born, but what will happen at puberty?

Extra Hormones Before Pregnancy

Perhaps the most chilling account of long-term effects of hormone exposure on women's ovaries and future children has been described by Professor Jean Jofen, a New York psychologist.[20] She discovered that some Jewish children of very intelligent parents had unexpectedly severe learning defects with IQs below 100. She discovered a common factor. All their mothers had been held captive during the war in the same concentration camp – Auschwitz. She did not find the same problem when mothers who had been in other concentration camps, suggesting that starvation alone was not the cause. Women who had gone to Auschwitz had stopped menstruating within ten days of their arrival. Hunger and stress take longer than that to affect the human system which has reserves of fat especially to cater for such emergencies. None of the mothers remembered any medical treatment or injections but some thought the soup had been 'treated'. Eventually Professor Jofen unearthed a secret document among the Nuremberg trial records. Greenhouses had been built in Auschwitz to grow a rare South American plant from which female hormones could be made. These were 'to lead to sterilisation of persons without their knowledge'.

The really chilling part of the story is that it was the women who were permanently affected. The men of Auschwitz later had children with normal IQs. And yet we are witnessing in the 1990s a social scene where smoking, drinking, pill taking and even drug addiction are becoming commonplace among younger and younger girls. Professor Jofen had found that *the lower the child's IQ, the younger the mother had been when she was first introduced to hormones*. Not all facets of intelligence were affected equally which is a typical finding among dyslexic children.

Although a Japanese chemical company developed a profitable new microbial method for making the pill from cholesterol, the Japanese Welfare Ministry was not prepared to lift the ban on the use of this type of contraceptive because of its ability to cause cancer and congenital abnormalities. Japan is famous among the world's 'rich' countries for having a low animal fat diet and an exceptionally low incidence of breast cancer. They are also beginning to lead the world in original scientific research.

Professor Jofen thought the best place to check on the pill's effect on children would be Puerto Rico where the pill was first used on a large scale. But the official, expensive and perfectly designed control trial carried out on 9,757 women between 1961 and 1976 came up with nothing – even the women taking the original high dose oestrogen pills had no statistical increase in thrombosis, metabolic upsets or cancer. Perhaps the fact that by 1976 only 26 active pill users were followed up might have something to do with these results.[21]

Not everyone, however, is happy about Puerto Rico's children. During 1978 and 1981 there was a striking increase in the incidence of precocious sexual development in children from as young as six months to eight years.[22] Dr Carmen Rodrigues, a paediatrician, came to London to lecture at the Royal Society of Medicine in 1984. She showed picture after picture of children with breast and sexual development – of girls who had started to menstruate when they had first started school and of boys who were also developing too soon. She suspected the oestrogenic substances, stilboestrol and zeranol, which are freely available in Puerto Rico and are used to improve the growth rate of chickens. The *Lancet* thought this unlikely but Dr Schoental suggested that perinatal exposure to pill oestrogens plus natural food oestrogens like zeralenone may have increased the children's sensitivity to future exposures to such food.[23,24] Our water supply is now contaminated by oestrogens, possibly from prescribed hormones, DDT or from industrial detergents.[25] Recently a woman professor from Texas showed us similar pictures, glibly commenting that perhaps these infant girls had swallowed their mothers' contraceptive pills. She had not asked if their mothers had taken the pill or fertility drugs during pregnancy and she now proposed to give these girls extra oestrogens or hormone stimulants.

Normally a girl should have had very little hormone stimulation until she is twelve or thirteen years old. Bleeding is the first sign that she has started her monthly rises and falls in oestrogens and progesterone. Brain hormones from the hypothalamus are secreted in pulses every hour or so and her pituitary responds by releasing FSH and LH to stimulate an egg follicle. Her cells are laden with receptors ready to respond to the new influx – the target cells are supersensitive. In some mysterious way, her biological clock is programmed to follow genetic instructions for forty years or so. By sending out waves of stimulating hormones nature arranges that triggered cells have time to recover. When all the receptors are used up, the cell needs time to make more and then is no longer sensitive.

At the menopause, the numbers of receptors decline and the ovaries stop responding. When hormones or oral contraceptives are taken continuously the cells become subsensitive and an early menopause can occasionally be the result. Continuous daily hormone stimulation is unnatural and, as has been found with HRT, can lead to addiction with higher and higher doses being given to suppress symptoms.

The contraceptive pill was never meant to be natural. A girl or woman taking the pill has suddenly been temporarily medically castrated.

There is one excuse only for this crime against humanity and that is the fact that the world's population is increasing at the rate of one million every four days. Only the fear that we are greedily or unwittingly spoiling our beautiful world by the demands of too many people can explain what has happened. In all of nature, millions of years of evolution and slow change have been invested in ensuring safe and accurate reproduction. Our genetic inheritance has been protected, mixed, enriched but not altered more quickly than it can be repaired – never until now.

Pill Discoveries

In 1836 a surgeon named Cooper published his observation that the stage of the menstrual cycle influenced the speed of growth and division of breast cancer cells.[26] They proliferated more rapidly in the early part of the cycle when the ovaries are secreting oestrogens. By 1896 the *Lancet* reported the experiments of Beatson who removed the ovaries of women with breast cancer causing their advanced disease to go into remission.[27] At the same time it was discovered that the secretions of the yellow cyst in the ovary prevented the release of any more eggs once a pregnancy had started. This gave rise to the idea that oestrogen and progesterone could be used as a contraceptive.

By 1932 it was known that oestrogens and progesterone could cause cancer of the breast, womb, ovaries and pituitary gland in experimental animals but the plans for manufacturing sex hormones were well under way.[28] In 1928 the German firm Schering had extracted oestrogens from pigs' ovaries but they needed four tons from sows just to get twenty-five milligrams of oestradiol! Hormones made from plant sterols are destroyed in the gut, so the race was on to make hormones that could be taken by mouth. Laboratories converted cholesterol derived from wool fat, cattle bile or plant sterols into artificial sex hormones.

In 1938 Professor Sir Charles Dodds and his colleagues discovered that the non-steroid compound diethylstilboestrol acted like an oestrogen. It does not have the complete four-ringed steroid structure but its molecules are arranged in such a way that it has the same key groupings. It locks into the oestrogen receptors so exactly that the cell is fooled into thinking that the body's own oestrogens are stimulating activity. Sir Charles warned of stilboestrol's power and cautioned against its use, predicting serious effects. Progestogens were first made by Allen and Ehrenstein in 1944 by a long and complicated method. In the fifties, the German firm Schering and the American firm Syntex were the first companies to produce these orally active hormones commercially. In Europe, the drugs were known as progestogens and in America, progestins. *These steroids are between 500 and 1,000 times more powerful than progesterone when taken by mouth.*

Animals reacted in a wide variety of ways when given the new hormone preparations. There were changes in their carbohydrate, fat and protein metabolism and alterations in their salt and water balance, demonstrating the overlap of adrenal steroid hormone actions. Animals given these progestogens in pregnancy sometimes produced offspring with abnormalities. Hormones are more likely to induce congenital abnormalities or cancer when there are nutritional deficiencies. But laboratory animals are given a diet with their essential nutrients added, so the hormones were causing these changes even though the animals had an adequate diet.

In spite of the animal studies, the decision was taken to go ahead with clinical trials of the pill. Because it was known that oestrogens could cause breast cancer, the original pill trials in America used progestins. The first progestins given to women by Dr John Rock, a Harvard gynaecologist, were impure and contained some oestrogens. When 'pure' progestins were given women complained of too much bleeding. It was then realised that to imitate the regular normal monthly period an oestrogen needed to be added. Dr Rock and Dr Gregory Pincus tried out the first 'Pincus pill' in the 1950s on a Harvard volunteer group and on some chronically ill mental patients. Both men and women took a high dose form of Enovid (10mg), which was more than enough to stop ovulation in women and sperm production in men. One of the men displayed shrunken testicles and the 'male pill' never recovered from the shock. As an eminent endocrinologist said, 'Any 'male pill' would have to be really safe.' The sudden deaths of three women in Puerto Rico from thrombosis did not seriously hamper progress of the contraceptive pill worldwide. By then millions of women were taking part in the greatest mass experiment in history and the spectre of overpopulation was thought to be finally on the run.

When I was a medical student in Dundee in the 1950s, we were told about the Pincus pill. At that time family planning had a low image and one professor joked about how women doctors in London spent their time fitting contraceptive caps. The Family Planning Association was still a voluntary organisation struggling to prevent married working-class women having too many children and wanting abortions (then illegal). There were very few abortions carried out in teenagers – it was much later in the 1970s that unmarried younger women began to be the main clients of family planning clinics. The depression of the 1930s and the Second World War meant very few of my class-mates in the 1940s and 1950s had more than one or two brothers or sisters. The main pre-pill methods of contraception were withdrawal before ejaculation of semen or the rhythm method, as natural family planning was then called. I thought the pill was probably a good idea, but when we heard that American doctors were giving their wives oestrogens to keep them young after the menopause, that seemed ridiculous. Divorce was very uncommon apart from among film stars. Women of my mother's generation did not have to try to stay artificially young to prevent their husbands going off with a younger model. It was only when use of the pill increased in the 1960s that divorce began to increase, until multiple partners became the norm in the 1970s. There have always been increases in venereal or sexually transmitted diseases (STDs) in wartime and increases in cervical cancer ten to twenty years later, but STDs and cervical cancers and terminations of pregnancies, especially in teenagers, have been increasing each year since steroid contraception became available. Now, far from family planning being a joke, it is nearly impossible for any young doctor, however well qualified, to be given a partnership with any group of general practitioners if he or she will not prescribe the pill. To object to prescribing the pill on health grounds is not to be tolerated.

In the 1950s oestrogens were prescribed. Stilboestrol was soon being given to as many as half of all new mothers to cut down or to dry up their milk supply if they chose not to, or were unable to, breast feed. Oestrogen cream was also given to postmenopausal women for vaginal dryness. Because of Sir Charles' warning, only a few thousand women in the UK were given oestrogens during pregnancy, if they had a history of previous miscarriages, but they were prescribed for millions of women in the USA. Later trials found no benefit but very serious consequences such as breast cancer in the mothers and vaginal cancer in the daughters.[29]

In 1959 I moved from Scotland and worked in obstetrics and endocrinology at University College Hospital, London. Dr Gerald Swyer had given pregnant women stilboestrol in the early 50s and he was now busy testing the new progestogens in his fertility clinic. He was finding out which doses prevented ovulation, delayed bleeding and whether infertile women could be helped. Dr Swyer was co-chairman with Dr Gregory Pincus of the oral contraceptive advisory group to the International Planned Parenthood Federation. He suggested to Dr Eleanor Mears, the Family Planning Association's medical secretary, that I could join her in the new 1961 oral contraceptive trials. Like Dr Swyer, Dr Mears had also given different pills to her own patients and was now organising nationwide trials. Each drug company contributed pills and money and the research body of the Family Planning Association started trials in London, York, Edinburgh, Liverpool, Birmingham, Newcastle and Glasgow. All the pill doses and combinations were to be tested in London where I saw the women, examined them and checked the changes in the lining of their wombs. Cervical smears were also taken and sent to a London hospital for assessment.

Already in the early 1960s the pill doses had been

reduced from the original 10mg Pincus pill to as little as 10 micrograms of progestogen. The actual dose is not so important as the biological dose. This is why I was testing the power of the different pill combinations on the lining of the womb. A 4mg dose of one progestogen may have the same actions as 0.5mg (50 micrograms) of a different progestogen. The results of the first trials are often discounted by saying that only high doses were tested and modern pills have lower doses. This is not true. In the 1960s we tested over seventy different combinations and doses of seven progestogens and two oestrogens. All contraceptive pills need a strong enough hormone dose to block ovulation and prevent irregular bleeding. Very low-dose weak pills – like those we discarded in the sixties – are now being prescribed. Any resulting unwanted pregnancy is blamed on forgotten pills or the antagonistic effect of antibiotics.

In 1961 women could not be enrolled for the pill trials unless they had the written consent of their husbands. The women had already proved their fertility and had more live children than miscarriages. Half of the women had become pregnant accidentally and the rest had mostly become pregnant as soon as they tried. They thought the pills would be much 'safer' than withdrawal, condoms or caps and were keen to volunteer. This view was a little misplaced as some women became pregnant on the lower dose pills. We gave 50 micrograms of oestrogen for the first fifteen days of a cycle as part of sequential regimes and too many women became pregnant including one who had twins. Very low doses of different progestogens were tested in Yugoslavia, again with rather too many unplanned pregnancies, to the annoyance of the local collaborating doctor.

At the headquarters of the Family Planning Association, my role was to take a careful history from each woman and give her a thorough examination. Weight, blood pressure, haemoglobin tests for anaemia, vaginal and cervical smears and biopsy samples from the lining of the womb (endometrium), were all taken before the women started taking any pills and then every six months. The idea was to scrutinise in detail small numbers of women on each pill, while larger numbers of women on a few types of pill were followed up in the other city clinics.

A year later Dr Mears and I published the results of the first pill we tested in the *British Medical Journal* in 1962.[30] We had kept coloured charts and marked every forgotten pill, headache, bleeding, the number of times the woman had sexual intercourse and anything else she liked to report. The first pill, Anovlar, was a fairly high dose of progestogen with a lowish dose of oestrogen. None of the first 100 volunteers became pregnant, they had regular scanty bleeding two days after stopping each course of pills. They had fewer cramps and premenstrual tension and some women noted their breasts were less tender. Cycle control was excellent with only two cases in one hundred of breakthrough bleeding. But other side effects were increasing – more women were complaining of full blown classical migraine, loss of interest in love making and depression. Other low-dose pills caused lots of bleeding, sore veins and sore breasts.

By chance, the pathologist who looked at the samples from the lining of the womb had decided to emigrate to Canada. I was given a microscope and asked to take over. I had the unusual opportunity to examine the cells and blood vessels of my own patients – the women I was seeing in the clinic every few months. We were testing such a wide range of hormone combinations that it did not take long to work out what was happening.

In 1964 I published a method for estimating the hormone balance of contraceptive pills.[31,32] There are three different types of pills. Side effects vary with each dose and balance and each individual's reactions to them.

1) Combined Oral Contraceptives

Each pill contains both a progestogen and an oestrogen.

Usually one pill is taken every day for three weeks and, if the progestogen dose is strong enough, a scanty withdrawal bleed starts two days later.

A normal cycle's growth and secretory phases are condensed into the first few days of pill taking. For the rest of the cycle, the womb lining remains thin and atrophic with a few dried-up glands. Cervical and vaginal secretions may also dry up.

In contrast, blood vessels, which normally only grow and widen at the end of a cycle in time to flood the womb with blood at the start of menstruation, can be unexpectedly prominent throughout the pill cycles. Although usually bleeding less, studies show that overall pill takers are more likely to have episodes of very heavy bleeding severe enough to need hospital admission compared with cap and condom users. Women who get headaches have the most over-developed small arteries.

When weaker doses of progestogen and oestrogen are equally balanced, samples from the womb lining show early secretory cells and dilated veins for more days in the cycle than usual. Such pills cause irregular breakthrough bleeding, escape ovulations and unplanned pregnancies. With these pills, veins dilate throughout the body increasing the risk of thrombosis.

If the hormone doses are too strong or a woman is supersensitive, she may not bleed. This absence of bleeding is known as amenorrhoea. It may persist as a sign of an early menopause. If these women are then given fertility stimulant hormones they have an increased chance of developing ovarian cancer. Other women with amenorrhoea have high prolactin levels, which are sometimes due to a prolactin secreting tumour of the pituitary known as a prolactinoma. One study found that if girls were given the pill because they had irregular bleeding they were 7.7 times more likely to develop a prolactinoma compared with those who had regular cycles and were given the pill for contraception.[33]

2) Progestogen-only Pills (POPs)

No oestrogen is added to the daily progestogen pill.

The womb lining is thin and dried up and irregular bleeding and escape pregnancies are more likely – three per 100 women-years compared with 0.5 with combined pills in the Oxford/FPA study.[34]

Norgestrel is a powerful progestogen: 30 micrograms are comparable to 350 of norethisterone or 500 of ethynodial diacetate (which is changed by the body into norethisterone).

We tested progestogen-only pills in Yugoslavia in 1969. Megestrol acetate 250 dose was too low to even change the endometrium or inhibit ovulation and half of the women became pregnant. However this low dose was powerful enough to change the cervical mucus – an early clue that the cells in the neck of the womb are especially sensitive to the influence of any dose of progestogen. The news of a sudden increase in early cervical cancer among pill users was just beginning to filter through from America.

Norgestrel was so much more powerful than the other progestogens that a mere 50 microgram dose gave a pregnancy rate of nine per 100 women years compared with pregnancy rates of twelve for a 500 dose of chlormadinone and four for a 300 dose of norethisterone acetate.[35]

3) Sequentials in Oral Contraceptives or Hormone Replacement.

An oestrogen pill is given alone for the first part of the cycle and progestogen is added later.

There is a lush growth of endometrium and enlargement

of blood vessels followed by secretion when progestogen is added. If oestrogen stimulation is excessive or merely continued for too long, there is an inevitable overgrowth of the womb lining (endometrial hyperplasia) which can change into endometrial cancer. Up to 13 days of a progestogen was given to ensure endometrial shedding and withdrawal bleeding when the pills were stopped.

Sequential oral contraceptives had an unacceptably high pregnancy risk if 50 micrograms of oestradiol or less was given. Higher doses of oestrogen were banned because of the increased risk of blood clots. Today's sequential contraceptive pills are made up of both hormones given simultaneously with sequential changes in dose during the cycle. Oestrogen is given alone as so-called hormone replacement therapy to women who have had their wombs removed but for women who still have a uterus progestogen is added for several days to reduce their risk of endometrial hyperplasia and cancer. *Some combined OCS and HRT regimes can contain identical steroids and doses in spite of the propaganda that HRT is different. Blood levels in women given identical doses can vary up to 50 times for oestrogens and 10 times for progestogens*[36, 37] See Appendix Three for trade names and doses.

How to Avoid Period Pains

The pill seemed to be achieving what every woman wanted – regular painless periods – or no periods at all, if they took daily hormones.

Very often adolescent girls have period pains – as many as six in ten girls take painkillers each month. Persuaded by drug companies and 'experts', general practitioners soon began to kill two birds with one stone. If they prescribed the pill to adolescents, the period pains would usually disappear and so would her chance of having an embarrassing teenage pregnancy, with the need to have an abortion, provided she remembered to take the pills each day.

Why do so many girls have period pains?

When a girl starts to menstruate at the age of twelve or thirteen, there is usually no pain. Primary dysmenorrhoea (period pains) often starts later – at age fifteen or sixteen. Why? At first a girl may not be ovulating and, like the pill cycles, these are usually pain-free cycles. The bleeding may be erratic with early or missed periods. Pain is connected with ovulation. When a girl's ovaries start to make oestrogen, she uses more zinc. At the same time, oestrogen makes her blood copper levels rise. Girls, boys and men have the same normal range of serum copper levels, but women have higher levels. The growing baby in the womb needs enough copper and oestrogen increases the amount of copper carried around in the mother's blood to even higher levels during pregnancy. Copper tends to lower zinc levels. This happens just when the growing girl and her ovaries are needing more zinc. Girls tend to become zinc deficient which affects other important chemical pathways. The commonest signs of zinc deficiency are period problems – pain, irregular bleeding and white spots on finger nails. Unfortunately, as the pill lowers zinc and raises copper levels, doctors have been adding to the problems of adolescent girls by prescribing contraceptive hormones which make these imbalances worse. Low magnesium in the womb muscle also causes painful cramps and lack of zinc interferes with the essential fatty acid (EFA) pathways. EFAs make the prostaglandins, the chemicals which orchestrate the bleeding and clotting during a period. If a girl is given enough zinc, magnesium, B vitamins and EFAs, like evening primrose oil, her problems may be solved by dealing with their root causes. If she takes aspirin, she blocks the prostaglandin pathways, and may bleed heavily.

Infection and endometriosis

Another cause of pain is infection. Early use of tampons or sexual intercourse is likely to introduce infection, which becomes trapped either in the tubes or in the cervix. Infection in the womb is less likely when the woman bleeds each month and the lining is flushed out. Very often women are unaware for years that they have infection and their future fertility may be damaged beyond repair before they are properly investigated and treated. Chlamydial infection of the tubes is known as the silent epidemic. One of the main reasons so many women attend test-tube baby clinics is because their tubes have become blocked.

Advertising, friends and even school swimming lessons persuade girls to start using internal tampons. Girls must be able to swim and exercise with complete freedom. But what happens? The tampons, pushed up against the neck of the womb, block the outflow of blood. Where does it go? It can backtrack up through the uterus, along both tubes and into the pelvic cavity. Tampon use together with magnesium deficiency affecting the contractions of the tubes, are likely to be common causes of endometriosis. In this condition, lumps of womb lining become attached to the ovaries outside the tubes and womb and even to the ovaries, bowel and bladder. Each month these isolated lumps of cells may bleed causing a great deal of pain. If a woman sleeps on her stomach with a tampon inserted, the blood can percolate straight down towards the pelvis. Another possible cause of endometriosis is wearing a cap or having sexual intercourse during bleeding.

Although most contraceptive pills shrivel the womb lining, the blood vessels distort and dilate which may encourage spread of endometrial tissue backwards through the veins. When the pill is given up, the misplaced tissue thickens and bleeds more profusely causing more monthly pain which eventually leads to the diagnosis. In the Oxford/FPA study previous pill takers had nearly twice the incidence of endometriosis compared with women who had never taken the pill.[38] Among these women starting the pill aged between 25 and 39, the peak ages for endometriosis being diagnosed was 35 to 44. Does this mean that women starting aged 15 to 24, who tend to take the pill for longer than older women and are more likely to have chronic genital infections, will be developing the disease when they are even younger than 25? It seems likely. In the Oxford/FPA study most cases were recorded two to six years after the women stopped the pill. Past IUD users also have a higher risk. Past pill and HRT users in the American Walnut Creek Trial had increases in both endometriosis and adenomyosis, where endometrial tissue is inside the muscle wall of the womb. The increase in endometriosis and adenomyosis are main reasons why so many women now have hysterectomies (removal of the womb) before they even reach the usual age of the menopause.[39]

The DES Action Group tell their members that oestrogen-exposed daughters are more likely to suffer from endometriosis. The narrowed cervix (cervical stenosis) and T-shaped uterus found in many DES-exposed women could facilitate backwards menstrual flow.

About half of all women investigated for infertility have endometriosis. Other symptoms include painful periods, painful sexual intercourse and painful bowel movements or even painful micturition (passing urine).

Recently Elizabeth, Prue and Irene came to consult me because they were having problems getting pregnant and each one had been told she had endometriosis.

Elizabeth
Now twenty-eight years old, Elizabeth had been given oral contraceptives from the age of nineteen to twenty-two. At twenty-three, endometriosis and an ovarian cyst were diagnosed. The following years were like a nightmare. Bouts of severe pain were treated by removal of her appendix, courses of antibiotics and removal of her left tube and ovary. Two pregnancies ended in early miscarriages. During three attempts at IVF two, three, and seven eggs were collected from her remaining ovary and three eggs were fertilised but failed to implant. No eggs at all were

produced after a fourth course of stimulating drugs. Elizabeth had been taking vitamins on and off for years. Her magnesium levels were low, as were some of her essential fatty acids, deficiencies which could be corrected with supplements. When tested, neither Elizabeth nor her husband had genital infections but the damage had been done.

Pru

Pru's periods started at the age of thirteen. At the age of sixteen she began to use internal tampons and her periods became painful after her first sexual intercourse at seventeen. She started the pill at twenty-one and took it on and off for the next eleven years, taking it for about half that time. She was changed to a stronger pill as the first one gave her break-through bleeding. Pru was now age thirty-eight. The year before a cervical smear was positive, cervical intra-epithelial neoplasia or carcinoma-in-situ grade two (CIN–2), and was treated by laser. Now, neither she nor her husband had genital infections but they were both deficient in zinc, magnesium and essential fatty acids. Pru had been taking the male-type hormone danazol for the past six months and she was short of fish oils (EPA) which is common in men. She had been unable to become pregnant in spite of trying for six years. An ovarian cyst was removed when she was thirty-two.

Danazol blocks the release of FSH and LH and prevents ovulation and rises in oestrogen and progesterone and should be avoided months before attempting to conceive. Danazol is widely prescribed but, like the pill, has a long list of side effects including male-hormone-like effects, migraine, flushing, emotional and menstrual disturbances, jaundice, benign intracranial hypertension, fluid retention and weight gain.

Irene

Now thirty-seven, Irene had never been pregnant. Given the pill at eighteen she took it on and off for the next six years. Then severe painful periods warned of endometriosis. She was given danazol, tamoxifen (an oestrogen receptor blocker), Cyclogest (progesterone) all to no avail. She was desperate – complaining of extreme tiredness, painful lumpy breasts, weight gain and PMT lasting nearly three weeks each month. She had tried nystatin for gut candida. Her zinc, magnesium and essential fatty acid levels were very low. Gradually, diet and nutritional supplements helped her to feel better but she did not become pregnant. Although her chlamydial antibody levels were raised, suggesting active pelvic infection, Irene's tubes were not blocked when last tested.

Endometrial Hyperplasia

In contrast to oestrogens and progestogens given for contraception and period pains, when oestrogen is given alone to older women at the menopause bleeding problems become very common. Oestrogen greatly overstimulates the lining of the womb and the overgrowth goes on to hyperplasia. This is treated with a D and C (dilatation and curettage) operation to clean out the uterus, or endometrial ablation. Instead progestogens may be prescribed to 'oppose' the oestrogen and shrivel up the lining of the womb. The sudden increase in womb cancer among HRT users in America caused alarm and oestrogens without progesterone, whether in the form of tablets, patches or vaginal cream, are now not recommended for women who still have their uterus.

Fibroids and Polyps

Fibroids are the commonest pelvic tumours and are formed from womb tissues. They can cause bleeding, pain or infertility; they are commonest in over-30-year-olds but tend to shrink after the menopause. Fibroids can grow rapidly in pregnancy and under the influence of extra oestrogen whether it is taken as a combined pill or as HRT. Zinc and magnesium deficiencies, by interfering with

51

ovulation and progesterone output, can prolong the time unopposed oestrogen influences fibroid growth. When a woman has infection, she may develop polyps in the entrance to the womb and fibroids in the womb itself. Both can cause irregular bleeding and the tumours are often removed by surgery. Both endometriosis and fibroids are also treated with a drug which blocks the receptors for the pituitary hormones, preventing the ovaries producing oestrogen for a few months. Oestrogens in the pill and HRT encourage fibroid growth. Details from the RCGP and Oxford/FPA pill studies[40] are given in Appendix One.

Ovarian Cysts

Many of my patients have ovarian cysts, possibly because of long-term zinc deficiency but mostly because they have been given pituitary hormone stimulating drugs for infertility. The anti-oestrogens clomiphene and cyclofenil are used to block oestrogen receptors and increase the output of FSH and LH when women are failing to ovulate. Side effects include ovarian enlargement and cysts, hot flushes, abdominal discomfort and blurred vision. As the ovary, a place of rapid growth, needs lots of zinc, when zinc is in short supply non-functioning cysts develop, which can become huge, and ovarian cancer may develop.

In one type of ovarian disease, multiple cysts make too much male hormone – presumably because lack of zinc prevents the conversion of testosterone to oestrogens. It is known as Stein Leventhal syndrome and women suffering from it grow hair on their faces and become rather masculine in appearance. There are two types of ovarian cysts, functioning or non-functioning. While women are taking the pill, they are unlikely to have functioning cysts as the point of taking the pill in a big enough dose is to stop the ovaries functioning. However pill users are more likely than non-users to develop the second type which are not functioning.

Ovarian and Endometrial Cancer

Ovarian cancer, like all cancers, is also more likely where there is zinc deficiency. Each time an egg bursts out of a follicle's protective covering the hole in the ovary must be repaired. Many ovarian cancers are now thought to begin when the repairing cells go on dividing out of control. Zinc is needed for normal cell division and healing.

There are many types of ovarian cancers. In one rare type, cells and tissues have been found which apparently come from male cells – some even have cells from different men – presumably due to sperm from different partners reaching the ovaries. An interesting study found a link with ovarian cancer and talcum powder, which can backtrack through the womb along the tubes and reach the ovaries, where it acts as an irritant like asbestos. Thirty years ago it was the custom to tell women to keep their caps dry by covering them in talcum powder! Galactose consumption, usually higher in vegetarians, has been linked to ovarian cancer.

Both ovarian and endometrial cancers are rare in young women. In spite of all we know, a pill selling point is the astounding claim that combined pills prevent both these cancers. How can this be? There is confusion because progestogens shrivel up the lining of the womb and are given to women with widespread endometrial cancer for this purpose. Another main confusion comes from the large-scale trials. A group of women with endometrial or ovarian cancer are asked how long they took the pill. A similar number of women, who may have anything else wrong with them but not endometrial or ovarian cancer, are also asked how long they took the pill. Usually women who went on to develop these cancers took the pill for a shorter time than those who did not. The immediate conclusion is that the pill is preventing womb and ovarian cancer.[41, 42] I am unable to make this jump in logic myself, because obviously it is the women who have side effects or problems such as irregular bleeding on lower dose pills or missed periods on higher dose pills who are those most likely to stop taking the pill earlier than the other women. The alternative, and I believe more reasonable conclusion, is that it is this group of more sensitive women, who are more likely to go on to develop cancer.

No one can now deny that oestrogen by itself makes endometrial cancer likely to develop within a very few years. Combined progestogen pills also contain oestrogen even if the oestrogen is not dominant. A Glasgow obstetrician, who likes to give women oestrogens, said at a recent meeting in London, 'Endometrial cancer is not very serious, it can easily be dealt with by removing the womb' – i.e. a hysterectomy. She was more concerned that adding progestogens to oestrogens gave premenstrual-type symptoms and spoiled the oestrogen feeling of well-being. This euphoria can be addictive and may need higher and higher doses of oestrogen to maintain.

Ovarian cancer is also more likely when oestrogen is taken. The large British HRT review had eight cases among the users including one who developed ovarian cancer after her ovaries had been removed – clearly from a remnant that had been left behind.[43] Women whose periods did not restart after they gave up the pill are more likely to develop ovarian cancer, especially if they are given fertility stimulating hormones.[44] Dr Peter Harper of Guy's Hospital says that women failing to conceive after having such infertility treatment may have a normal or up to 250 times more increased risk of ovarian cancer.[45] Only time will tell as years of excessive ovarian stimulation is a new phenomenon.

Although it has been reiterated *ad nauseam* that the pill prevents ovarian cancer, the world's largest cohort study by the Royal College of General Practitioners has actually found no difference in the incidence of ovarian cancer between the majority of its pill users (those taking the pill for up to four years) and the rate in the control group.[46] Again, with the combined progestogen-oestrogen pill, women with ovarian cancer take the pill for a shorter time than average and this is called prevention. The perverse logic assumes that as fewer longer-users of the pill get endometrial and ovarian cancer the pill must be preventing these tumours developing. This fails to take into account that it is the women who are most likely to give up the pill and HRT because of side effects who may have more risk of cancer unless their deficiencies are corrected. Progestogens can shrivel some tissues but, unlike oestrogens, which stimulate the immune system, progestogens are highly immuno-suppressive. Progestogens also develop blood vessels which may encourage the spread of cancer. Women who are given huge doses of progestogens for advanced endometrial cancer do not have good survival rates and many develop blood clots.

The good news is that it is now possible to have an early warning blood test. Our bodies have many protecting and correcting mechanisms and we can help by making sure we have enough anti-oxidants – the correct levels of our essential minerals, vitamins and essential fatty acids. For many women the last thirty years have been grim but the future could look better.

KEY POINTS

- If taken in early pregnancy oestrogen feminises males and progesterone or testosterone masculinises females.
- Effects of hormone imbalance or zinc deficiency on brain development include homosexuality, mental illness, hyperactivity and dyslexia.
- Actions of combined contraceptive pills, progestogen-only types or oestrogen HRT-like sequentials on bleeding patterns.
- Period pains, infections, endometriosis and hysterectomies increased among ex-pill-takers.
- Fibroid growth stimulated by oestrogens.
- Ovarian cysts and ovarian cancers increased by hormone stimulants used for infertility.
- Endometrial cancer caused by oestrogen HRT.

Chapter Three

Controlling Your Blood Vessels

HOW TO AVOID HEADACHES, MIGRAINE, FLUSHING, PRE-ECLAMPSIA, HIGH BLOOD PRESSURE, STROKES AND HEART ATTACKS

Young adults are usually healthy so why were young women on the pill more likely to develop blood clots, strokes and heart attacks? What was going on?

With the first pill we tested, more than half of the volunteers complained of severe headaches. One woman was so desperate to use this 'safe' method of contraception that she tried four different pills only to finish up bedridden each time with migraine. Changing pills may get rid of headaches but different symptoms can appear instead.

Thrombosis

The most 'notorious' pill side effect in the 1960s was thrombosis. Startling and sometimes fatal, it gained massive newspaper and television coverage. One of the first cases was described in the *Lancet* by a Suffolk general practitioner, whose patient, a nurse, had suffered clots in both lungs.[1] Thrombosis simply means a blood clot. Clots can form in either arteries or veins blocking the blood circulation. Clots can cause strokes, paralysis, heart attacks or severe abdominal pain. A common site for clots is the leg veins and this is potentially dangerous because the clot can travel up to the lungs as a pulmonary embolus. Sudden damage to the lungs can be as much an instant death sentence as a heart attack.

Thrombosis is one of the commonest causes of death for the elderly but is rare in young people. This may have accounted for the publicity, although cancer kills twice as many women under fifty-five as vascular disease, hormone-induced cancers usually take years to appear. The pill was claimed to be safer than pregnancy, but, in the 1960s, the number one cause of maternal deaths was a clot in the leg followed by pulmonary embolism due to oestrogens. Nearly half of all new mothers were given oestrogen in the form of stilboestrol (DES) to suppress lactation soon after childbirth when they did not have enough milk or if they chose not to breast feed their baby.

Doctors may not be aware of the true incidence of serious side affects. In America in the early 1960s, although only a few cases of thrombosis were initially recorded, when newspapers carried the story of this side effect of the pill the number of cases reported increased dramatically overnight. Few doctors report drug side effects to the Committee on Safety of Medicines in the UK.

My clinic secretary had several notifications of thrombosis coming in from other family planning clinics, including one about a woman who had her arm amputated following a blood clot in her artery. One day, I was dismayed to hear that my secretary, herself, was in hospital. She had taken a combined pill for two years. She was carrying a suitcase when she had a sudden sharp pain at the top of her right leg. She was rushed into hospital where they diagnosed a thrombosis in her iliac artery. When I went to visit her, she was on a drip having intravenous fluids because her gut muscles had become paralysed. Like many doctors, I thought such life-threatening events were unusual and if we tried enough different combinations, a safe one would be found. Years later my secretary tried oestrogens, this time as HRT for her menopausal symptoms, and immediately had pains again in her right leg.

It is not my experience that serious side effects from exogenous hormones are rare. In fact, the third patient we enrolled suffered a brain haemorrhage and thrombosis, while the twelfth went on to develop benign intracranial hypertension – a rare condition, known to happen in people taking steroids.

Mrs C

Mrs C had a large family and a difficult husband, so she was delighted to be free from the fears of yet another pregnancy. Four years after she started a low-dose oestrogen pill, her blood pressure was 140/90 but two years later had rocketed to 210/140. She had gained about 20lb and was complaining of tiredness, depression, irritability and headaches. She also had womb fibroids and needed a hysterectomy. Against my advice, Mrs C went on taking the pill. Six months later she was suddenly rushed to Guy's Hospital with a brain haemorrhage which had followed a cerebral artery thrombosis. The vessels in the brain at operation showed thickening and clots – changes very similar to those I was seeing in the womb blood vessels of many pill takers.

Mrs C was like too many other women, too frightened to stop taking the pill, even when she knew it was making her ill.

Mrs JR

After 70 cycles on the pill Mrs JR had gained 28lb in weight. She was admitted to the Atkinson Morley neurosurgical hospital because of headaches and visual disturbances. She had raised pressure in the brain ventricles and papilloedema (swollen vessels in the back of the eye).

Benign intracranial hypertension can happen when steroid therapies such as cortisone or prednisone are stopped but it can also develop when steroids like the pill are being taken.

Sticky Platelets

When I worked in the Obstetrics department of UCH, Dr Helen Payling Wright was busy counting tiny fragments of blood cells called platelets. She found the platelets of the new mothers increased in number and stickiness each day after delivery until they reached the tenth day when thrombosis was most likely.[2] This is why women are now encouraged to get up and move around as soon as possible after childbirth. It was not until 1969 that my lecturer from Dundee, Professor Sir Alex Turnbull, then in Oxford, published the connection with taking stilboestrol.[3] He told me that some obstetricians used to give large amounts of oestrogens to induce labour. The risk of post-partum (after childbirth) thrombosis is three times greater if oestrogens have been prescribed.

I learned more about platelets from Dr Kitty Little, also in Oxford. She had spent many years investigating the effects of steroids on the bone marrow.[4] Red and white blood cells and tiny platelets are made in the marrow of our bones. Giant cells, called megakaryocytes, are responsible for the tiny platelets. One of the effects of progestogen-oestrogen pills on the marrow is to distort these developing cells, leading to a greatly increased production of abnormally sticky platelets. In her experiments, masses of tiny clots were found in the bones, liver, spleen and kidneys in rabbits. These effects are exaggerated by the adrenal stress hormones and Dr Little is convinced that HRT (oestrogen and progesterone) prescriptions will eventually cause more osteoporosis than they prevent, because of micro-thrombi in all the bones.

Thrombosis is also more likely after any surgical operation and women are advised to stop hormones beforehand. Smoking and cancer increase thrombosis. Biolab has a sticky platelet test – available to anyone. It is very interesting to see how quickly platelets usually become less sticky when the patient stops taking hormones, gives up smoking and instead takes extra fish oils (EPA) and vitamin E.

Thrombosis happens when there are changes in the blood such as sticky platelets, and alterations to clotting factors, the blood flow and vessel walls. Amongst pill users, vein complaints were more likely with progestogen pills which had either a higher dose or a higher balance of oestrogen and these pills tended to dilate the endometrial veins. Dilated veins mean blood stagnates and the circulation back to the lungs and heart is slowed down.

Most pill publicity focuses on oestrogens causing thrombosis but it is both sex hormones given together in combined pills which change the blood vessels most dramatically. It is hardly ever mentioned that target organ blood vessels, those of the womb and the ovaries, are likely to be affected, threatening a woman's future fertility.

Eye Problems

In 1965 Dr Frank Walsh in Baltimore had reviewed the international literature of sixty-three cases which involved brain or eye complications among pill takers.[5] Brain syndromes included twenty-five strokes, and eye problems were mostly due to artery or vein thrombosis. There were four cases of benign intracranial hypertension and another developed with a sixth nerve paralysis one month after the steroids had been discontinued.

Multiple Sclerosis

Dr Walsh found the eye symptoms were also caused by damage to nerves or blood vessels. There were eight cases of optic neuritis which is usually an early sign of the demyelinating disease known as multiple sclerosis (MS).

MS is thought to be a disease of the nervous system, but the earliest damage to the myelin or nerve sheaths is caused by changes in the small blood vessels around the nerves. Two of his cases did develop widespread symptoms of the disease. One of the women developed loss of vision one month after starting norethynodrel and mestranol for heavy periods and was later diagnosed as suffering from a 'fulminating demyelinising problem.' During the period 1963 to 1978 the number of hospital admissions for MS among men remained the same but amongst women nearly doubled. By 1992 four times more women than men were attending a London hospital MS clinic. This may well be a result of the pill since in experiments MS was found to be increased by the progestogen-only medroxy progesterone acetate (MPA).

HORMONE BALANCE AND BLOOD VESSEL CHANGES

Thickened Arteries

Soon after I began to examine my patients' biopsy specimens, I was surprised to discover that in some samples groups of thick-walled small arteries, known as arterioles, dominated my view down the microscope. I discovered that women with well-developed blood vessels were also having migraine attacks.[6] Often women who had headaches before they took the pill had small groups of arterioles in their pre-pill samples, which became thicker and much more obvious on the pill when their headaches got worse. Although most contraceptive pills dry up the lining of the womb and shrivel its glands, the blood vessels tend to overdevelop. *This has long-term implications as the increased vasculature can encourage the spread of endometriosis and cancer besides matching the incidence of headaches and thrombosis.*

I remembered that Dr Edris Rice-Wray had reported

seeing strange vascular patterns in the Mexico pill trials. Dr Kitty Little, an Oxford scientist, found that the male-hormone-derived progestogens, the nortestosterones, developed animals' blood vessels so that they became thicker and more irregular than usual, but the other progestogens also had this effect.[4] Perhaps this is one of the reasons why men are more susceptible than women to sudden, unexpected heart attacks. Since men's hormone levels do not fall each month headaches are less likely to warn of something wrong. Oestrogens increase immunity, and immune responses such as antibody production and allergic reactions to foods, so women are more likely to get headaches. Progesterone and testosterone do the opposite and suppress immune reactions.

Younger men, up to the age of fifty or sixty, have far more heart attacks than women. I think this is because they can tolerate lower zinc levels, more cigarette smoking and higher alcohol consumption than women can, before being warned by troublesome headaches or mood changes. Men are more likely to have underlying blood vessel changes which are symptomless. A lower normal range of zinc levels is traditionally given for men than women but, as men need more zinc, they are often deficient. Each time a man ejaculates he loses a lot of zinc – incidentally, his wife gains what he loses if they are trying for a baby! Alcohol increases the loss of both zinc and magnesium in the urine and interferes with the vital essential fatty acid (EFA) levels. Men also lose essential fatty acids in the semen and many men are deficient of the oils derived from fish, needing to take extra fish oils (EPA) in their diet to prevent clotting. This is more natural than taking aspirin which can cause bleeding. Smoking, besides increasing the risk of vascular disease, also increases the amount of cadmium in the body and cadmium antagonises and replaces zinc.

Progestogen-dominated contraceptive pills make women's hormone balance more masculine.

Switching Doses

As we went on testing more contraceptive pills, once more a pattern emerged. While most pills gave women more headaches than before, others produced fewer. The highest dose of both oestrogen and progestogen suppressed headaches and mood changes but caused too many missing periods. Lower doses caused irregular bleeding or dilated veins. The middle dose combinations caused most headaches but the differences are subtle. *A change in dose as small as 15 micrograms of oestrogen or half a milligram of progestogen can mean the difference between a pill which causes a lot of headaches or very few.*[7, 8]

When the most reactive women are changed to different pills they just get different side effects. One woman stopped having migraine when she was given less progestogen, and she was less depressed, but she had sore veins and dizziness instead. In her endometrial sample arteriole groups had been replaced by numerous small dilated veins. As the years went by, it was clear that women who had previously not reacted often, suddenly began to react with a full range of side effects and their blood vessels had changed – dilating and thickening.

Dilated Veins

Pill volunteers complained to me of distended, painful veins and leg cramps which sometimes woke them during their sleep. Under the microscope, their biopsy samples showed lots of dilated sinusoids (tiny veins) and the women with the muscle cramps had a thick layer of cells round the sinusoid walls. I wondered if this thickening was being reflected in the veins of the calf muscles, where waste products of cell metabolism were being trapped and unable to enter the blood stream. If so, the night cramps could be explained. During rest, waste products accumulate, whereas movement speeds up the return circulation. We now know pill users are often magnesium deficient.

Taking extra magnesium helps the blood circulate in the limbs and helps to prevent cramps. I published the results in the *British Medical Journal* in 1969.[9] The longer that women took the pills, the more of them had dilated sinusoids and the more chance they had of serious vascular accidents. By 1979 we had 12 cases of thrombosis among 797 new patients completing 16,892 cycles. This equals 9 per 1000 women per year. But for the 174 women completing 3027 cycles on low-progestogen-high-oestrogen pills, the thrombosis rate was 26 per 1000 per year.

Oestrogen Dose Curtailed

About the same time, the Committee on Safety of Medicine published evidence that thrombosis was more likely with a high dose of oestrogen. *All pills containing more than 0.05mg oestrogen were promptly withdrawn.*[10] But oestrogen makes women feel happy and older women especially had taken these higher balance oestrogen pills for longer, which partly explains the current HRT craze. It was also found that women over thirty-five were more likely to die of thrombosis. Throughout the 1970s there was a switch in the ages of pill takers, with teenagers becoming the main pill starting and using group by the 1980s. Women over thirty-five were advised to use other forms of contraception, a decision which temporarily stemmed the increase in breast cancer for that age group but gave pill-taking teenagers a greater future risk of this cancer.

Sweden also reduced the oestrogen in pills in 1968 and by 1980 the incidence of venous thrombo-embolic disease had fallen by 30 per cent, but there was no improvement in the incidence of arterial complications or mortality rates.[11]

In 1970 three Washington DC army pathologists studied the blood vessels of twenty young women who had died while taking oral contraceptives for as little as five weeks to thirteen months.[12] Recent clots were found in vessels *all over their bodies* including the lungs, liver, abdomen and legs of these twenty-year-olds. Most of the vessels had

65

thickened patches in the inner layers of the artery and vein walls – sometimes nearly filling the entire vessel. One had gone blind due to an arterial thrombosis in her eye. Another two had knobbly arteries and localised thickening of all three layers of the pulmonary artery – something unusual in non-pill-users. One of these women was not known to have been on the pill and had been chosen as a control but it was later discovered that she had taken an oral contraceptive for six weeks before her death.

In 1977 US Air Force gynaecologists examined the main womb artery taken from women having hysterectomies.[13] Nearly all of the forty-four patients who had taken either combined pills, or so-called 'natural' HRT oestrogens or medroxy progesterone (POP), had moderate to severe thickening of the inner layer of their arteries. The women who had never taken hormones before their hysterectomies did not have such changes. Most of the pill takers had used the pill for less than five years, but those who had taken the pill for longer had more severely affected vessels. Most had stopped the pill several years before. These changes did not relate to hypertension or smoking. Two of the HRT oestrogen users also had cancer of the endometrium.

The increased risk of haemorrhage in the tissues round the brain has been estimated as 6 times for pill users and 22 times for pill users who also smoke.[14] Weak areas in blood vessels may be present from birth and can form a sac known as an aneurysm, but the situation is aggravated by the pill and neurosurgeons have become used to operating on young women who have bled from aneurysms (subarachnoid haemorrhage) after taking oral contraceptives.

The pill can cause high blood pressure and harden artery walls. Pills which induce a lot of headaches and artery changes in the womb vessels are especially likely to cause high blood pressure. The longer a woman takes any pill, the greater the chance of her blood pressure rising. The hormones controlling the blood pressure are altered by the pill and vessel damage in the kidneys can in turn cause more blood pressure. Tiny clots in the kidneys' blood supply cause dead areas and scarring which cause a reflex rise in the chemicals responsible for raising blood pressure. Another cause of high blood pressure is kidney damage from urinary infections which are more likely to become chronic in pill takers. Many women who need kidney transplants could have had their kidneys damaged by taking the pill.

Although the majority of Western doctors in general practice prescribe the pill, very few have published detailed records and even fewer have looked directly at the blood vessel changes which so often match the symptoms. When I listed our patients alphabetically, irrespective of which pill they were on, nine out of ten women developed multiple complaints, and serious life-threatening symptoms and signs were recorded for *one women in every ten*.

In 1982 Professor Victor Wynn of St Mary's Hospital, London, published the results of a study using the lowest-dose combined pill available. After three years only 8 per cent of the original 210 women were taking it. Out of thirty-nine women entering the third year, two developed deep venous thrombosis and one had superficial thrombosis.[15]

The claim that oestrogens prevent heart attacks is non-sensical. Professor MacGillivary gave Glasgow women, who had previously had their ovaries removed, a very small dose of oestrogen, only 20 micrograms of mestranol. Within twelve weeks, 18 per cent of the women had developed thrombosis.[16]

Large-scale Trials

The results of the world's large-scale trials have given some clear insights but also helped to confuse the situation. The advertisements say that 'oestrogens' at the menopause prevent heart attacks and women who take HRT are less likely to die early: obviously not true. What has happened? At the end of the 1960s hormones, especially oestrogens, were thought to be too dangerous to give to women over thirty-five. Now women of all ages are told they are safe. A leading female endocrinologist from the Royal Free Hospital in London has published her view that most, if not all, women should take HRT. Have oestrogens suddenly changed into something quite different? Have they been metamorphosed from outer space? No – they have been sanitised by clinical trials.

Epidemiologists are people, often not medical doctors or basic scientists, who sit in offices and analyse and add up data. They may not know what the data means exactly but their 'learned pronouncements' are widely publicised. Sometimes, as with the sex hormones, their conclusions from huge multicentre trial data are the equivalent of rediscovering the wheel and finding that it is square.

The world's three large-scale pill trials were started in 1968. Details of these trials and their results are given in Appendix One. The two trials in the UK were run by the Royal College of General Practitioners and an Oxford group of epidemiologists with the results from Family Planning Association Clinics. The American study was known as the Walnut Creek trial as that was where the data was collated. The idea in these cohort trials was to follow up, for as long as possible, two groups (or cohorts of women) with only one group of women taking the pill while the other acted as a control.[17,18,19]

The reality was much more muddled.

A key confusion is that women who already had a history of illness, by then known to be made worse by the pill, were likely to be in the non-user or control group. This means the pill women were healthier from the start than the control women. Some of the controls later became pill takers and some used HRT.

Although a careful attempt was made to trace every single death, ten years later by 1979, the Oxford/FPA study listed only half as many pill users dying as would have been expected from the overall published death rate for England and Wales. There were half the deaths from cancer, half the deaths from vascular disease and less than a third of the deaths from accidents and violence.[20] After twenty years the death rate had increased and deaths from cancer had doubled.[21] (See page 278.)

The RCGP study also recorded fewer deaths among pill users and fewer cancer deaths, but they found more vascular deaths than in the general population. Only 42 per cent of their women had been followed up for symptoms, but the deaths could be checked from the national register.

The same has happened in the UK national HRT study published by the Oxford group. Women on HRT were less likely to die than in the population as a whole, and half as likely to have heart attacks. At first they were even half as likely to die of breast cancer. Wonderful!

This optimistic view of hormone risks results from starting with a healthier group of women, of higher social class, better fed, less likely to smoke. These women may also be less easily persuaded to keep taking the hormones if they feel ill and therefore less likely to go on to the bitter end. Often optimistic claims from studies are meaningless because so few women remain as long-term takers.

Dr Valerie Beral, an Australian, had noticed that more young women were dying in her country since the pill was introduced and she wrote to the *Lancet*.[22] She said it was a cause for concern that women who had ever taken the pill had 39 per cent more chance of dying of vascular disease or suicide from the RCGP data in 1974. By 1977 further RCGP data found deaths from vascular disease, mostly heart attacks or brain haemorrhages, were nearly 5 times more likely in pill takers and 10 times for those who continued to be exposed for five years or longer. Four out of every five deaths were in pill takers over thirty-five. Older non-smokers had 10 times more risk of a vascular death than younger pill takers and older smokers increased their already higher risk 5 times.[23]

A review of many international pill studies gave the

following results by 1980.[24] Pill takers had 1.5 to 11 times more risk of an embolism, 1 to 14 times more risk of a heart attack and 2 to 26 times more risk of a stroke due to either thrombosis in a brain artery or a haemorrhage in the membranes round the brain (subarachnoid haemorrhage).

Martin Vessey from Oxford said the very large differences given in the reports depended on the accuracy of the follow-up, the ages of the women given the pill, their smoking habits and the types of women chosen as 'controls'.

The only true controls would be healthy, non-smoking women, who had never taken any type of exogenous prescribed steroid hormone or fertility drug. Such women are increasingly hard to find. The second-generation effect is now coming into play whereby men and women's health is being compromised by their mother's use of hormonal steroids.

Heart Attacks

All three of the world's main pill cohort studies, set up to compare what will happen to takers with a similar group of 'never takers', have tended to exclude the most sensitive women at enrolment, and use women of higher social class who have a better than average life expectancy. The longer the study groups are followed, the more deaths are likely. Vascular deaths happen mostly to recent users and they often have warning symptoms but cancer deaths can occur up to ten or even forty years after taking hormones. The Oxford/FPA data now shows an increase in fatal heart attacks extending to women who stopped the hormones six years before.[25] In view of this finding it is strange that in a 1992 study women stopping ten years previously are being listed as non-users, probably a deliberate boost to their numbers because there are now so few never-ever-takers.[26] Such reports help to give the impression that the risk of vascular disease has declined or disappeared, although the authors do point out that they expect fewer pill deaths from heart attacks since *fewer older women (over age thirty) now take the pill and the risk of strokes or heart attacks increases ten times for older women.*[23] If a woman develops 'high risk factors' such as high blood pressure, diabetes, thrombosis or chest pain, 'better supervision and selection of users' ensure less pill taking. Advising against taking a poison doesn't make it less toxic for those who still do.

There is no evidence that prescribed hormones have become safer, other than the fact they are given to younger women.[27] Indeed seven case-control studies conducted in Britain, elsewhere in Europe and in the USA throughout the 1980s found heart attacks up to 4 times more likely among recent or past pill takers.[26]

Usually women have a lower risk of heart attacks than men. While some women begin to develop atherosclerosis about fourteen years after their menopause, the sharpest increase in heart attacks in men occurs between ages of forty and sixty. Oddly, the rate of increase tends to flatten off perhaps because older men lose their receptivity for testosterone, or perhaps the men most at risk from heart attacks have already died prematurely. Pill deaths in young women are not due to hardening of their arteries (atherosclerosis) but due to the other vascular changes I have described already. The male hormone – testosterone – lowers a protective fraction of cholesterol and so do progestogens. Oestrogen tends to raise cholesterol and other blood fats. Because oestrogens do not lower the protective fraction (high density lipoprotein – HDL_2), doctors began to believe that oestrogens, given at the menopause, would actually prevent heart disease. This betrays an amazingly simplistic approach and a ridiculous dismissal of all the many vascular changes and metabolic upsets, such as raised cortisol (stress hormone) induced by oestrogens.

Although up to 50 per cent of women in the USA have been given oestrogens as HRT, very few women over the age of sixty still take them and five years is regarded as long term! The average woman has stopped by nine months. Rather pathetic if a woman's ovaries are removed, as is increasingly happening, by the age of thirty-five.

In October 1985, the prestigious *New England Journal of Medicine* published two papers. One, from Harvard, gave results which claimed to support the hypothesis that post-menopausal use of oestrogens reduced the risk of severe coronary artery disease.[28] In this Harvard Nurses' Study, younger women, nurses aged thirty to fifty-five, were surveyed by post at two-yearly intervals. After six years the proportion of deaths due to confirmed coronary disease was small. The nurses taking oestrogens were five times more likely to have lost their ovaries and nearly twice as likely to have previously taken the pill than the non-oestrogen-taking nurses.

At each survey, as women who had already got coronary disease might alter their pattern of hormone use (that is stop taking oestrogens) and, as they were at 'increased risk of progression of the disease', they were excluded from further follow-up. There was no reduction in total mortality once women with cancer at base-line were eliminated. The paper concluded that the beneficial effects on osteoporosis or menopausal symptoms had to be weighed against the increases in endometrial and breast cancers. By 1993 only 9 per cent of the nurses were listed as current HRT takers but 43 per cent were taking vitamins. *Nine out of ten women did not believe that HRT was beneficial.*[29]

The second 1985 paper, the Framingham Heart Study, reported that their post-menopausal oestrogen users had 50 per cent more heart disease and twice as much cerebro-vascular disease as non-users.[30] In the Framingham study older women, aged between 50 and 83, were examined carefully and their electrocardiogram readings were checked. At the last examination about 17 per cent of the women in their 50s, but only 2 per cent of those over 70 were still taking hormones. Sixty per cent had taken oestrogens for three years. *Oestrogen users had a higher risk of vascular disease which was independent of other main known risks such as early menopause.* While oestrogen users weighed less and had lower-risk cholesterol profiles than the control women, they also had had these advantages *before* they started taking oestrogens. In other words, *lower-risk women are selected for oestrogen hormone replacement therapy.* Women selected may either have had no obvious side effects on the pill, or if they did have problems, they might be unaware that these have been caused or exacerbated by the pill. Although nearly a third of the oestrogen users had had a surgical menopause (and the Walnut Creek data showed significant increases in hysterectomies, pelvic and ovarian disease among young pill users) the women likely to get pelvic disease may not be the ones who are most susceptible to vascular disease. Pelvic disease increases with greater numbers of previous sexual partners.

British HRT Study

The British data was published in the *British Journal of Obstetrics and Gynaecology* in 1987.[31] Although called a cohort study, there was *no control group.* All 4,544 women surveyed had already been given oestrogens and had taken them for *at least a year* at twenty-one specialist menopause clinics around Britain. Between 1963 and 1983 the average length of time the women had taken *175 different formulations* of a few oestrogens was sixty-seven months – five and a half years. Nearly half had also been given added progestogens to 'oppose' the oestrogen stimulation of the endometrium and reduce the endometrial cancer risk. The deaths and number of cancers were compared with the national England and Wales rates. We have already seen that, by this criterion, the Oxford/FPA oral-contraceptive study had very low rates – about half for deaths and causes of deaths – although the main causes of death including vascular diseases had increased in pill users compared with their own matched controls.

73

Now that there were no matched controls, the finding that, once more, the study group had just over half (0.58) the chance of dying compared with other women in the nation, was hailed by the HRT pushers as showing that oestrogens save your life!

In spite of this artificially low death rate, cancer of the ovary was increased by 1.43 (which could be nearly 3 times for the general population), and suicide or suspected suicide was up by 2.53 (or 5 times for the country as a whole). Endometrial cancer was up 2.84 (or nearly 6 times in line with known national increases in the USA). Breast cancer was increased 1.59 (or 3 times). Only twenty women had heart attacks which was half the number expected nationwide.

One of my neighbours should have been part of this study. The forms arrived but she would not send them back. She had gained several stone in weight when taking the oestrogens and some months after stopping she suffered a temporary stroke, losing the power to move her right hand and leg. She did not want to fill in the forms as she said she felt a fool that she had taken these dangerous hormones for such a frivolous reason as trying to stay younger looking! Like my friend, one in five women did not return the forms.

By 1990, the death rate from breast cancer in the British HRT study had increased from 0.5 to 1.5. These women who had been thought to have a lower death risk now had a 50 per cent greater risk of dying of breast cancer, which is the commonest cause of death among these HRT 'ever-users'.[32]

Several reasons for the lower overall death rate of the women in the study were given in the 1987 publication. There had been a dramatic fall in HRT prescribing between 1977 and 1980 due to adverse publicity because more evidence was being published that prescribed hormones cause breast cancer and the national incidences of breast cancer were continuing to rise in hormone consuming countries. Most women had been to one of only ten clinics and started oestrogens between 1974 and 1981 when they were aged between forty-five and fifty-four. Half were younger than the natural age of the menopause and 36 per cent had already had a hysterectomy – 2 to 2.5 times more than in the British population. Sixty per cent of this age group had never taken the pill. Importantly, twice as many women belonged to social class 1 and 2 as in the country as a whole (46 compared with 23 per cent). At least 31 per cent were smoking but as up to 60 per cent women in the other social classes smoke, a lower heart attack risk would be expected among these higher class women. Most important of all is the fact that none of the most sensitive women, those who gave up HRT within twelve months and were more likely to have reactive blood vessels, were included in the follow-up. According to recent surveys *70 per cent of women discontinue HRT within a year and only 7 per cent last 8 years*. In the world's case-control studies very few women take HRT for long.

In spite of the lack of valid evidence, other than the fact that oestrogen dilates blood vessels, prevention of heart attacks is given as a reason for prescribing HRT and listed as a cost benefit, while smoking is blamed for most of the vascular deaths. It was decided women had very little chance of dying from a clot or haemorrhage if they didn't smoke. It is true that the effects of the steroid hormones on the clotting mechanisms or over-reactions of the blood vessels are greatly exaggerated by smoking but an important point, nearly always overlooked, is that hormone takers who don't smoke are more at risk than smokers who don't take hormones. This fact was obvious in the 1960s but became obscured by the 1990s due to the scarcity of never-takers.

Mrs K
I know several women who had heart attacks while taking oestrogens and have been well since giving them up. A patient, Mrs K, told me the other week that her doctor

didn't believe the chest pains radiating down her arms even merited investigation. The doctor believed that oestrogens prevented heart attacks and had decided that this lady was simply neurotic. Mrs K was fifty-one and had smoked twenty cigarettes a day for twenty-four years in spite of having asthma. She was given HRT in the form of patches stuck on to her skin slowly releasing oestrogen. For the first six months she didn't feel too bad and then she had violent palpitations and anxiety. Her oestrogen dose was actually *increased* from 50 to 100 micrograms. She then had violently severe headache and chest and arm pains. A pharmacist told her to reduce the oestrogen dose gradually. Mrs K had attacks of hot flushes alternating with cold spells and she was sure her aorta was thumping in her abdomen. All these symptoms were at their peak when she was using the patches and improved when the patches were removed although Mrs K went on smoking. Dissatisfied with her general practitioner, she changed to a well-known female general practitioner. The new doctor (who tragically soon after this was taken ill with cancer) said she took HRT herself and, in her opinion, Mrs K would not be better unless she restarted the oestrogen. Investigation at Biolab showed Mrs K was suffering from severe shortages of magnesium in her sweat, hair and red cells, chromium deficiency in her sweat and serum, while her hair showed high copper due to the oestrogens, and abnormally low manganese and low cobalt (in vitamin B12) due to tobacco smoking. Further tests showed deficiencies of protective essential fatty acids and excesses of more harmful fats, including cholesterol. Mrs K's imbalances can cause arterial disease and explained how appropriate supplements and a low-allergy diet would help her to stop smoking and soon make her feel better. The irony is that Mrs K has not yet reached the menopause. Since taking the nutritional supplements her periods have become regular and her hormone levels normal.

Preventing Headaches, Flushings and Raised Blood Pressure

By the mid to late 1960s I was convinced that exogenous hormones would soon be taken off the market. Surely doctors could not continue to be allowed to prescribe such dangerous drugs! I was also informed that I 'knew too much' for family planning work and that I should stick to research instead. My publications on migraine interested the Migraine Trust – a large charity which organises prestigious international conferences and runs migraine clinics. Dr Marcia Wilkinson, of St Bartholomews Hospital and the City Clinic, asked me 'if the pill is causing migraine in women, what is the cause in men?' By the late 1970s, after working in migraine clinics at Guildford and Charing Cross Hospital, London, we had published some of the answers. Smoking turned out to be the main culprit causing tension headaches or migraine in men. Seven out of ten men patients smoked compared with one in three women. One in three men and one in five women were addicted to ergotamine which had been prescribed for the most severe migraines.[33] One in three women were taking hormones, mostly the contraceptive pill, as HRT had not yet been vigorously pushed. In the 1980s and 1990s more older women on HRT are going to migraine clinics. In the 1970s most of my patients were either smoking, taking ergotamine or using so-called low-dose pills. *When persuaded to stop these practices, both men and women had ten times fewer headaches and migraine attacks over the next three months.*[34]

The Charing Cross Migraine Clinic, now known as the Princess Margaret Migraine Clinic, runs an emergency service. Anyone can walk in off the street and be treated. When these acute, self-referred patients were compared with doctor-referred patients, a difference emerged. Few non-users needed emergency treatment. One in three of smokers, both men and women, had needed acute treatment, half of the hormone takers, but six out of ten women who took hormones *and* smoked, had been treated during a migraine attack. The average duration of smoking was 25 years for men and 23 years for women. But the average duration of hormone use was only 4 years for non-smokers and 3 years for smokers. Clearly, *exogenous steroid hormones were causing more severe migraine attacks, in a much shorter time than smoking,* presumably because of their more direct action on blood vessels and the neuro-transmitter chemicals.

The same difference applies to heart attack risks – coronary disease incidence takes off when smokers have smoked 200,000 cigarettes on average or 20 cigarettes for 25 years. *But less than five years of hormone exposure is enough to induce an episode of serious vascular illness in susceptible women, either while the hormones are being taken or in the years immediately following.*[35]

Migraine research is also confused by the prescription of other drugs. If a patient had just headaches, they were diagnosed as 'tension headaches' and the patient given Valium or a long-acting type – Ativan. If they complained of sickness or visual disturbances they were prescribed ergotamine. Dr Wilkinson realised that ergotamine often made patients worse. About one in every two people given an ergot drug becomes so ill with so much nausea and vomiting that they refuse to take ergot again. For the rest, ergot can seem like a magic cure – nothing else can make their excruciating headache disappear so quickly.

Ergot is a fungus. In the Middle Ages, St Antony's Fire sometimes raged through the population. When the weather had been damp and the grain had gone mouldy, it became very toxic. Moulds like the ergot fungus constrict blood vessels causing severe headaches, heart attacks and even gangrene. The Romans knew the importance of drying their grain and used under-floor heating in their grain stores.

Why do ergot drugs sometimes help? The theory is that in common or classical migraine, the early sickness and disturbances in vision are due to dilatation of blood vessels. As ergot constricts, there would be immediate benefit. For anyone whose main problem is blood vessel constriction, ergot would obviously exacerbate the headache. Moulds and fungi tend to act like oestrogens, so women, taking the pill or HRT, who also smoke and take ergot, have the most severe and frequent migraines. Ergot is so addictive that even those patients who can tolerate it at first usually become dependent on taking it daily or several times a week in an attempt to prevent severe daily migraines. This takes an average of about five years to achieve.

It seems amazing that doctors were relying on a variety of highly addictive drugs rather than trying to get the patients to stop taking exogenous hormones or to stop them smoking. Of course, it is much easier to write a prescription than to struggle with addiction, or to find alternatives for contraception and menopausal symptoms, but, it seems the only logical course of action. I was especially concerned that so many women, in their child-bearing years, were given drugs which could cause infertility, miscarriages or damage their babies. In the same way, there is little regard for the effect these drugs may have on sperm development, quality, motility or numbers. There is also little attention paid to the importance of headaches and migraine as warnings for both men and women that they may go on to develop serious vascular complications like heart attacks and strokes.

We do not have deficiencies of aspirin, paracetamol, codeine, Valium, ergotamine and so on, but we can and do often have deficiencies of our essential and vital nutrients. In the 1980s the message about smoking began to get through, but most doctors are as keen on exogenous hormones as ever in the 1990s.

By 1979 I had published in the *Lancet* what happened when patients, who still had headaches after stopping smoking and taking hormones, followed Dr John Mansfield's low-allergy rotation diet, avoiding grains, dairy products, yeast, tea, coffee or any other food which caused a pulse change or symptoms after four days of lamb and pears.[36, 37] The results were dramatic. Headaches disappeared and raised blood pressure levels fell to normal. *All (100 per cent) of these hospital patients improved and 85 per cent remained headache-free, needing no further medication.*

To this day no more effective way to treat migraine has been published as far as I know. Avoiding precipitants is in theory very simple and yet an array of drugs continue to be prescribed. The excessive reactivity of a migraine sufferer can be prevented by ensuring adequate levels of essential nutrients.

A severe attack of classical migraine, preceded by spots before the eyes and sickness, is one of life's most painful experiences. Why are some people susceptible and not others? Sufferers often have a family history of migraine and know they have headaches if they become over stressed or eat too much cheese or chocolate or drink red wine. Three times more women than men are affected. Women's headaches usually come on each month just before their periods as part of the premenstrual syndrome (PMS), when the high levels of oestrogen and progesterone in the last half of the cycle suddenly fall. Doctors have given women oestrogen or progesterone with no lasting benefit because hormone-level changes are not at the root of the problem. There is no reason why changes of hormone levels in a healthy woman should precipitate headaches. It is a man or woman's inability to metabolise and deal with changes in brain chemicals – the neurotransmitters – which causes the flashing lights, vomiting and excruciating pain.

Headaches are a warning that something is wrong. The brain has become overexcited and there are changes in its electrical discharges. Blood vessels in the brain's surrounding membranes dilate and constrict excessively. The same chemicals control blood vessel reactivity and the transmission of messages in the brain. Normally these chemicals, such as adrenaline and serotonin, are regulated automatically – excessive rises or falls in their levels are avoided. The enzymes facilitating these pathways have weak points. They need to have enough zinc, magnesium and B vitamins. When these essential co-factors are in short supply it is as if we have become stuck in the wrong gear and headaches or mood changes can be the result.

Deficiencies of Zinc and Magnesium

When I compared fifty men and women who got regular headaches with fifty who rarely did, there were significant differences in their sweat and blood levels of zinc and magnesium. The average values for those complaining of headaches were below the Biolab normal range. All were either zinc or magnesium deficient and most were deficient in both. There were no differences in the other essential minerals measured. When headache sufferers are supplemented, their zinc and magnesium levels usually rise into the normal range.[38] This doesn't mean that they will no longer get headaches or hangovers from alcohol, but they have become much less susceptible, compensating for the familial tendency which probably stemmed from nutrient deficiencies during early development.

Taking prescribed hormones compromises these automatic systems and alters the development and reactivity of our blood vessels whether or not we have side effects. For most young and middle-aged men and women there is no need to suffer from headaches or migraine. Flushing or cold sweats are also signs of vascular over-reactivity. These symptoms are most noticeable at the menopause, when a woman loses the suppressive action of her steroid sex hormones. They are not an indication for HRT, which will make her underlying problems worse but usually indicate zinc and magnesium deficiences. Instead changes in lifestyle and diet are a better bet for future health.

Vascular disease is the commonest cause of death among the elderly and eventually the human body wears out but it is estimated that in the UK three to 6 million working days are lost due to migraine with economic losses of up to £300 million annually. In 1979, my *Lancet* paper had showed that most of the suffering and excessive costs are unnecessary. But for those who continue to take drugs and exogenous hormones, simple preventative methods are usually ineffective in the long term.

KEY POINTS

- Pill hormones change blood vessels – dilate and thicken arteries and veins in the womb, legs, eyes, brain and throughout the body causing migraine, palpitations, high blood pressure, clots, strokes and heart attacks.
- Very small dose changes switch type of side effects.
- In 1969 pills with more than 50 micrograms oestrogen were withdrawn but 20 micrograms caused thrombosis in one in five women hysterectomised within 12 weeks in one study.
- Risk of pill-induced vascular death (strokes or heart attacks) is 10 times higher for women over age 35.
- Misleading low overall death rates in pill and HRT trials while deaths from main causes increase.
- Prescribed hormones cause serious vascular illnesses sooner than smoking (4 years compared with 25 years).
- Avoiding prescribed hormones, smoking, drugs and changing diet dramatically prevents migraine, headaches, reversible high blood pressure and other forms of vascular over-reaction such as menopausal flushings.

Chapter Four

Preventing PMT, Post-natal and Menopausal Depression

Glowing Well-being or Moody Blues?

A healthy mother-to-be glows. She feels well, looks well, walks with a proud carriage and has a sparkle in her eyes as she looks forward to the birth of her baby.

Oestrogens give this feeling of well-being. Nowadays, women who are nearing or who have passed the age of their natural menopause, or those who have had their ovaries removed surgically before they are fifty, try to emulate a pregnant woman by taking oestrogens. Older women on HRT have pregnancy-like high copper levels. But is this good for them?

Young women, before they are ready to start their families, are given ovulation blocking hormones to dry up their secretions. Low doses of progestogens and oestrogens are substituted for their own higher fluctuating hormone levels. This results in young women mimicking older women past the menopause. No wonder the world's largest pill study lists 'neurotic depression' as the commonest reason for giving up the pill.

> Oestrogens lift the mood.
> Progestogens can cause depression.

These facts of life have become so obvious to doctors

promoting oestrogens as HRT that they are reluctant to add a progestogen to prevent endometrial cancer developing in 'those women unlucky enough still to have a womb', as a leading HRT expert said on national television. Another gynaecologist thought it was worth taking the chance of womb cancer rather than have women put off their HRT by the return of premenstrual symptoms which accompany the addition of a progestogen to the oestrogens.

By 1968, we had published the details of the mood and enzyme changes caused by the different oral contraceptives.[1,2] One drug company tried to buy enough copies of the paper to supply every doctor in Australia and New Zealand in order to advertise the fact that fewer women became depressed on their mostly oestrogen-sequential pills compared with the usual combined pills. The *British Medical Journal* declined to print so many reprints. Nowadays, the pill depression problem has been dealt with in two ways. Lower doses are given to very young women who are less likely to become depressed. These lower-dose pills can cause irregular bleeding in up to 20 per cent of cycles. In the 1960s we regarded 6 per cent breakthrough bleeding as the safe contraceptive limit so now there are more unplanned pregnancies.

Women are More Moody than Men

It has been known throughout history that women are likely to become moody and unpredictable at certain times each month. So close is the time-worn association of strange behaviour with monthly cycles, that is has become part of our language. The word lunatic is derived from the Latin word for moon.

Apart from when a woman is taking prescribed hormones, depressive mood changes are more likely when the levels of both oestrogen and progestogens fall.

1 PMT – premenstrual tension.
  Pent-up feelings of irritability, anxiety and depression

84

are common a day or two before a period, affecting seven out of ten older women. These feelings are often suddenly relived when the bleeding starts.

2 Post-natal depression.
During pregnancy there are high levels of both hormones which suddenly fall when labour and delivery are underway. For some months after delivery, while a woman is breast feeding, she has lower oestrogen levels and no rises in progestogen as she is not ovulating.

3 Menopausal depression.
Again hormone levels fall. Ovulation ceases so progesterone levels are minimal and oestrogen levels sharply decline. But not all older women are depressed so it is the sudden fall in hormone levels that seems to cause depression in some susceptible women.

Brain Essentials in Our Food

It is the same brain chemicals which control both blood vessel reactivity and mood changes. Once again shortage of zinc, magnesium and B vitamins prevent enzymes from coping with chemical changes. Women with PMT or PMS (when headaches, distention, bloating, fluid retention, breast pains are added to irritability) have lower than normal levels of these essential minerals and vitamins.[3] Low levels of the key essentials fatty acids, like those obtained from evening primrose oil, are also found in men and women with depression and schizophrenia and in women with PMS.[4]

What do Cheese, Chocolate and Red Wine Have in Common?

In the early 1960s it was accidentally discovered that a drug which blocked the action of the monoamine oxidase (MAO) enzymes prevented depression.

The brain's chemical messengers – neurotransmitters – are made from breaking down proteins in our diet. Proteins break down to make amino acids and amines which have a powerful and often immediate action on the brain. Cheese, especially the mouldy variety, is packed with tyramine; chocolate has lots of phenylethylamine, and alcoholic drinks like red wine can be high in histamine. Headaches are induced in susceptible people if they eat too much of any of these, especially those who are short of zinc and magnesium and B vitamins which are needed for the enzymes in the breakdown pathways. Several enzymes are also involved in the breakdown, including MAO enzymes.

If the MAO enzymes are very active the amine levels may fall too low and cause depression.

Progestogens stimulate MAO and can cause depression.

If the MAO enzymes are too inactive, amine levels may rise too high causing headaches or migraine or high blood pressure or a manic feeling.

Oestrogens suppress MAO giving a feeling of well-being.

The first MAOI, monoamine oxidase inhibitor drug, was given to treat tuberculosis. There was surprise and excitement when the TB patients, who were also depressed, became quite happy. MAOI drugs soon became widely used in psychiatry to treat depression. Then some of the treated patients began to complain of excruciating headaches and some even developed brain haemorrhages. These reactions were found to be especially likely if the patients had eaten cheese, chocolate, yeast extracts used in gravy, or drunk alcohol. Because the MAO enzymes were blocked, the amine levels had risen too quickly, causing spasm, rupture and haemorrhage. Since then all patients are warned to avoid these foods and drinks if they are taking MAOI drugs. Other drugs commonly used in psychiatry such as the tricyclics also change amine levels, making heart attacks more likely. When given with oestrogens, their action can be made more powerful, sometimes with tragic consequences.

Mrs MK

Mrs MK had been taking oestrogens for years. She was given 'natural' mare's oestrogens when she felt ill after a hysterectomy and removal of her ovaries in her late thirties. When she tried to do without the hormones she became breathless, so she restarted the oestrogens and felt well again.

She looked young for her age, her hair and skin were lovely, she dressed well and she was happily looking after her children. But gradually Mrs MK became more and more anxious, restless and upset. She became worried about the children, felt trapped in her beautiful home and felt life had no future for her.

By now she was seeing a psychiatrist who was giving her anti-depressants. Neither she nor the psychiatrist believed that her condition was affected by taking oestrogens; they both thought her problems were mental. She had been told that oestrogens were given to treat menopausal depression and she was sure her symptoms were due to lack of oestrogens if she didn't take them. The anti-depressants made her much worse, however. She became violent and, sadly, her second suicide attempt ended with her death.

Mrs P

Just this week I saw a patient who was taking an MAOI drug. As soon as I opened the door, I noticed she seemed withdrawn and unresponsive. She had tried many doses and types of anti-depressants with little benefit. However Mrs P was managing to work and maintain a fairly normal lifestyle but she was complaining of headaches, lasting for several days every month. Her zinc and magnesium levels were low and she had gut candida – a yeast overgrowth. Her headaches cleared and her energy returned following a low-allergy diet and taking supplements and anti-candida treatment.

Dr John Howard and Dr Adrian Hunniset, of Biolab, find that if the mineral levels are low, especially zinc and magnesium, the vitamin levels are also usually low and there tend to be imbalances in the essential amino acids in the blood and urine.[5] More rarely, patients can have normal mineral levels and only have deficiencies in B vitamins. The first vitamin deficiency to be recognised in oral contraceptive users was pyridoxine B6 and it is known that deficiency in B6 alone can cause depression.[6]

Mr D
Recently I was asked if I could help a young man. His friends were worried on his behalf as he was attractive and likeable but inexplicably depressed. His illness had started when he was shooting up in his teens to a height of over six feet. It is quite common for tall young men to be zinc deficient when they are growing, sometimes even leading to suicide when pressure of studying is blamed. Mr D was too depressed and lethargic to work on his PhD thesis. He had convinced himself that it was no good and would never be any good. I told him he was likely to be short of zinc and magnesium so he made an appointment to be tested at Biolab straight away. His doctors were going to give him anti-depressant drugs if he didn't improve soon. Much to my surprise, his mineral profile was completely normal. Luckily, he had had his vitamin profile checked and there was the answer – abnormally low vitamin B6. After a few weeks of taking supplements, the PhD thesis seemed easy and previous doubts were soon forgotten. I reminded him to keep taking his vitamins in case his deficiency recurred and his depression returned.

Stress also affects the amine pathways by producing cortisol from the adrenal glands and dropping zinc levels. High steroid hormone levels minimise the stress effect and when there is a fall in steroid hormone levels – in women, each month, after a baby or at the menopause – mood changes and vascular reactivity are increased.

But it is quite complicated as high steroid levels suppress many reactions including allergic-type reactions to food – so many different changes are happening when steroid hormone levels fall. A further complication is that taking exogenous prescribed hormones raises cortisol levels, stimulating the stress amine-break-up pathways and shunting them in the wrong directions. The result is shortages of minerals and vitamins and the production of abnormal chemicals, including carcinogens which are secreted into the urine.

When I first started testing hormones for contraception in 1961, the background biochemistry was still to be discovered, but we already knew about premenstrual tension. For decades scientific papers had established that women were more likely to have accidents or commit crimes before or during their periods. Since 1931 supplements of magnesium and calcium had been used in the USA to treat PMT, but it has taken fifty years to establish exactly how important magnesium is in preventing irritability and fluid retention. Graham Greene's brother, Dr Raymond Greene, described the premenstrual syndrome in 1953.[7] He emphasised that water retention was an important part of the syndrome and said this was a sign of adrenal hormone overactivity. Progesterone relieved the symptoms in some women and Dr Greene's assistant Dr Katherina Dalton has continued to prescribe progesterone for PMS with great enthusiasm.[8] Dr Greene remained doubtful that progesterone therapy was a universal panacea and he was very interested in my pill discoveries of changing blood vessels and moods with different balances of hormones.

Dr Dalton investigated the effects of PMS on women. One previous publication had reported women air pilots were more likely to crash, while another described how French women prisoners, convicted of violent crimes, had committed 85 per cent of their offences in the critical premenstrual phase. Dr Dalton repeated the French study in England and found that women were more likely to commit crimes before a period. She took the matter further and found that children's illnesses can also depend on their mothers' cycles. Not only are women more likely to be off work, sick or admitted to hospital at period times, but their children are also more at risk of being taken to a doctor or admitted to hospital. Some mothers realised they had been unnecessarily violent with their children just before their periods when their feelings of tension were unbearable.

When reviewing Dr Dalton's book for the *BMJ*, although admiring her work on the symptoms of PMS, I disagreed that progesterone should be prescribed to suppress them.[9]

Mood Changes with the Pill

PMT increases with age, marriage and number of children, and about four in every ten of our pill volunteers usually had some symptoms each month. With the first high-dose-progestogen-low-oestrogen pill, 26 per cent experienced less tension, 11 per cent said it was worse and 5 per cent felt no different. Daily doses of pill hormones mask PMT. Instead of the normal sudden change in brain chemicals just before a period, the chemistry is changed throughout pill cycles and particular symptoms can intensify.[10]

What was soon very clear was that different pills caused different mood changes. Some pills made women depressed and lose interest in love making, others caused tiredness, fatigue and irritability.

A paper in the *Lancet* at that time described how there were changes in MAO activity in the lining of the womb just before a woman's normal cyclic bleeding.[11] By then I had realised that the pills causing immediate depression and loss of libido were progestogen-dominant. The late secretory phase was prolonged from the normal two or three days to as long as two or three weeks. I wondered whether these depression-inducing pills increased MAO activity more than others. With this question in my mind I rushed off to see Professor Martin Sandler who had been helping me investigate the pill headaches in the Department of Chemical Pathology at Queen Charlotte's Maternity Hospital. He was not impressed, but his pathologist colleague, Dr John Pryse-Davies stepped in to help by promising to stain our endometrial samples to see whether the MAO activity was strong, weak or moderate.

I collected samples in the usual way and froze them immediately for their journey. The little bottles were put in a thermos and a special delivery boy took them on the back of his motorcycle to Queen Charlotte's. Apart from one day when the thermos exploded and we lost the specimens, we were to carry out this regular chore for two years until we had six groups of results.

Besides MAO, two other enzymes – alkaline and acid phosphatases were also measured. At that time I did not know the significance of the other two enzymes but we now know that alkaline phosphatase is important for absorption in the gut and possibly connected with the development of food allergies.

These results were even more conclusive than I had imagined. *All three enzymes were altered by oestrogen and progesterone.* My suspicion that the very depressive pills might cause greater MAO changes in the endometrium was confirmed. Sure enough, these pills induced high MAO activity for most of the month. These results were even more conclusive than I had imagined.

This was very exciting, because once more it seemed obvious that what was happening in the lining of the womb was going on elsewhere in the body, especially in the brain. One in four women became depressed on high-dose progestogen pills combined with a low 50 microgram dose of oestrogen. Of 214 women taking these pills, 28 per cent had depressive mood changes compared with only 6 per cent of 301 women taking the oestrogen sequentials. The rate for 702 women taking other pills was between 16 and 20 per cent, but these weaker combined pills caused more irregular bleeding. One high-dose pill, with high MAO levels due to the progestogen, only depressed 3 per cent of the women taking it because it was combined with a high dose of oestrogen. The lower-dose progestogen and low-oestrogen pills now commonly used can cause depression in about one in ten women depending on their age and susceptibility.

It became clear that oestrogen increases amine production and prevents depression but too much progestogen causes depression, presumably by increasing amine breakdown and lowering tissue levels. Tiredness and irritability were more likely with the weaker doses but these, of course, also cause more irregular bleeding, and increased pregnancy risk. What we were suggesting was not eagerly greeted. We sent our results to a clinical biochemical journal in the United States to have it returned, about a year later, with the comment that it was 'ludicrously unscientific to suggest that a chemical change in the womb could be connected with brain changes'. Eventually our paper appeared in the *British Medical Journal*.[2]

When Dr Sandler saw how well our results had worked out he agreed to measure MAO biochemically, and in 1967 we were ready to publish the changes in the normal cycle. We had discovered that the rise in MAO activity was dramatic, ranging from below 1,000 to more than 20,000 units of activity.[12] The high levels were only found in the late secretory specimens – meaning that women have to cope with a twenty times change in enzyme activity just before a period. MAO activity in the blood increases, then falls before the period begins. The latest research, thirty years after our discovery, makes the connection between brain and womb changes more likely.

The sequential pills, oestrogen only for the first eleven or fifteen days, had low MAO throughout the cycle. Adding a progestogen for the last ten or fifteen days did not increase the MAO activity and few women became depressed taking these pills.

In women it is known that oestrogens are converted into highly active 'catechol' oestrogens which control amine metabolism in the sensitive areas of the brain and in target organs like the uterus and ovaries. It is not ludicrous to suggest that womb changes might give a more direct indication of changes in the brain than measurements of blood levels.

Animals Too

Techniques now available show how different areas in the brain respond to hormone and amine stimuli. The natural hormone progesterone has been shown to alter brain MAO in animals and particular areas are being mapped out in animals' brains according to their reactions to hormone and amine stimuli.

In the 1960s Dr Richard Michael, working at the Institute of Psychiatry, gave progesterone to female monkeys and found that they were less interested in the males who, incidentally, became less interested in them. He discovered that vaginal secretions contain copulins which are made by normal vaginal bacteria. Progesterone changed the vaginal cells, just as it alters the cells in the womb, and the bacteria produced less copulin. Dr Michael also discovered that the same process happens in women taking the pill.[13]

Sensitive Women

Some women develop symptoms with any prescribed hormones. This is what happened to three of them.

Mrs NL
Mrs NL took a very-low-dose-progestogen-high-dose-oestrogen pill (ethynodiol diacetate 0.1mg + mestranol 0.1mg) for nineteen months. She asked to change to something else because of heavy irregular bleeding with cramps and numbness in her feet. Her endometrial biopsy showed lots of dilated sinusoides.

She changed to the 1mg dose of the same pill. Her leg and feet symptoms disappeared and her periods became very scanty. This time she wanted to stop after only three months because she had lost interest in sex, in spite of the high dose of oestrogen. Although this pill was strongly progestogenic the effect of the oestrogen dose made some women have vein symptoms and two out of thirty women developed thrombophlebitis.

Mrs NL then tried a sequential pill with the same high dose of oestrogen for twenty-one days and a progestogen (chlormadinone 2mg) added for ten days. She still complained of depression and loss of libido and changed once more to the 0.25mg dose of ethynodiol diacetate plus mestranol. She took it for fourteen months but had irregular bleeding for eleven of these cycles.

Mrs ID
Mrs ID started on the same low (0.1mg)-progestogen-high-oestrogen pill but after twenty-seven months bled continuously for thirty-five days. She changed to the 0.25mg dose but bled for fifteen days after seven cycles and she complained of dizziness. Her next pill was the 0.5mg dose which she took for thirteen months before stopping it because of headaches, dizziness, severe cramps in her right leg and putting on fourteen pounds in weight.

Of the twenty other patients trying this particular pill, one collapsed with severe chest pain, one was admitted to hospital for an acute anxiety state and another for abdominal pains.

Mrs VO
Mrs VO took three different doses of norgestrel with a low (0.05mg)-dose oestrogen. She was thirty-seven and had ten children but no miscarriages.

She had suffered premenstrual tension, depression and headaches before her periods and occasional leg cramps. She started with 0.1mg of norgestrel and after nine cycles she had two irregular bleeding cycles, more leg cramps than usual and her varicose veins had burst on two occasions.

She then took the 0.25mg dose for twelve months and gained nine pounds in weight. She was changed to the 0.5mg dose because the lower dose had been discontinued for causing too much breakthrough bleeding. Twelve months later she stopped the pill altogether as she had developed swollen fingers and ankles, was fainting and had feelings of tightness in her chest.

If the dose of a progestogen is increased from 0.1mg to 3mg and combined with a same dose of oestrogen (for example, 50 micrograms of ethinyloestradiol), women's symptoms can change from breakthrough bleeding to vein effects such as distended leg veins, leg cramps, thrombosis, to arterial effects such as headaches and hypertension and on to depression and loss of libido and weight gain. So-called 'neurotic' symptoms like tiredness, anxiety and irritability are most severe with lower dose progestogen pills with a higher balance of oestrogen.

Pills which rapidly change both arteries and veins cause most weight gain, anxiety, aggression and violence. One pill, similar to some still on the market, had severe mood effects including aggression, violence and loss of memory.

Mrs N

Mrs N was twenty-three. She had been happily taking a pill for two years when she began to change. Gradually over the next ten months she got more irritable. One day she exploded with anger at her husband and threw a frozen chicken at him. Luckily he was unhurt, but he had to tell her about the attack as she had lost her memory and couldn't remember what had happened. Another woman on the same pill threw a large biscuit tin at her husband. Although this pill did not depress, it seemed particularly likely to cause violent mood swings. Similar pills to Mrs N's are still being prescribed.

There are other mood changes too, including some *increased* libidos – not entirely surprising as most of the pills have male-hormone-like actions. One patient, a beauty therapist, complained of growing dark body hairs. Another pill, with male-hormone-like actions in animal tests, and a slightly higher balance of oestrogen, had a peculiar effect on sex drive and mood. One woman, for example, went on a bus trip and had to suppress an over-whelming desire to hug and kiss the driver! This was quite out of character, she said.

Some HRT proponents are actually giving women testosterone as HRT and Germaine Greer gives an amusing account of the effect this had on her.

The switching of symptoms with different doses and balances of the sex hormones is not surprising, as the same neurotransmitters are involved in the control of mood, behaviour and blood vessel reactions. Mood changes are not only caused by combinations of progestogens and oestrogens. Although oestrogen is commonly used to treat depression, either oestrogen or progesterone given alone can cause many serious metabolic upsets, including dramatically raising levels of blood copper in susceptible women – those who have a tendency to manic depression or schizophrenia.

The Copper Enzyme

There are two main amine breakdown pathways. When we are excited or frightened, we make adrenaline as part of the fight or flight reaction in the catechol amine pathway. An important enzyme involved in this amine breakdown is catechol-o-methyl transferase (COMT).[14] At the Guildford Migraine Clinic we found that patients suffering from the most severe attacks, usually those taking ergotamine, oestrogens and/or progestogens, had lower or higher COMT levels in their red cells than normal.[15] COMT is a copper-dependent enzyme. We now know that copper levels can be pushed too high by infection, and perhaps by oestrogen-like fungi. When the copper stores are being depleted, copper levels can be too low.

In 1968, Halsted and his colleagues had published the fact that both oestrogens and progestogens increase the circulation of proteins in the blood plasma.[16] One of the plasma proteins, ceruloplasmin, carries copper, and blood copper levels rise. At the same time zinc levels fall. For balanced mental health, zinc and copper influences need to be equal. The phrase 'mentally unbalanced' has real meaning! High-dose pills can change the colour of plasma to green, as we spotted in blood banks. Professor Carl Pfeiffer, in 1972, reported that some schizophrenics had high blood copper levels and these could be three times higher than even normal pregnancy levels if they took contraceptive pills.[17]

Blood copper can rise due to a few years of pill or HRT use, long-term infection in the cervix or tubes or use of the copper containing intrauterine device (IUD) or due to ovulation-stimulating fertility drugs. When copper levels in serum, sweat and hair have been forcibly elevated for too long, zinc levels are forced down and copper stores become depleted. The first sign is a fall in serum copper. This is followed by lower sweat and later by lower hair levels. At this point extra zinc supplementation will lower both zinc and copper levels. A small amount of copper, 3mg, is given on alternate mornings for three weeks only, while zinc, 30mg, is given each night. This restores the copper/zinc balance, which is essential for mental stability, by switching back on the liver metabolism.

Steroid hormones including hydrocortisone, progesterone and oestrogen exaggerate the effect of adrenaline on an individual. In 1969 Kalsner reported this was because the steroids blocked the action of COMT.[18] Other investigators found depressed women were more likely to have low COMT activity than depressed men.

Vitamin B6 is involved in both amine breakdown pathways, so shortage of B6 will also lead to lack of mental balance. In 1969, David Rose, working at St Mary's

Hospital in London, discovered that oestrogens, oral contraceptives, cortisol (stress) and pregnancy divert the amine pathways so that more vitamin B6 is needed and B6 becomes deficient.[19] Low levels of the key amines in the brain cause depression and women who were depressed on the pill improved when vitamin B6 was given. Vitamin B6 is involved both in the production of key amines and in their break-up.

On the one hand, prescribed oestrogens may treat depression by raising some amine levels, but, by increasing amine breakdown and by causing co-enzyme deficiencies, oestrogens can actually induce more mental upsets and uncontrolled blood vessel reactivity. For this reason prescribing oestrogen to depressed women is not sensible.

In the last few years, 'crusading zealots' for HRT have been anxious to prove the well-being of women taking oestrogens. Trials have shown that oestrogens improve post-natal, premenstrual and menopausal depression and yet the average duration of HRT use in the UK is only four to five months, and less than one in three women given oestrogens continue to take them. The experience of most women would not be recorded in the British HRT trial as only tougher women managing to tolerate oestrogens for at least twelve months were included. When higher than expected rates of attempted suicide and violent deaths were recorded among HRT takers the excuse was that more women suffering from depression are put on oestrogens in an attempt to treat them. The fact that the fatalities from mental illness are increasing with longer oestrogen exposure shows how wrong the doctors are who pursue these optimistic but shallow beliefs to the bitter end.

Results from large-scale studies are given in detail in Appendix One. *The three pill trials and the British HRT study all record increased mental illness and violent deaths among hormone takers including more suicides among women taking oestrogen HRT.*

I am always reluctant to prescribe mood-changing and

often addictive drug treatments to anyone but especially to women in their childbearing years. Partly because I don't think they get to the root causes but also because some medications can cause foetal abnormalities. Lithium is taken by one in every thousand women and while it effectively prevents suicide over the long term, it can induce heart abnormalities in babies if taken during pregnancy. MAOIs, tricyclics and some tranquillisers can cause vitamin B deficiencies, which, in turn, can cause congenital abnormalities. If the women's problems are due to food allergies, genital infections or gut candida, antidepressant drugs are not going to treat these. Most migraine patients also have depressive symptoms before starting the lamb and pears diet but rapidly feel better when their allergens are excluded. A course of tetracyclines can improve premenstrual symptoms in women with pelvic inflammatory disease and antifungal diet and treatment are perhaps the most effective ways of treating mental illness.[20]

Hormones taken by the mother in early pregnancy can cause cancer or genital abnormalities in her children. The stilboestrol (DES) studies inform us that babies subject to exogenous oestrogens in early foetal life are more likely to develop mental illnesses and become suicidal.[21] Offspring of animals given oestrogens are more likely to become violent.[22]

A review paper in the *Lancet* suggests that oestrogens may be addictive, saying that dependence on some drugs can be hard to recognise.[23] Drugs that promote a feeling of well-being are suspect. Oestrogen binds to numerous sites in the brain and often drugs of abuse share some of the same sites. Father-and-daughter team, Drs Bewley and Bewley, think that women at the menopause might be especially likely to become addicted to their prescribed oestrogens.

They say that, as ageing affects the ability of the receptors in the cell nucleus to bind oestrogen, giving older women extra oestrogen continuously switches off the receptors. The result is more and more oestrogen is needed to raise amine levels. Very high oestrogen levels have been measured in 3–15 per cent of women who have been implanted under their skin with pellets of oestrogen. (Blood oestradiol levels in women taking tablets, patches or implants varied from 60 to 2,900 units in one report.) Oestrogen withdrawal symptoms, such as flushing, recur with falling but still very high oestrogen levels.

In a series of letters to the *Lancet*[24] Dr Whitehead wrote that these very high oestrogen concentrations were due to too frequent reimplantation of 50mg and 100mg oestradiol implants every four to eight months. Dr Compston said only 30 per cent of women go on taking the HRT they have been given, while Dr Ginsberg, who wanted most women to take HRT, said the average use in the UK was four to five months so oestrogens could not be addictive. Mr Studd added that some women returned for oestrogen implants more frequently than advised and some self-medicate with extra oestrogen tablets or skin patches. He said symptoms return four to eight months after an implant even though the oestradiol levels are normal. Women with a psychiatric history, including PMS and menopausal depression, and those with signs of 'an addictive personality' such as heavy smokers, were more likely to be unsatisfied with the usual doses and want higher levels. These women would then be at more risk from breast cancer. I wrote in giving the figures for the large overall increase in breast cancer with the increasing prescription of sex hormones.

Drs Bewley and Bewley reminded us that naturally occurring substances could be addictive. The brain produces morphia-like substances – endogenous opiods. Enkephalin, a brain opiate peptide, is thought to be released with exercise and partly accounts for the euphoria runners experience. Anabolic steroids, banned in athletes, also produce dependence. Women who are worried about their increased risk of cancer can have great difficulty giving up their HRT.

Mrs B

Mrs B has tried many times to manage without her oestrogen patch. Every time her withdrawal symptoms are desperately severe within a few hours of taking off the patch. She suffers from hot flushes when she pours with sweat, stays awake all night, feels exhausted and is tender and sore in her vagina and vulva. Nothing else except oestrogen will help. After trying to stop a dozen times she usually gives in and sticks on another patch. In Mrs B's case, she had already been having her levels of minerals, vitamins and essential fatty acids measured and has been taking supplements to try to counteract the HRT-imposed changes. In spite of this she seems unable to give up the HRT. She may be suffering from gut candida which, although at too low a level to make alcohol after glucose loading, could still be why she becomes more sensitive to foods and chemicals on HRT steroid withdrawal. She benefits from antifungal therapy.

Mrs C

In contrast, Mrs C removed her oestrogen patch and was immediately and dramatically better. Mrs C is a journalist and came to see me about HRT. She is only forty-eight, still not at the menopause and has a son aged five, but had been given oestrogen patches two years ago. She had been troubled with acne and neck stiffness. She had found her skin was better if she avoided dairy food and apple juice. Three years ago, she had been to Biolab. Her zinc and magnesium levels were too low and she had gut candida. Since then she was given a course of antifungal therapy and had been taking nutritional supplements. In the course of the interview, she said she was worried about 'memory black spots' which, as a journalist, she found especially disconcerting. She suddenly developed three breast lumps – one large and two smaller. Mrs C went to the HRT clinic and was told she needed an immediate mammogram (breast X-ray) which was booked for the following day. That night, probably because she had already interviewed me about the rising breast cancer incidence, she peeled off her oestrogen patch. When she woke up the next morning she couldn't believe it – the lumps had disappeared. She went for the mammography and the staff couldn't believe it either. No sign of trouble! Mrs C returned to Biolab. Zinc levels were just normal but copper was too high in her sweat, hair and serum due to the prescribed oestrogens. The breast-protecting 6-series fatty acids, such as those obtained from evening primrose oil, were deficient. She was still producing some alcohol in her gut in response to a loading dose of sugar – a sign of yeast overgrowth or gut candida. The good news was not only did her breast lumps disappear but her memory was completely restored, much to her delight.

Yeast overgrowth, candida, is notorious for causing mental symptoms and many patients taking hormones have gut candida and strong reactions to yeast in their diet. Very few women with either mental symptoms or headaches can tolerate alcohol. I see very few alcoholics as most sensitive women have already discovered for themselves that they have severe and unpleasant reactions, because of the yeast content, to even one glass of any type of alcoholic drink.

While gut candida can cause mental dullness so can taking sex hormones. I recently saw a woman being treated and neutralised for food allergies in an Environmental Clinic. She said her mind was in a blur. Her doctor had concurred with her continuing to wearing an oestrogen patch while being treated but when this lady had taken a pregesterone for irregular bleeding her mind had been in a similar dwalm, as we say in Scotland.

Smoking is not a big problem among higher social class older women but more younger, lower social class women are smoking now than ever before. Clearly, tobacco is highly addictive with most smokers reaching twenty cigarettes each day. Smokers always say they need to smoke to calm themselves. In fact, the additional mechanism works by releasing adrenaline which gives a buzz. When the adrenaline levels fall, another cigarette is needed. At Charing Cross Migraine Clinic many of the 'tension' headache patients were smokers and one in five were taking Valium. When smokers had given up cigarettes, their need for tranquillisers was much less as only one in ten ex-smokers were taking them. Ergotamine, Valium and its long-acting version Ativan are addictive. One woman took a year to be weaned off Ativan. As hormone users are also more likely to want tranquillisers, more women than men become addicted and many of the women continue to be addicted long after they have changed to another method of contraception.

So what is the answer? Obviously it is important to avoid potentially addictive drugs and to make sure levels of essential brain nutrients are adequate. Dr Alan Stewart tested women with PMS at Biolab. Like my headache patients, the women had very low average sweat zinc and magnesium levels and poor vitamin B6 activity. These deficiencies were improved with supplements taken for four months. Seven out of ten women noticed an improvement in their complaints.[3] Nutritional supplements alone are not enough. Mental symptoms are a common response to eating some common foods and drinks. Wheat, corn, yeast, milk and cheese often cause brain allergies. Alcohol is notorious for causing mental reactions including aggression and violence. Consultant psychiatrist, Dr Graham Sheppard, found that among twenty-four women and nine men with major depressive illness nearly all were severely deficient in sweat and serum zinc and in red cell magnesium.[25]

Anyone who has low levels of zinc, magnesium and B vitamin is also likely to be deficient in essential fatty acids. Essential fatty acids, like linoleic acid, are obtained from vegetable oils, especially olive oil and evening primrose oil (available in capsules). They make prostaglandins (PGEs) which, like amines, are powerful mood regulators.

Platelets from depressed patients make less PGE1 than normal, while manic or euphoric patients make more than normal. Prostaglandin means secretion of the prostate, and although most tissues can make PGEs, semen contains especially large amounts of PGE1.[4]

Dr David Horrobin has suggested that variations in PGE1 levels may hold the key to alcohol addiction. Although alcohol stimulates platelets to make PGE1, it can also cause a shortage by blocking production at an earlier stage from the essential fatty acid – linoleic acid (LA). Even if an alcoholic is taking adequate amounts of vegetable oils containing LA, the individual will run short of PGE1 and keep drinking more alcohol in order to feel good. Alcohol prevents LA being converted into GLA (gamma linolenic acid). But this block can be overcome by giving GLA in the form of an oil made from the seed of the evening primrose. The Latin name for the plant, *oenothera biennis*, means 'healer of the effects of wine'. Not only can a few drops of the oil prevent a hangover, but Doctors Iain and Evelyn Glen in Inverness have evidence that evening primrose oil relieves alcohol withdrawal symptoms. Also in their tests abnormal liver enzyme levels returned to normal significantly faster than in their control group.[26] The normal conversion of LA and GLA needs adequate amounts of zinc, magnesium and B vitamins.

The occurrence of mental symptoms in response to hormone changes is not a sign of shortage of hormones[27] but warns instead of imbalance and deficiencies in essential nutrients. With the help of modern laboratory investigations such abnormalities can and should be easily corrected.

KEY POINTS

- Depressive mood symptoms are linked to a fall in sex hormones and a rise in stress steroids – before periods, after pregnancy or at the menopause.

- Symptoms likely when zinc, magnesium, B vitamins or essential fats or amino acids are deficient and copper is high.
- Mood changes are caused by the pill and HRT (oestrogens or pregestogens) distorting amine pathways and altering enzyme actions.
- Prescribed hormones also cause depression by increasing food allergies and causing gut candida.
- Studies show both pill and HRT takers are more likely to commit suicide.

Chapter Five

Maintaining the Balance

PART ONE: ZINC AND PROTEINS

Each of our cells takes in food, grows, divides and puts out waste. The process is automatic; all we have to think about is eating and drinking. In a romantic 'Garden of Eden' scenario the fruit hangs on the tree ripe for picking. For millions of years, as the human brain was evolving its amazing capabilities, we were eating a Stone Age diet. Hunter gatherers ate fresh fish, game, vegetables, fruit and nuts uncontaminated by hormones, antibiotics, pesticides or artificial fertilisers. We kept fit by physical exercise and a well-balanced diet. Humanity prospered and reproduced mostly unhindered by plagues or diseases. Protected by an immune system against invading viruses or bacteria, the fittest survived to threaten the world's resources by today's population explosion.

About 10,000 years ago the first settled communities appeared and wild grasses began to be cultivated as regular crops in the surrounding fields. The grains could be stored and ground into flour for making bread. Grains, however, can grow mouldy and bread is levened by yeast – also a fungus. One story of the earliest neurosurgery is that a hole was bored through the skull bone to let out evil spirits or was it to relieve migraine headaches? Dr Gina Schoental, the distinguished veterinary scientist, described how mycotoxins in grains, especially those with oestrogen-like actions, have always been a powerful cause of disease. Moulds can powerfully suppress the immune system, encouraging cancer growth and congenital abnormalities.[1]

We have become accustomed to seeing pictures of starving men, women and children in Africa and watching the people whose leaders won the race to be first in outer space as they now queue in empty shops. It is more difficult for governments and doctors to believe that so many of us in Britain and America, countries where every type of food glistens from supermarket shelves, are also poorly nourished and measurably lack essential nutrients in our bodies. It is hard to imagine that the overweight, the aerobically fit, or the international football player with a hamstring injury might all be suffering from cell starvation.

One of the great geniuses of this century, Dr Alan Turing, a code breaker during World War Two and the inventor of the computer, always had lines on his nails. Were they white horizontal stripes – the sign of zinc deficiency? He was bored when he was at school. As a young man he had homosexual relationships and had a tendency to be suicidal. He was found dead at the age of forty-two. Was he suffering the effects of zinc deficiency?

Professor Bryce-Smith, whose efforts went a long way to having lead removed from petrol in the UK, believes that the higher the intelligence, the more zinc is needed during development, and lack of zinc can lead to mental instability. I think to some extent this is true. Among my patients it often seems that it is the more intelligent and sensitive who are the most vulnerable to mental illness. Obviously, a more active brain uses more zinc.

Dr Elizabeth Lodge Rees, a paediatrician, who measured minerals in the 1960s in California, says you need as much food to give a lecture as to take physical exercise. Dr Lodge Rees published one of the first papers showing that children with learning or behaviour problems had high levels of toxic metals – lead, cadmium and aluminium, in their hair.[2] Her findings have been confirmed many times since, but it was only using Dr John Howard's sweat test that zinc deficiency was shown to be so common. Nearly all the children we have tested suffering from dyslexia (specific learning difficulties) have been zinc deficient in their sweat.[3] Sweat zinc gives an excellent measure of cell zinc status. There is a mechanism for conserving zinc lost in sweat. When the cells are short of zinc less is excreted into the sweat. It takes about fourteen days of extra supplements to return the sweat concentrations into the normal range if the zinc is absorbed properly.[4] Sometimes, when there has been long-term zinc deficiency, likely in women who have taken the pill for several years, problems in the gut and pancreas prevent absorption and need to be treated separately.

Protein Metabolism

Metabolism means change. Metabolism describes the chemical processes which maintain life. There are metabolic pathways in our cells – chains or cycles of reactions breaking down or building up materials, using up or releasing energy.

The male hormones, androgens, mostly testosterone, promote cell growth and the build-up of proteins and muscles – known as the anabolic effect. Anabolic steroids are the subject of controversy in sport. Some competitors illegally take extra hormones to increase their muscle development, strength and endurance, in spite of longer term dangers.

Meat and fish are first-class proteins. They are made from all the essential amino acids we need. If we eat them, provided our pathways are working properly, we should be able to digest and absorb the key building blocks our cells need to carry out their own functions. Before the pill hormones came into general use by nearly all young women, vegetarianism, the refusal to eat meat, was fairly unusual. The pill hormones interfere with the protein-breakdown pathways and women have turned more and more against meat, starting a 'vegetarian epidemic'. If you are tired it is easier to digest and absorb a carbohydrate meal. Bread, cheese and cereals can always be at hand. Most patients I see in their twenties and thirties eat the same diet. Cereals for breakfast, cheese sandwiches for lunch and vegetable pasta for supper. If they can still tolerate alcohol they may add some wine, and herb tea is popular for the rest of the day. Invariably they have been 'on the pill' when younger and many became vegetarian when they were taking the pill. If fish is eaten, it is usually tinned tuna once weekly and meat is chicken – taken, at the most, once or twice a week. The husbands or partners are often on this same poor quality diet and they are usually pleased when I prescribe a high-protein diet.

Most of my younger patients are referred from Foresight, the charity for preconception care, and most have either fertility problems or a history of recurrent miscarriages. Both men and women are often deficient in their sweat in zinc and magnesium with some of the women having particularly low blood (serum) zinc levels. When zinc deficiency has been severe for a long time the usual controls that keep serum zinc within a fairly wide normal range have become inadequate and infertility or recurrent miscarriages are more likely.

Ex-pill users who become pregnant with low zinc status may be damaging their children. We have evidence that there has been a sharp fall in their children's sweat zinc levels in the 1980s. In 1971 only 9 per cent of single women had taken the pill but, by 1981, 90 per cent of women had been on the pill before they had their first child. These mothers are often out at work and, in spite of fridges and freezers, fall into the habit of not buying fresh whole food and cooking at the end of their working day. Automatic fridges can harbour harmful moulds and need regular sodium bicarbonate washes.

Children are becoming less used to proper meals either

at home or school. Concern about animal fat causing heart attacks and bowel and breast cancer has helped vegetarianism develop the status of a religion. Oddly enough, cheap storable cheese, pure animal fat, maintains its fashionable status. Children, seeing wildlife films on television, are encouraged to refuse to eat animals, often to the detriment of their own growth and development. Vegetables have second-class proteins. That means you have to eat several vegetables together to be sure of ingesting the full range of essential amino acids – those that our bodies must take from our diets because our cells are unable to make them.

There is another reason why vegetarians are more likely to be zinc deficient than meat eaters. Professor Noel Solomons of Harvard tested how much zinc was absorbed from different foods.[5] Oysters, long known to be an aphrodisiac, are by far the best source of zinc (which is needed for functioning sex hormones). In tests, 120 grams of oysters raised serum zinc levels by 140 mcgm/dl. Then Noel added beans to the oysters – the rise in zinc was reduced by half. When he added corn to the beans and the oysters, there was no increase in zinc levels at all. Some foods interfered with zinc absorption. When Professor Solomons tested a bacon breakfast, zinc levels rose, but a cereal breakfast plus coffee caused zinc levels to fall lower than they were before. Coffee and tea block zinc and iron absorption, while cereals, especially those containing phytates, actively remove zinc.

No wonder we had such excellent results at Charing Cross Migraine Clinic. Patients taking Dr Mansfield's lamb and pears every meal, three times a day for five days, not only avoided the common grass family, dairy products and yeast allergens, but must have been boosting their low levels of zinc and magnesium. For those with iron deficiency, both iron and zinc can be absorbed from red meat, whereas iron and zinc tablets can't be taken at the same time as they antagonise each other.

Our body is unable to store zinc, but attempts to prevent

losses in our sweat. Tea, coffee, alcohol, colours and additives like tartrazine, increase zinc excretion in the urine. Dr Neil Ward made the interesting discovery that it was only the already zinc deficient hyperactive children who lost more zinc in their urine when given tartrazine. There was no change in the healthy children's blood or urine levels.[6] At a Society for Environmental Medicine Conference Dr Doris Rapp described how, when hyperactive children were given foods they reacted to, their blood immediately showed changes denoting impaired magnesium-dependent pathways.

Children's Development

In the 1960s and 1970s, many studies discovered that problem children had high toxic metals in their hair.[7] Very low hair zinc concentrations were recorded in young children who had poor growth – small and short for their age.[8] In long-term severe zinc deficiency, hair zinc levels can fall very low, but zinc is needed to make the proteins in the hair. Lack of proteins means hair stops growing and toxic metal levels rise. Zinc and other essential mineral levels also rise giving an artificial impression of normal zinc status. Sometimes hair zinc levels are exceptionally high. I have seen this pattern more in teenagers and adults, and I think they have been zinc deficient for most of their lives. When supplements have been absorbed for three to four months, the hair essential mineral levels return to the normal range and the toxic mineral levels fall. Fifteen thousand analyses of serum, sweat and hair at Biolab showed that essential mineral levels tend to fall with age while toxic metals tend to rise.[9] It is worrying to find so many children with low zinc levels.

Vegetarian mothers tend to have lower zinc and higher copper levels than meat eating mothers and they have lower-birth-weight babies. As more mothers are given hormones during pregnancy, and more become zinc deficient, more children are unable to grow properly and more of them are being given growth hormones. I think it is intolerable that some children are prescribed growth hormones before they have been properly investigated and treated for nutritional deficiencies. Lack of zinc inhibits protein build-up and stops growth. Extra hormone stimulation can make zinc deficiency more severe, causing cancer, malabsorption, interference with immunity and adversely influencing brain development.

Children's growth is regulated by growth hormone from the hypothalamus and thyroid hormones. Down's syndrome children have particularly low serum zinc levels and poor thyroid hormone production. When they are given zinc supplements the output of their thyroid hormones becomes normal.[10] In turn thyroid hormones help to maintain serum zinc concentrations. The adrenal glands of both men and women make androgens, with women converting smaller amounts of their adrenal androgens into active testosterone. Anabolic hormones stimulate the formation of sugars and proteins inside cells, leading to vigorous cell and blood vessel growth. The cell walls become flexible, allowing easy transport of materials.

Halting Growth and the Stress Hormones

Our genes contain growth regulating instructions, and, if our nutrition is adequate, we stop growing when we reach our inherited height and body shape. In her book *Bone Behaviour*, Dr Kitty Little describes how adrenal steroid hormones can have anabolic blocking effects – anti-anabolic instructions halt cell division.[11]

The stress hormones, adrenal glucocorticoid steroids, are released during stress and temporarily stop cell metabolism. This is known as the catabolic effect. Dr Little writes, 'The hormone balance may approach the catabolic during the later stages of pregnancy, after childbirth, after the menopause, during old age, when corticosteroids are given for therapeutic purposes, or as a result of oral contraceptive agents.' When exogenous sex hormones are taken, a mixture of anabolic and catabolic effects happen. Cortisol levels may be abnormally high, encouraging thrombus (blood clot) formation and changing cell membranes. While anabolic hormones encourage the cell membranes to allow easy transport of metabolites, catabolic hormones make the cell walls rigid. Sodium is retained inside the cells and potassium is kept outside. The important sodium potassium pump is impaired and nerve cell metabolism is particularly hindered. Large doses of cortisone or prednisone can cause emotional imbalance, irritability and depression and even a schizophrenia-like psychosis or temporary madness. Everyone can suffer from stress if it is prolonged or severe enough – as was discovered in the trenches during the First World War.

These steroids have been widely prescribed to suppress the inflammatory reactions which are the body's response to injury, infection or immune changes. Although steroids are used to bring temporary relief for illnesses like asthma and arthritis, their side effects can be devastating, including high blood pressure, changes in fat and water metabolism with obesity and a round 'moon' face. Catabolic hormones cause osteoporosis (thin bones) by interfering with bone cell metabolism. They increase sticky platelet formation and masses of small thrombi form in the bones of old people with senile osteoporosis. Women taking HRT oestrogens are more likely to have blood clots and have high cortisol levels. They actually have lower bone activity – lower levels of bone alkaline phosphatase, the bone cell enzyme which needs zinc as a co-factor, than other women of the same age. Patients taking catabolic steroids have less defence against infection and are less able to deal with carcinogens because of impaired liver function.

Our stress mechanisms, adrenal steroid release and adrenaline release were meant to either temporarily halt cell metabolism or stimulate other reactions during an emergency or time of change. Artificially stimulating stress responses for prolonged lengths of time is not a good idea.

In Chapter Four the effects of oestrogens and progestogens on protein and amine metabolism have been described. The two main amine pathways can be shunted in the wrong directions while essential nutrient deficiencies exaggerate the resulting loss of control over mood and blood vessel reactivity. Exogenous hormones have also caused problems with excessive weight gain, excessive weight loss and the general control of appetite.

Anorexia Nervosa and Bulimia

Anorexia, the refusal to eat, seems to be a modern disease affecting mostly teenage girls and young women in their twenties but younger children are also being affected. The Victorians called it neurasthenia – thin, nervous and pathetic. While mentioned in novels, neurasthenia or anorexia were not commonly diagnosed before the 1960s. How much of our modern epidemic is an extension of the zinc deficiency induced vegetarian epidemic? How much is due to early use of sex hormones perhaps for painful or missed periods? How much is due to a mother taking hormones or being zinc deficient in pregnancy affecting her daughter's ability to cope with her own hormone changes at the menarche or her son's growth? Anorexia is also to do with low self-esteem, typical of zinc deficiency, and with a distorted body image. Girls become obsessed by their appearance. They dislike their shape, look in the mirror and want to be thinner. This may be partly media induced – a woman is worthless unless she looks like a model. Partly, it is fashion. Painters like Rubens would not have thrilled to paint many of today's photographic models. Some anorexics vomit everything they eat and become thinner and thinner until they need to be admitted to hospital. Some girls alternate between anorexia, not eating, and bingeing. Bulimics stuff themselves with food and immediately vomit, even rushing to the bathroom in the middle of a meal. Meals become less regular, to be replaced by compulsive eating at any time or dieting during the day and bingeing during the night.

Normal appetite, sated by three regular meals, becomes a distant memory. Laxatives may be used in bigger doses. Some sad cases even eat toilet paper, risking an operation for gut obstruction. Hair and teeth can fall out and stomach acid, regurgitated, can cause narrowing and stricture of the oesophagus (gullet) or they can choke on the vomit. Increasingly, severe zinc deficiency means more risk of infections and cancer. One of my friends, a general practitioner, thinks that anorexia often starts after first sexual intercourse. She thinks that it is a revulsion at the ethics of the promiscuous society – instant gratification for men and the degradation of women. Of course more teenagers are being encouraged to go on the pill at younger and younger ages and without their parents' knowledge. The pill lowers their zinc levels when they still need extra zinc for growing and coping with the stress of the menarche. Psychiatrists, treating anorexics with psychotherapy or drugs, tend to ignore the underlying biochemistry.[12] All right, they say, even if anorexics are zinc deficient, they are short of food and when persuaded to eat regularly again, their patients make dramatic improvements. But it is much more complicated than that. The brain control centres for both the sex hormones and appetite are interconnected in the hypothalamus. Changes in a woman's metabolism happen when her periods begin at the menarche and during pregnancy in order to feed her baby. Food cravings are a well-known feature of early pregnancy. We know that lack of zinc during early development in animals can mean changes in the brain and even different brain catechol amine levels. Zinc deficient offspring have impeded brain control systems.

At the Migraine Clinic in the 1970s we measured serum zinc and copper and tested liver clearance – how long the liver took to metabolise antipyrine, an aspirin-like drug. Liver clearance was too fast or too slow in patients with low zinc and high copper levels. These patients also reacted to most foods when tested on a rotation diet.[13, 14] Both the pill and antibiotics cause gut candida which also increases allergic reactions to both foods and chemicals making everyday life difficult. Many doctors treating anorexia seem unaware of these results and tube feed their patients with common allergens.

Susan

Susan came to see me when she was thirty-five years old because she had recently lost a baby. She looked big, strong and healthy and had been a policewoman. Her father had a tendency to be depressed, her brother had been psychotic and had been treated with lithium since he was fifteen years old. Her sister got migraine. Family life during Susan's childhood had been stressful and her periods had been heavy since her menarche at thirteen. At age sixteen she became vegetarian and anorexic. When she was 'stressed' she binged and vomited. She was prescribed oral contraceptives at the age of eighteen. Her weight went from twelve stone down to seven stone. Susan had a mental breakdown and was admitted to hospital for three months. She says it was disgusting. She was force fed sweet milk (cane sugar and cow's milk commonly cause unpleasant reactions) and given Largactil. She felt doped and ill. Susan was married when she was twenty and had problems becoming pregnant but conceived her daughter when she was twenty-seven. She had been given 'massive doses' of ovulation-stimulating drugs until she had ovarian cysts. She left the police as she found coping with violence was too stressful, stress making her cysts enlarge and become painful. Her daughter, now aged eight, was born with one leg shorter than the other. Susan's first husband left after their daughter was born, when she was suffering from post-natal depression including an episode of psychosis. Susan then discovered she reacted to cow's milk and cheese. She used to binge large amounts of cheese but now she only took skimmed milk. She also took some daily minerals and vitamin supplements and her zinc, magnesium, manganese and iron were low normal. She was still vomiting occasionally and had three miscarriages with a new partner. I prescribed a high-protein, low-allergy diet plus extra supplements. Susan's partner had a heavy haemolytic streptococcal infection in his prostate and urine and the last miscarriage may have been due to this infection. Susan had learnt how to help herself by reading health books and was now coping very well.

KEY POINTS

- Normal protein metabolism needs an adequate supply of essential amino acids and zinc.
- Best sources of both are meat and fish.
- Prevents delayed growth, learning and behaviour problems, anorexia, malabsorption and food allergies.
- Prescribed pill and HRT sex hormones interfere with protein metabolism and increase vegetarianism.

PART TWO: CARBOHYDRATE METABOLISM

Refined sugars – corn, cane and beet sugars, honey and maltose (in beer) are rapidly digested and absorbed. The blood sugar (glucose) level rises and the pancreas secretes insulin, which turns any extra glucose into saturated fatty acids. The blood cholesterol is increased and fat deposits in the tissues.

Complex carbohydrate foods, starchy vegetables, fruits and unrefined grains, are digested and absorbed slowly and are less likely to be turned into fat. They contain the vitamins and minerals they need to burn cleanly into carbon dioxide and water.

In diabetes, any extra glucose is spilled over into the urine because the pancreas has failed to make enough insulin. If too much insulin is produced, the blood glucose falls too low, and low blood sugar (hypoglycaemia) causes craving for sugar. The rapid absorption of ingested sugar stimulates more insulin secretion and sugar-craving cycles and obesity can result.

When the blood glucose goes too low, the adrenal glands secrete cortisol to block the insulin-secretion and make glucose from proteins. Both the pancreas and the adrenal glands can become exhausted, resulting in diabetes and stress diseases. The adrenals can no longer respond adequately to any occasional stress. This is what happens to women taking oral contraceptives or HRT oestrogens – they have too high continuous cortisol production and become 'stressed out'. Hypoglycaemia can become severe because the overworked adrenals fail in their blood-sugar-raising function. Symptoms such as depression, dizziness, crying spells, aggression, lack of sexual interest, insomnia and even blackouts can be blamed on the menopause when they are really due to adrenal exhaustion. In 1966 Professor Wynn had found the most striking change induced by oral contraceptives was raised blood pyruvate – due to an increase in the women's own cortisol production.[15]

It is unfortunate that HRT enthusiasts use the analogy of diabetes. They say both diabetes and the menopause are deficiency diseases. Diabetes is due to the pancreas failing to secrete insulin while menopausal symptoms are due to the ovaries failing to make oestrogen. An unfortunate analogy, because prescribed oestrogens in contraceptive pills or in HRT increase the chance of a woman developing diabetes. Oestrogens prevent insulin lowering a woman's blood sugar.

Professor Wynn expected oestrogens and progestogens to cause diabetes because they were being used to mimic pregnancy, when some women spill out sugar in the urine.

Since 1966 when the St Mary's team published their findings that nearly one in five women taking different oral contraceptives had abnormally high glucose levels,

Professor Wynn has often seen maturity-onset diabetes caused by oestrogen and progestogen combinations.

Lowest Doses

In 1982 Professor Wynn published a study on the lowest-dose combined pill then on the market. Three years before, he had given 210 healthy young women, mostly aged between twenty-five and thirty, 150 micrograms levonorgestrel and 30 micrograms ethinyloestradiol. After fifteen months, 60 per cent of the women had stopped taking it and after three years only 8 per cent were still using it, 42 per cent having been lost to follow-up. Only 10 per cent were known to have stopped because they no longer required contraceptives.

Of the thirty-nine women who started their third year, two (5 per cent) developed deep vein thrombosis and another woman had superficial venous thrombosis. Four had a sustained rise in blood pressure after one year of use, which reverted to normal when they stopped the pill, and one woman developed an abnormal electrocardiogram. Six women developed abnormal glucose tolerance tests and some of the women deteriorated into the diabetic range with continued treatment, improving when they stopped. One woman made this jump twice. Just over a quarter of the women stopped the pill for 'minor' side effects – weight gain, headaches, depression, diminished libido, breakthrough bleeding, amenorrhoea and nausea – while another 11 per cent asked for a change of pill.[16]

Progressive Deterioration

During this study, even women who seemed well had a progressive deterioration in their glucose tolerance. This means a woman's metabolism becomes more abnormal the longer she takes the pill, whether she has symptoms or not. The insulin secretion rose at first but eventually did not keep up with the rising glucose values. Professor

Wynn's conclusion was that this combination of steroids was too strong for contraceptive use. Conjugated oestrogens used as HRT also cause progressive deterioration of carbohydrate metabolism and are more powerful in this respect than synthetic ethinyloestradiol.

Since 1970 it has been known that injections of large amounts of progesterone (300–400mg per day), which is similar in amount to the endogenous progesterone secretion in the latter third of pregnancy, causes changes in carbohydrate metabolism. The glucose tolerance is impaired, as in diabetes, and there is an increased resistance to insulin – injections of insulin are less likely to lower the blood sugar. Professor William Spellacy's group in Chicago found that oral microdoses of a progestogen with male-hormone-like actions, given as oral contraceptives, can alter carbohydrate metabolism as much as these large doses of progestogen given by injection.[17-20] From the doses used it can be worked out that megestrol acetate, norethisterone and ethynodiol diacetate are roughly 1,000 times and norgestrel 5,000 times more powerful than progestogen in this effect. The chance of the pill causing diabetes is increased by its male-hormone-like actions, but is also increased by the oestrogen which is added to most pills. Oral androgens, anabolic steroids and danazol, used to suppress breast lumps, can have similar adverse effects on glucose tolerance and are particularly antagonistic to insulin.

Too much or Too Little Testosterone?

When Professor Wynn reported that even a low dose of norgestrel was causing metabolic changes, interest swung to the weaker desogestrel which has a progesterone-like action but almost no androgen or anti-oestrogen effect. The results of trials of Marvelon – 150 micrograms desogestrel and 30 micrograms ethinyloestradiol – were reported in 1983 at a workshop on oral contraception. The effects on metabolism were those of the accompanying oestrogen – the blood fats were raised as well as the plasma proteins. There was still impaired glucose tolerance and insulin resistance, although the levels of testosterone were very low.[21]

Most oral contraceptives lower the levels of free testosterone. Normally women's libido peaks at ovulation in the middle of their cycle but oral contraceptives take away this peak effect. Pills like Marvelon, with no androgen activity, are given to treat acne and hairiness and polycystic ovary disease. A Swedish professor commented, 'We have a hard time keeping our women on some of the various experimental models of treatment.' It seemed that these women preferred to be hairy, keep their libido and not take drugs! He also noted that the Swedish Regulatory Board, heavily dominated by very active women, is very sceptical of any combination that decreases testosterone levels. Hirsutism is claimed to be very common among pill users, and some Swedish investigators think that the powerful androgenic progestogens, like norgestrel, can cause hairiness by displacing binding sites and releasing endogenous testosterone.

During the workshop, concern was expressed over the prolonged action of desogestrel which made it difficult to get patients to menstruate unless they were given extra oestrogen. (This progestogen is in pills prescribed for adolescent girls' acne, but not for boys who are more likely to suffer from acne. It is simpler and safer to treat acne in either sex with zinc supplementation, fish oils and a low-allergy diet.) The speaker also felt there was a need for a suitable pill for hirsute women particularly since the earliest non-androgenic pills had been removed from the market for causing breast lumps in beagle dogs in the 1960s.

Forty years on and the oral contraceptive scene is still going round in circles. Even taking the same pill, the levels of some critical controlling enzymes go too high or too low. It is a game of swings and roundabouts. Individual variations of the enzymes in the gut wall and liver mean blood levels of pill progestogens can vary up to *ten times*.[22] Self-medication with large doses of the usually beneficial vitamin C has the effect of upgrading a pill from a low to a high dose of oestrogen.[23] Oestrogen blood levels in HRT users vary up to 50 *times*.[24]

In 1992 Ian Godsland, Victor Wynn and their team published further results on pills with 30–40 micrograms of oestradiol.[25] The progestogen doses included the lowest doses we had tested in the 1960s.

Progestogens: Lowest doses used	1960s	1990s
norgestrel	50	30
(or norgestrol)		
desogestrel		150
norethisterone	300	350
ethynodiol diacetate	100	500

The lowest doses were not marketed in the 1960s because they were too weak to prevent irregular bleeding and unplanned pregnancies, even when given with the larger 50 micrograms of oestrogen. Ian Godsland found most of these low-dose mixtures deteriorated sugar tolerance and insulin resistance while increasing insulin secretion from the pancreas. The desogestrel combination slowed down the elimination of insulin from the blood, probably by impairing kidney function.

Professor Wynn emphasises that raised insulin levels increase arterial disease as insulin stimulates the artery wall muscle to thicken and lay down cholesterol. All the changes in fat and carbohydrate metabolism plus the pill-induced increase in blood pressure mean hormone takers have a higher risk of coronary artery disease. These changes happen whether they smoke or not. The so-called diminished risk with modern pills is because they have been given to much younger women who are less likely to develop atheroma – not because the pills are really any safer or indeed very different. Studies in the 1980s find up to three times more heart attacks among pill takers with the risk known to be continuing for at least seven years after the pill has been discontinued.[26]

Pancreatic Function

Oral contraceptives affect the pancreas and insulin production or excretion.[27] Insulin is produced in isolated islands of cells called the Islets of Langerhans. The rest of the pancreas makes enzymes which are secreted into the bile and help to digest our fats, proteins and carbohydrates. When a person is zinc deficient, the production of digestive enzymes is decreased. It can take up to two years of zinc supplements and good normal zinc levels before the pancreas is able to function properly again.

Biolab provides us with a gastrogram – graphs showing how much acid the stomach glands are producing and how the pancreas is performing. Nearly all the women I have screened, who had used oral contraceptives for more than five years and had stopped within the last ten years, had half the normal amount of pancreatic secretion and half the usual amount of zinc in their sweat. Some patients appear to have a familial pancreatic insufficiency problem, for example, both mothers, daughters and sisters may be affected. In my experience, women with familial pancreatic insufficiency are unlikely to take hormones for more than a few weeks because they are soon aware of unpleasant side effects.

KEY POINTS

- Prescribed sex hormones raise levels of stress hormones.
- More diabetes occurs with longer exposure.
- Microdose progestogens are 1,000 to 5,000 times more powerful than natural progesterone.

- Blood levels of progestogens vary up to 10 fold and oestrogen levels vary up to 50 times among women prescribed identical hormone doses.
- Hormone-taking often decreases pancreatic enzyme secretion and causes malabsorption.

PART THREE: FAT METABOLISM

Fat is a 'feminist issue' or so they say, although beer bellies are a common sight on older men. In general young men seem to have less trouble with energy balance than women. When girls start to menstruate their raised hormone levels encourage fat to accumulate in their breasts, hips and thighs. Nature tries to make sure that women have stores of extra energy for pregnancy. At the menopause 'middle-aged spread' may be due to the raised cortisol catabolic effect. Many women need to be careful with their intake of calories in their teens, during pregnancy and after the menopause.

Weight Gain and Heart Attacks

When women take progestogen-oestrogen pills their gain in weight depends on the doses and balance of these hormones and how each pill alters their blood vessels.

Half of the women taking 50 micrograms oestrogen combined with 1mg of norgestrel gained an average of ten pounds within twelve cycles, but gained less if they took either higher or lower doses of the same progestogen. This combination caused most headaches and vascular changes which suggests an allergic component to weight gain. I later published how to lose weight safely on a low-allergy diet.[28]

Both oestrogen and progesterone cause weight gain. Some women taking progesterone by suppository or injection become huge as both muscle and fat increase and fluid is retained. Not all women are affected equally. Some gain weight rapidly, others only put on weight slowly and may not link their obesity to taking the pill or HRT.

Professor Victor Wynn investigated anabolic steroids in the 1950s at St Mary's Hospital in London. They altered protein, carbohydrate and fat metabolism. He predicted that as oral progestogens were very similar to the male hormone testosterone they would act the same way.

In his 1966 publications, Professor Wynn found the oestrogen in the combined pills raised blood fat levels. The higher the dose or balance of oestrogen in the pills, the greater were the increases. Oestrogens also increase cortisol output from the adrenals (indicated by rises in blood pyruvate), which means extra oestrogens cause biochemical stress.[29] At first Victor Wynn was puzzled that oestrogens were raising blood fats because young women are much less likely to have heart attacks than young men. After the menopause a woman's chance of having a heart attack increases but is still half that of a man, although her cholesterol may be higher. The answer turned out to be that some fats actually protect against vascular disease and these are lowered by male hormones and by the progestogens in the pill.

The Greek word for fat is *stea*, and the saturated fat stearic acid is abundant in beef, lamb, pork and dairy products. When we eat too much of these saturated fats they tend to stick together and deposit in our tissues especially if we are short of protecting minerals, vitamins and essential oils. Fat sticks on the inside of arteries mixed with proteins and cholesterol. Sugars and starches can also be converted into saturated fats. We now know that a diet high in animal fat, sugar and starches is likely to give us heart disease.

Dietary fat from meat, fish or vegetables is mostly in the form of fatty acids, chains of carbon atoms with two hydrogen atoms attached to each carbon. Three fatty acid chains are usually fixed to a glycerol molecule forming a triglyceride. Fats are insoluble and need to attach to proteins to be carried around in the blood stream. The fat-protein complexes become denser as they pick up more protein: changing from very low-density lipoproteins (mostly triglycerides), to low-density lipoproteins and then become high-density lipoproteins which are mainly protein.

Fat interacts with artery walls forming fatty plaques and the walls become thicker. The high density complexes, bulging with protein receptors, circulate in the bloodstream mopping up the damaging fat as they go by, and carry fat from the tissues to the liver. There it is excreted in the bile into our gut. Both testosterone, the male hormone, and the male-hormone-like progestogens, lower the blood levels of these mostly protein high-density complexes, depriving younger men and pill users of their protection.

As little as 35 micrograms of norgestrel or 350 micrograms of norethisterone given alone lowers high density lipoprotein levels, while 30 to 40 micrograms of ethinyl oestradiol raises very low-density lipoprotein (triglyceride) levels.[30]

Hormone Replacement Therapy

At the menopause women's ovaries no longer make progesterone. Residual oestrogen plus increases in stress hormones (cortisol) elevate blood fats, including cholesterol in older women. Giving oestrogens as HRT will further raise cholesterol and triglyceride levels increasing the risk of heart attacks.

Some women have large surges in their blood fats when given oestrogen HRT perhaps as part of a stress or immune response. When progestogens are added to the HRT a woman's protective fats will be lowered. Taking hormones further increases the output of adrenal stress hormones, all adding to the risk of thrombosis. When twenty-five Glasgow women, aged forty-six to sixty-two, were given a mere 20 micrograms of mestranol after their ovaries had been removed, 16 per cent developed thrombosis within

120 days, while the remainder had impaired glucose tolerance and a rise in serum protein-bound iodine.[31]

Ageing

Why do cholesterol levels tend to increase with age in both men and women? Besides having changing hormone profiles older people become increasingly deficient in essential nutrients. Fifteen thousand hair mineral analyses at Biolab show that mineral deficiencies increase with age. Lack of zinc, magnesium, chromium, too high or too low copper levels, low cobalt, low vitamins, low essential fatty acids, especially fish oils, all make arterial disease more likely. Toxic metal levels – lead, aluminium, mercury and especially cadmium from tobacco smoking – increase with age, combining to lower essential mineral levels.[32] The best protection for healthy arteries in old age is excellent nutrition – not hormones from the outside. Lack of minerals and vitamins and infections interfere with the protective essential fatty acids and block their pathways even if the diet is adequate.

Older people have more problems with digestion and absorption. Years of zinc deficiency and chromium deficiency (from too much sugar in the diet) can cause lack of stomach acid and a fall in the output of digestive enzymes from the pancreas or changes in gut flora.

These absorption problems can be diagnosed by a simple gastrogram test at Biolab. Treatment with acid pills and pancreatic enzymes can improve the absorption of essential nutrients. Available today, these are valuable screening tests for prevention of heart attacks. Stopping smoking and drinking alcohol and changing to a low-animal-fat diet can lower cholesterol levels and decrease the risk of vascular disease.

Gall Bladder Disease

Another consequence of oestrogens raising blood fat levels is an increase in gallstones and gall bladder disease. While oestrogens raise cholesterol levels, progestogens delay gall bladder emptying – both making cholesterol gallstones more likely.[33, 34]

Alison

A young mother of two children, Alison was thirty years old and she looked healthy, bright and cheerful. She was a statistician and I asked her to help me when I was preparing the results of the London pill trials for the *BMJ*. She calculated that the differences in numbers of women having headaches, thrombosis or depression were highly significant with different pills. This means that the symptoms had not just happened by chance but were more likely than not caused by the different doses of hormones.

Our daughters were in the same class at nursery school so we visited each other for tea. One summer day I brought Alison a large strawberry cream cake. She looked at it longingly and said, 'That looks great but I can't eat fatty foods. I'm going to have my gall bladder taken out in a week or two.' I commiserated with her but then suddenly thought to ask her if she was on the pill. Alison said she was. On my advice she stopped the pill at once. The surgeon was amazed that the gallstones he had seen on Alison's X-rays disappeared before he could operate. Many years later Alison still has her gall bladder and she has no difficulty coping with fatty food since stopping the pill.

Others among our young pill-research volunteers were developing gallbladder disease in the early 1960s. These were the first notifications the Committee on Safety of Medicine received but soon other cases were reported in Britain. Gall bladder disease was no longer just for the 'fair, fat, fertile, female and forty' but was becoming more common in younger women than ever before. The RCGP study found that gall bladder disease is twice as likely with higher doses of oestrogen but any exogenous oestrogen increases the risk for young women.

Essential Fatty Acids

There has been so much anti-fat propaganda that the message seems to be fat is bad news. True, too much animal fat can clog up our arteries and make us obese but we can't survive on a fat-free diet. Much of our brain and most of the membranes in each of our cells is made of fat in the form of essential fatty acids (EFAs). Named essential because we are unable to make them in our bodies and we have to take in enough fish and vegetable oil from our food.[35, 36]

Essential fatty acids are abundant in linseed oil which is extracted from flax. The Romans were aware of the importance of flax and described it as being 'most useful' – *linum usitatissimum*. The two most essential of the fatty acids are *linoleic* and *linolenic* acids.

Flax was cultivated in Babylon around 5,000 BC. Hippocrates, in the 5th century BC, described how flax could relieve inflammation of the mucous membranes and diarrhoea. In the 8th century AD the Emperor Charlemagne ordered its consumption by law. It has been given to animals to improve their health since antiquity – until the end of the Second World War. Then flax and linen for clothes fell out of fashion. Linoleum for floors was superseded by cheaper synthetic coverings. Inferior oils with longer shelf life were sold for cooking. The problem is that linseed oil goes rancid quickly. The best health-giving oils are unsaturated and rapidly destroyed by light or heat.

The chemistry of the essential fatty acids is described in Appendix Two. Animal fat is mostly saturated but essential fatty acids are unsaturated. Saturated fatty acids have two hydrogen atoms attached to each carbon atom. In contrast unsaturated fatty acids have given up a few of their hydrogens and where this has happened the carbon atoms are linked by double bonds. These are unstable and easily form new bonds with other chemicals. The short-chain saturated fatty acid found in butter, butyric acid, has four carbon atoms all with attached hydrogen atoms. It is very stable even when heated and is good to use for cooking food. The essential fatty acids, abundant in flax, fish oils and brain tissue are unstable, being composed of unsaturated fatty acid chains from 18–24 carbon atoms long with two or more double bonds. They rapidly distort when heated.

In the human body nutrients guard our essential fats against distortion by heat or light which is known as oxidation or free radical damage. Protective antioxidant nutrients are B complex vitamins (B1, B5 and B6), vitamin C, the sulphur-containing amino acid cysteine and sulphur-rich proteins, zinc, selenium and vitamin C's bioflavinoid co-factors.

Cell Membranes

Cell membranes make use of both saturated and unsaturated types of fatty acids. The stable saturated fatty acids make the membranes rigid, while more unstable and reactive unsaturated fatty acids make the membranes flexible and responsive. Both types should be in balance in a healthy body.

The messages brought by hormones in the blood stimulate the essential fatty acids in the membranes to release local hormones – prostaglandins and leukotrines. Prostaglandins keep our blood vessels open and repair any damage, while leukotrines help organise our immune system and the movements of our scavenging white cells.

There are two families of essential fatty acids which belong, like BMW cars, to a 6-series or a 3-series. The difference is important as men tend to be short of the 3-series EFAs which are obtained from fish oils, while women often need to take evening primrose oil to make sure they have enough of the 6-series.

The two most essential fatty acids, linoleic acid (LA) and alpha linolenic acid (ALA), have 18 carbon atoms and they are lengthened in our bodies to more active and powerful family members with up to 24 carbons. Linoleic acid keeps our skin moist but otherwise it is its conversion to ALA, to longer fatty acids, that is important. In theory, if we have enough of both we can use enzyme-aided pathways to make all the EFAs and prostaglandins that we need. In reality, there are several reasons why these vital pathways become blocked, the most important of which is taking steroids including the pill and HRT.

6-Series EFAs and Evening Primrose Oil

Linoleic acid has two double bonds. A slow acting desaturase enzyme adds an extra double bond and forms gamma linolenic acid (GLA). *This crucial desaturase enzyme is easily blocked by steroids, stress and common nutritional deficiencies.* Most people seem to be getting enough linoleic acid in their food but 6-series pathway deficiencies are common. Taking extra supplements of evening primrose oil, and extra minerals and vitamins if also deficient, can help bypass any blocks. (See page 288.)

Females are more likely to be short of these 6-series fatty acids than males. Among my patients *one in two women* and *one in four men* have 6-series deficiencies.

EFA 6-series deficiency symptoms include eczema-like skin eruptions, loss of hair, behavioural disturbances, excessive thirst and sweating, drying up of glands, increased susceptibility to infections, failure of wound healing, delayed growth, miscarriage in females, heart and circulatory problems and liver and kidney degeneration.

Supplements for the 6-series EFAs are usually given in the form of evening primrose oil (EPO) which is rich in both linoleic acid and gamma linolenic acid and was traditionally used by the Indians of North America.

Evening primrose oil is now widely available and is famous for preventing period pains, benign breast disease and for treating premenstrual symptoms. GLA is present in mother's milk, borage and blackcurrent seeds, storage oils of algae such as spirulina and in various fungi.

3-Series EFAs and Fish Oils

Similar enzymes change both series of EFAs in the 3-series pathway. Alpha linolenic acid (ALA) is converted into eicosapentanoic acid (EPA) and docosahexaenoic acid (DHA). Again, blocks in this pathway are common in spite of an adequate diet. We found that *three out of four men* and *one in four women* were deficient in fish-oil-type 3-series essential fatty acids.

The 3-series fatty acids were discovered when Eskimo diets were investigated. Eskimos were eating high fat diets but not getting heart attacks because the fish blubber was high in 3-series fatty acids. The Eskimos were found to bleed longer if they were cut. If we take just enough extra EPA to bring our platelet stickiness into the normal range we do not risk prolonged bleeding. Even small doses of aspirin, by knocking out prostaglandin production and causing gastritis, can increase the risk of bleeding from the gut or elsewhere.

EFA 3-series deficiency symptoms include delayed growth, weakness, tingling in arms and legs, impaired vision, learning and behaviour problems and uncoordinated movements.

Supplements for the 3-series EFAs are given as EPA, made from fish oils obtained from fish like sardines, mackerel and salmon. Men need these fatty acids in sperm production and may need up to three times more EPA in their diets than women to maintain normal levels. Among both my men patients and also among 'apparently healthy' Foresight husbands, seventy-five were deficient in their 3-series pathways when tested. Most had enough ALA but not enough to convert into adequate amounts of EPA and DHA.

It is very important to correct these deficiencies with high doses of EPA capsules given up to three times each day. EPO capsules also need to be given as fish oils taken alone can drop the 6-series EFA levels. Besides measuring these essential fatty acid pathways in red cells, Biolab also tests platelet stickiness. Low 3-series EFAs result in platelets becoming too sticky, risking thrombosis.

Saturated fatty acid levels tend to rise when essential fatty acids are deficient and fall when fish oil and evening primrose oil supplements are taken.

Mr S

A heart attack in his early forties led Mr S to become very interested in nutrition, to the point where he actually became a college lecturer in the subject. He stopped smoking, gave up alcohol and by strictly avoiding all animal fat managed to reduce his blood cholesterol to a respectable level. He was dieting so strictly that he lost a lot of weight and became very thin but he was still suffering from angina so he asked for my advice. He went to Biolab to be investigated. He was severely zinc deficient in his sweat and serum. He was also short of chromium, magnesium, vitamin E and n–3 fatty acids. In spite of eating lots of oily fish, there was a block between ALA and EPA and his platelets were dangerously sticky. Mr S also had increased gut permeability, causing malabsorption, likely to be due to food allergy.

Mr S had been keen on the Pritikin low-fat high-fibre diet, but when I asked him to avoid wheat completely his angina disappeared. This happened twice. For some reason it is very hard for people to believe that wheat, well known for causing coeliac disease in children, causes so much masked allergy and malabsorption in adults. The surgeon Mr Dennis Burkitt had promoted wheat bran but he told me his own wife was intolerant to wheat and took rice bran instead.

Mr S soon felt well and his deficiences were corrected with supplements. He was delighted to find that he could now walk up a steep hill without experiencing chest pain.

Receptor Sensitivity – Altered Response to Hormones

While EFAs usually increase the activity of our cell membranes, they also prevent some harmful over-reactions. If we have enough EFAs, our cell receptors are less likely to accept sex hormones. *If we are short of these key fatty acids, and they are replaced by saturated fats and cholesterol, our cell membranes can have an exaggerated response to even normal amounts of circulating hormones.* Oestrogens and testosterone become more powerful when they are combined with saturated fats. Women can have more breast disease and men more prostatic disease. Blood vessels may over-react causing headaches at times of hormone changes.

Cholesterol increases the number of serotonin receptors. The brain needs enough serotonin to prevent depression and harmful behavioural impulses. Several trials have shown that lowering cholesterol levels can decrease heart disease but increase deaths from suicide and violence.

EFAs prevent our receptors being too sensitive to peptides like angiotensin which can raise blood pressure. They also prevent us becoming too receptive to opiates whether addictive drugs like opium or natural opiates like wheat and milk which release brain endorphins making us feel good to the point of becoming addicted. Withdrawal of common foods can cause surprisingly severe symptoms especially when EFAs are deficient.

Smoking and Alcohol

Both tobacco smoking and alcohol drinking increase cholesterol levels. Tobacco lowers zinc and raises cadmium levels, lowers vitamin C, chromium, magnesium and cobalt levels, interfering with normal fat and essential fatty acid metabolism. Alcohol dissolves in cell membranes, making them more fluid. The cells respond by manufacturing more cholesterol to restore the membranes to their less fluid state. When the alcohol wears off, the membranes harden and some of the excess cholesterol is removed. It is hooked up with linoleic acid (LA) and shipped off to the liver to be changed into bile acids provided there are enough vitamins and minerals. But alcohol drinkers pass out their zinc and magnesium in their urine and tend to be deficient. They are usually short of B vitamins too.

Bile acids help with fat digestion and are then removed in the body wastes, provided that the foods contain sufficient fibre and the bowel action is regular enough to prevent the bile acids being reabsorbed and recycled. Breast cancer, related to the intake of dairy fats, is more likely in women who are constipated. Constipation is more likely when vitamin C, magnesium and essential fatty acids are deficient or if the diet is high in allergens such as wheat or cow's milk. Fibre is best obtained from foods with a lower risk of allergy.

Alcohol Addiction and Brain Performance

Why is alcohol so addictive? Alcohol stimulates the release of the anti-inflammatory prostaglandin PGE1 which makes us feel good. Another reason for alcohol's popularity is that it makes us less self-critical! But besides loosening inhibitions, alcohol also makes our cells flabby. Alcohol depletes linoleic acid from our cells and our cell membranes become more fluid. Prolonged drinking damages the pancreas and liver, interfering with both absorption and general metabolism. At first more PGE1 is made, but as the production pathway gradually blocks, the levels start to fall. When alcohol is withdrawn there is a sudden catastrophic fall in PGE1.

Lack of PGE1 causes brain damage and impairs brain function. A woman who drinks is likely to be short of essential fatty acids and more likely to be infertile, miscarry or give birth to a baby suffering from learning difficulties, or even full-blown foetal alcohol syndrome. 'Safe' daily alcohol amounts are meaningless for an individual. Supplements of evening primrose oil improved both liver and brain function in people giving up alcohol. Ex-alcoholics can be helped to be safer drivers as their memory and visual-motor coordination have improved with EPO supplements.

Also important for better brain performance for children with learning problems or for older people with cerebro-vascular disease is the role EFAs play in keeping our cell membranes more fluid. Red cells are too big to pass through our smallest capillaries and need to be flexible and bendy. Lack of EFAs mean stiff red cells and our tissues can become short of oxygen. Tobacco smoking and ageing make cell membranes stiff while EPO supplements can restore fluidity. Even old people, who have had several brain infarcts (damage following blood clots), have had improved brain function on supplements.

Biolab measures the essential fatty acids in serum and in red cell membranes. A third of the fatty acids in membranes are EFAs and the rest saturated fats. People who take daily alcohol are often short of essential fatty acids and their red cells are too high in saturated fats even when they are vegetarians eating very little animal fat. Levels of saturated fats such as stearic acid rise when essential fatty acids are deficient and fall when fish oils and evening primrose oil supplements are taken. Twenty per cent of the dry weight of our brain is made of essential fatty acids. As Becky said to John Wayne in the film *True Grit*, 'I don't want a thief to steal away my brain.'

Quality of Semen

Semen in very rich in essential fatty acids and their by-products the prostaglandins which were first isolated from prostatic secretions. As men need more zinc and EFAs than women they are particularly likely to become short of both and risk damaging not only their own health, but the health and the intelligence of their future children. It is absurd that specialists in infertility are still saying they do not know why so many men can only produce small numbers of mostly abnormal sperm, when they are not taking the trouble to test for and treat these crucial deficiencies of essential nutrients or the hidden genital infections which block the EFA pathways.

Women's Treatment

Twice as many women as men need extra EPO, perhaps because previous pill taking has left them short of zinc, magnesium, B vitamins and pancreatic enzymes. EPO is extensively promoted for women's problems – sore breasts, period pains and PMS. Again both EPO and EPA supplements are needed as some women develop EPA deficiencies after taking only EPO because the balance in their essential fat metabolism had been upset. Conversely, if only fish oils are taken, the 6-series fatty acids can become deficient. Dr David Horrobin, pioneer of essential fatty acid research, discovered that infections, including viruses, stop the EFAs being produced. When routinely checking preconception couples for unsuspected genital infections, I find most patients with prostatitis or cervicitis also have essential fatty acid deficiencies.

Reasons for Blocks in EFA and Prostaglandin Pathways

In both sexes EFA deficiencies are usually due to blocks in pathways rather than to poor diet. The pathways should be producing a balance of various prostaglandins in both sexes. About thirty prostaglandins have been discovered so far. They are like short-lived hormones and they regulate cellular activities moment by moment. Prostaglandins control blood vessel reactivity and thrombosis. They include PGE1 which is anti-inflammatory, PGE3 which is anti-thrombotic and PGE2 which is inflammatory.

Prostaglandin production can be blocked or imbalanced by alcohol (as already discussed), prescribed steroids including sex hormones, aspirin-like drugs, stress or excess copper or vitamin A, or due to lack of essential nutrients.

Dr David Horrobin writes that 'drugs which block the formation of prostaglandins are among the most widely used of all therapeutic agents.' *Steroids also block prostaglandin release and, as steroids include sex hormones, the pill and HRT, an instant feeling of well-being can explain the popularity of such prescriptions among doctors and their patients who disregard the longer term implications.*

Steroids

Steroids, cortisone or prednisone, block the release of arachidonic acid from the membranes and its conversion to the inflammatory prostaglandin (PGE2). While this may give instant relief to arthritis sufferers, steroids also unfortunately at the same time block the release of the beneficial dihomogamma-linolenic acid (DGLA) which in turn prevents anti-flammatory PGE1 formation. Steroids also block the formation of EPA and anti-thrombotic PGE3. Patients on long-term steroids, which include sex hormones, the pill and HRT, are more likely to have sticky platelets and more chance of thrombosis, heart attacks and osteoporosis due to microthrombi in the bones.

Mental and physical stress, OCS and HRT use elevate natural cortisol levels. Cortisol or stress also lower zinc levels. Low zinc and raised steroid cortisol levels both help to block the EFA pathways and disturb prostaglandin production. EFA deficiency exaggerates hormone actions causing over-reactivity and undesirable side effects. Eating too much fat and sugar also releases cortisol.

Menopause

Vitamins A and E are needed to keep our essential fats intact and to prevent them being destroyed by oxygen and damaged by free radicals in our body before they can perform their important functions. Vitamins E prevents platelets being too sticky.

Younger women have the same vitamin E levels as men but post-menopausal women have higher levels of vitamin E. Fat levels rise after the menopause when the effect of any natural oestrogen production is no longer modified by cyclic progesterone. Older women have less risk of thrombosis due to having extra protection from higher levels of vitamin E, 3-series essential fatty acids and high density lipoproteins. Even though older women tend to have higher cholesterol levels than men, they are half as likely to die from heart attacks because of this extra protection.

If women are given extra oestrogens as HRT and especially if progestogens are added, raised copper levels and the many other changes already described, including raised cortisol levels, will increase their chances of vascular disease. The current fashion for prescribing oestrogens to women with heart disease is crazy. It is based on misleading epidemiology and the fact that oestrogen dilates blood vessels. But that is why prescribed oestrogens caused clotting in the first place and where we came in thirty-five years ago.

KEY POINTS

- Cholesterol makes steroid hormones, vitamin D, bile acids and helps essential fats (EFAs) regulate our cell membranes.

- Cholesterol is secreted by the glands in the skin and protects against dehydration, cracking, ageing and sun damage aided by natural antioxidants.
- Oestrogens, combined OCS, and HRT raise the levels of blood fats, cholesterol, triglycerides and some fatty acids.
- Testosterone lowers the levels of the protective HDL2 fraction of cholesterol and the protective 3-series EFAs.
- Combined OCS and HRT plus progestogens also lower protective fats while elevating the artery-clogging fats giving the worst risks from both men and women.
- Taking EFA supplements reduces the risk of diseases of brain, heart and blood vessels, breast, prostate, liver and skin, and helps tissues to stay healthy.
- Normal EFA levels reduce over-reactivity to hormones and drugs.
- EFA pathways are blocked by steroid hormones, stress, aspirin, infections, common nutritional deficiencies, smoking and alcohol.
- Exogenous hormones, whether OCS or HRT, interfere with our ability to maintain the balance of these complicated fat interactions.

Chapter Six

Staying Young Naturally Without HRT

In the world's rich developed countries, women are being pressurised into taking HRT – so-called hormone replacement therapy – at the menopause. The advertising propaganda, to doctors and women alike, gives the impression that the menopause is a kind of disease and not perfectly normal. The usual age when a woman's periods stop and she becomes infertile is round about fifty-two. Although contraception is advised for older women until two years after the menopause, some women, especially if they are zinc deficient, smokers, or alcohol drinkers, may undergo a very early premature menopause. Women exposed to extra hormones in their mother's womb, as the pill, or as fertility stimulants, may stop ovulating in their twenties or thirties. At the menopause, the eggs in a woman's ovaries are used up and fresh follicles can no longer be stimulated by her brain hormones. The result is her ovaries stop making oestrogen and progesterone. Then women are interested in their grandchildren and are often relieved that their own childbearing years are over. As we grow older the important question is are our cells properly nourished and not what are our hormone levels. A woman's adrenal glands and fat tissues continue to make a small amount of oestrogen and she goes on looking like a woman. Women outlive men and are half as likely to die from early heart attacks before their Biblical three score years and ten are up. A great deal of nonsense is spoken about life spans. The average life expectancy has increased dramatically because so few babies now die in infancy. Some people have survived to ripe old ages for thousands of years. Old age is not an invention of the twentieth century.

Can men or women stay healthy as they age? Ageing is in our genes. We are programmed to age, die and be replaced by new generations. Genetic engineering is capable of changing this. Women can be given ovarian implants containing young egg cysts to prolong the time when their ovaries can respond to brain hormones. In the future it may be possible to go on living for centuries or even thousands of years. As overpopulation of our planet is of great concern, such a scenario may not seem welcome. What is happening now is far removed from this revolution in nature's laws – just the opposite. While average life spans have been increasing so far, the predictions for young pill takers are not good and our years of disability are increasing. More people are being crippled by heart disease, arthritis, osteoporosis, cancer and other degenerative diseases. Pollution, drugs and inappropriate diet, an excessive dependence on grains – the grass family – wheat, corn, rye, cane sugar and dairy products cause hidden allergies, interfere with the absorption of nutrients and even cause the excessive excretion of essential nutrients. For nearly everyone, a modern diet and lifestyle means extra nutritional supplements are needed to avoid deficiency diseases. The Japanese, traditionally small and intelligent on their diet of fish and magnesium seaweed, are changing. As the young Japanese are brought up eating hamburgers and drinking cow's milk, they are growing taller but dying younger of degenerative diseases. Big is not always beautiful.

At the menopause some women simply stop bleeding and that's all there is to it. Other women have severe hormone withdrawal symptoms – hot flushes being the most troublesome characteristic sign. What is not well known is that hot flushes are a result of an allergic reaction. High steroid hormone levels tend to suppress some vascular reactions which become obvious when hormone levels fall. *Hot flushes are not a sign of oestrogen deficiency.* Some women have been given implants of oestrogen. When the effect of the oestrogen begins to wear off the hot flushes come back. The women return to their doctors sooner and sooner for their next implant. Their oestrogen levels rise and rise with some women having fifty times higher concentrations in their blood than other women. But *a fall in these extremely high levels can bring on flushing*.

Flushes are very similar to headaches, migraine and rises in blood pressure. At the Charing Cross Hospital Migraine Clinic, I asked my patients to find out for themselves which food or drinks gave them reactions. Many men and women know they get headaches if they eat cheese, chocolate, oranges or alcohol but very few people are aware that they react to wheat, corn, milk, yeast, tea or coffee. These are known as hidden allergens and they need to be unmasked. Unmasking is a bit like sudden hormone withdrawal – perhaps stopping milk and beef is sudden hormone withdrawal although the UK government deny that! Dr John Mansfield has worked out a lamb and pears diet. As he had found few people reacted to these foods, he asked his patients to eat only lamb and pears plus sea salt and spring water for every meal for five days. The result is usually dramatic. After withdrawal symptoms such as headache, backache and 'flu-like symptoms which begin on the first night and intensify on the second and third days, the patient starts to feel like a new person. The clean fresh feeling is amazing. Headaches and migraine vanish and raised blood pressure levels usually fall to normal. For arthritis patients too much red meat may cause inflammation, and Dr Mansfield has found they do better with fish and root vegetables for a week or two.[1] Only about one in fifty people are allergic to fish. Their allergy may be only to shell fish or fish protein and they may be able to tolerate the important fish oils like those in EPA capsules.

After five days when a new food is introduced the patient can test his or her pulse before eating and every fifteen minutes for an hour after eating the new food. Milk, wheat, yeast, eggs, corn and oranges are the commonest foods causing an immediate pulse rise. Drinks likely to cause reactions are orange juice, tea, coffee, soft drinks containing colours and additives and alcohol. Occasionally the pulse falls as a sign of a reaction. We should be able to eat and drink without precipitating these vascular reactions, stomach pains or other symptoms. Foods causing reactions can be omitted for a few weeks. Some patients, especially those who have taken steroids for years, react to every single food they test. Clearly they can't just stop eating, but they can eat only one type of food at each meal and have a different food at the next meal. This 'total allergy syndrome', in my experience, is often a result of taking either sex hormones or adrenal steroids for years.

The more severe the essential nutritional deficiencies, the more foods and chemicals are likely to cause reactions. The opposite is also true – restoring the essential nutrient levels to normal decreases the number of foods causing reactions. Steroid and sex hormones raise copper and lower serum zinc levels, and interfere with liver function and the metabolism of food. This means that women who are given extra oestrogen after the menopause are likely to have even more flushings, headaches, raised blood pressure and vascular reactions when they stop these extra hormones than they did before they took them.

In spite of its tendency to cause addiction, a recent Osteoporosis Review published by a drug company asks the question 'Hormone Replacement Therapy: Why do so few women use it?' Drs Hall and Spector from St Bartholomew's Hospital in London say that oestrogen has been readily available for the treatment of climacteric (menopausal) symptoms since the 1960s but very few women in the UK are taking extra hormones. Massive government-backed advertising campaigns and promotion have not exactly taken off so far.[2]

Among nearly 7,000 women questioned, only one in ten had ever taken HRT and only one in a hundred women aged forty-five to sixty-five is taking it. Most stop after one or two years. These British doctors wondered if the word 'hormone' was the reason for non-acceptance. They said that the word hormone conjures up a picture of hirsutism (hairiness) obesity and bad skin. They suggested we should replace 'hormone' with 'oestrogen' as the Americans do.

Women also associate HRT with the oral contraceptive pill and its side effects, and friends becoming ill. When I first heard that nearly half of the women in the USA were taking or had taken oestrogens at the menopause, I was amazed. How can so many women be so gullible especially if they have already tried several different oral contraceptives in a usually vain attempt to escape side effects?

But women can be persuaded that HRT is 'different from the pill' and that they must take it to avoid osteoporosis and fractures in their seventies or eighties. The clearly fallacious 'prevention of heart attacks and strokes' is repeated to the point of idiocy when the opposite is true.

One of the main proponents of HRT in the UK said on television that women who still have their uterus are unlucky. The 9 per cent of women aged forty-five to sixty-five who have had their womb removed are the lucky ones. They can take oestrogen without the risk of endometrial and cervical cancer. The 3 per cent who have also had their ovaries removed are even luckier – in theory they should have no risk of ovarian cancer. But to be really lucky they need to have their breasts removed as breast cancer is also hormone-dependent and has greatly increased since the 1960s, especially in the USA. Women who still have a uterus must also be prescribed progestogens each month. Regular withdrawal bleeding decreases the otherwise inevitable overgrowth of the womb lining and reduces the greatly increased endometrial cancer risk. In the USA endometrial cancer increased twelve times among oestrogen users.

Among 2,500 women aged forty-five to fifty-five prescribed HRT in North America, most never started taking these hormones or gave up within nine months. In the UK, even among women whose abnormally thin bones were diagnosed by X-rays, most gave up. Only 40 per cent were still taking the hormones for six to twelve months.

Many GPs, quite rightly, do not believe that HRT prevents vascular disease as they have seen the identical hormones cause thrombosis, embolism and high blood pressure. Too many of their patients are developing breast and cervical cancers. Unless they are blinded by high pressured advertising and confused through drug company lunches, they are in a position to see the evidence for themselves.

REASONS FOR EARLY REMOVAL OF WOMB AND OVARIES

In most HRT studies, up to a third of the women have had their womb removed before the natural age of the menopause. Removal of the womb alone should not lower hormone levels but the blood supply to the ovaries may be interfered with, affecting a woman's natural hormone production. The reasons for the hysterectomy, such as infection and essential nutrient deficiencies or imbalance, may be themselves causes of a premature decline in natural hormone production. Wombs and ovaries are removed because of infection, fibroids, endometriosis, ovarian cysts, and cervical, endometrial or ovarian cancers. All these conditions are increased in hormone users although they are often diagnosed after contraceptive hormones have been discontinued.

Fibroids are the most common pelvic tumours and the

most common reason for hysterectomy, usually diagnosed when women are in their forties as they tend to shrink after the menopause. Obese women get more fibroids perhaps because fatty tissue produces oestrogen. Infection also irritates the womb tissue leading to abnormal growth and fibroid formation.

In the RCGP women taking a lower dose of the progestogen pill were more than twice as likely to develop fibroids. Further trial details are in Appendix One

The Walnut Creek study, which started with more older women than the British studies, found that women who had ever taken oral contraceptives had more uterine fibroids; the oldest longer users having most risk. *Women takers of oestrogen HRT had six times more fibroids.* Fibroids cause heavy bleeding and they are usually discovered in wombs removed by hysterectomy. The Walnut Creek study found *both menstrual disorders and hysterectomies were more common among pill and oestrogen HRT users.*

Women with heavy bleeding are now being offered endometrial ablation as an alternative to hysterectomy. A laser is inserted inside a tube (endoscope) and dragged over the lining of the womb to vaporise the tissue. The womb lining can also be cut away using a cutting tool in the endoscope. This is like an old fashioned D and C – dilatation and curettage. Less dilatation of the cervix is needed and the cutting is done under direct visual control. Women are first given danazol as an anti-oestrogen. These procedures reduce heavy bleeding in most women for at least three years but in one survey 15 per cent of the women needed further treatment or a hysterectomy.

Among my patients I find heavy bleeding is often due to infection or magnesium and essential fatty acid deficiencies, especially lack of 6-series fatty acids. Treatment of cervical infection with cervical cautery, appropriate antibiotics and nutritional supplements, especially evening primrose oil, are all that is usually required. Infections in partners also need to be investigated and treated.

149

Aspirin or food allergies during menstruation can cause heavy bleeding. The same foods which are most likely to cause headaches are most likely to cause bleeding in sensitive women, especially in those who are deficient in zinc and magnesium.

Mrs E

Aged forty-six, Mrs E was about to have a hysterectomy for heavy bleeding when she asked me what else could be done. The swab of the inside of her cervix showed no sign of hidden infections but the Biolab screen discovered the common deficiencies. Mrs E's hair mineral pattern showed raised concentrations of toxic elements especially cadmium, and abnormally high zinc levels due to long-term zinc deficiency and reduced hair growth. When the hair growth is poor, minerals accumulate. The sweat sample confirmed zinc deficiency and both the sweat and red cells were short of magnesium. Toxic metals were not high in the serum. The essential fatty acid profile showed adequate amounts of the 3-series fish oils but low 6-series linoleic acid and arachidonic acid levels. These deficiencies were corrected with zinc, magnesium and evening primrose oil supplements and the bleeding returned to the normal menstrual amounts.

Mrs H

Mrs H was referred to me by a local gynaecologist. He had removed her womb the year before because of fibroids and heavy bleeding. At the same time both ovaries were taken out because they were cystic. Mrs H was now forty-four years old and she still felt ill. She had taken the pill when she was thirty-two but stopped within a few months because of weight gain, depression and migraine. She had two healthy children but her husband had numerous sexual partners and Mrs H suffered from repeated infections and pelvic inflammatory disease. The pelvic pains did not stop after her hysterectomy but became worse when she was given HRT – Prempak and norgestrel. She had pelvic congestion, sore breasts and throbbing legs. She had food allergies and had found out that cream gave her migraine, while wheat, sugar and eggs made her sneeze, made her chesty and brought on a cold. I advised her to stop HRT and immediately her breasts, legs and lower abdomen stopped feeling painful. Biolab mineral analysis showed severe magnesium, selenium and chromium deficiencies. Her serum iron was below the normal range while her sweat and serum copper were above normal because of the oestrogens. Her hair results showed low magnesium concentrations and low sodium and potassium levels, believed to reflect increased stress cortisol such as can be produced by extra oestrogens. Mrs H felt much better with on low-allergy diet and nutritional supplements. A bowel fermentation test was positive for alcohol and, like many ex-HRT users, she needed anti-candida treatment. Mrs H has regular mineral screens to check that her levels are now normal. This lady's experience demonstrates that surgery does not necessarily cure all the underlying problems.

The Walnut Creek study found twice as many past users of the pill had hysterectomies compared with never-users in the 18-39-year-old age group and past users age forty to forty-nine also had a higher risk. Current oestrogen users had *'a pronounced increased risk for every condition of the genital tract under study' including pelvic congestion, endomentrial hyperplasia, adenomyosis and endometrial cancer.*

Adenomyosis, when endometrial tissue is seen penetrating the womb muscle, is usually diagnosed in hysterectomy specimens. The Walnut Creek doctors found past users of the pill were 2.5 times more likely to have adenomyosis in all the age groups. Endometriosis was also more likely in past users compared with never-users. It is strange in view of these results that progestogens are usually given to 'treat' endometriosis when treatment of hidden infections and nutritional deficiencies would be more helpful for long-term benefit.

OSTEOPOROSIS IN TWENTY- OR EIGHTY-YEAR-OLDS?

Why is there a panic about osteoporosis? How much of it is due to poor nutrition? As people age they tend to 'grow down' and become shorter. Very old people are often bent nearly double with fragile, easily broken bones. Their hip, vertebrae or forearm may break spontaneously without a fall or trauma. The bone mass is reduced and the skeleton fails – a frightening picture.[2]

Ninety per cent of hip fractures in women over seventy-five years old are the result of a fall. Many of these falls should be preventable by earlier treatment of cataracts, physical therapy for impaired mobility, safety measures in the home and avoidance of drugs such as sleeping pills which impair brain function. Extra magnesium supplementation will help to ensure that an older person is calm, can sleep and has improved muscle and joint function and greater bone mass. Zinc, chromium and selenium supplements help to prevent lens opacities and cataract development. Fractures are often due to steroids such as prednisone. Given long term, the risk of fractures can increase nine times.

Professor Christiansen in Copenhagen studied 178 'healthy' post-menopausal women aged forty-five to fifty-four in 1977 and followed them up twelve years later.[3] Thirty-three were excluded due to diseases or use of drugs known to influence calcium metabolism and 24 were lost or dead. The remaining 121 women had become shorter and heavier and lost 20 per cent of the bulk of their forearm bone on average. Twenty of the women, those losing bone most quickly, had had compression fractures in their vertebrae. The seven women who had had arm fractures had lower bone mass at the menopause than the other women. After the menopause, bone can be lost at the rate of 2 per cent each year.

This is an abnormal group as healthy women should not have an early menopause which is a sign of ovarian failure and not a sign of good health. Long term (five years or longer) taking of oral contraceptives leads to decreased pancreatic function, persistent zinc deficiency and an early menopause becoming more likely.

Bone Density in the Young

Clearly bones are heavy and need a lot of feeding. Our bone mineral density (BMD) depends on our diet and absorbing enough minerals.

A study of young women aged thirteen to twenty showed great variation in bone mineral density. The women with the thickset bones were heavier and had good hormone levels – oestrogen and testosterone. Those with the lowest oestrogen concentrations were underweight for their height. Thin women who regularly engaged in strenuous activity were especially likely to be amenorrhoeic (absent menstrual bleeding and usually not ovulating). These women are particularly predisposed to osteoporosis and fractures later. Women with a history of anorexia, which is accompanied by amenorrhoea and ovarian cysts in prolonged and severe cases, due to zinc deficiency, can have a poor skeleton for the rest of their lives and more risk of premature osteoporotic fractures.

As oestrogens and progestogen in the form of oral contraceptives induce earlier menopauses with more chance of early osteoporosis, so more and more women are being persuaded to take oestrogen and progestogen in the form of HRT. The inner lining type of bone, called trabecular, which tends to diminish after the menopause, needs a good blood supply but can be impaired by tiny blood clots developing in pill and HRT takers as by described by Dr Kitty Little.[4] Both trabecular and outer cortical bone tends to diminish in men as well as women over age seventy unless their nutrition is adequate.

NUTRITIONAL REASONS FOR OSTEOPOROSIS

Dr Alan Gaby and Dr Jonathan Wright have reviewed the relationship between nutrition and osteoporosis in the *Journal of Nutritional Medicine*.[5] They estimate that nearly one-third of all American women will develop osteoporosis severe enough to cause a fracture. Bone mass in many women declines at thirty-five years of age. The loss accelerates rapidly for eight to ten years around the time of the menopause and then continues at a slower rate. While oestrogen slows down the rapid bone loss when it is being taken, Dr Law illustrated in the *British Medical Journal* that the bone-loss acceleration after oestrogen is stopped.[6] If a woman manages to tolerate extra oestrogen for five years after the menopause, and then discontinues it, by ten years her bone loss is the same as that of a woman who never took HRT.

Calcium

In animals, lack of calcium causes soft bones but it is lack of magnesium which causes thin bones – osteoporosis. There is a widespread belief among women and their doctors that calcium supplementation is very important but calcium deficiency is rare and difficult to diagnose. In spite of the very prevalent belief, white spots on finger nails are not due to lack of calcium but to lack of zinc. I have yet to see a low serum calcium level among my patients. Only one hypothyroid patient was calcium deficient in a muscle test performed by Dr Howard. Urinary levels may be more useful and urinary excretion of calcium, phosphorus and zinc are included in Biolab's osteoporosis profile along with serum bone alkaline phosphatase tests.

As much as 2gm per day of calcium supplements for two years, given to post-menopausal women, did not significantly reduce bone loss in one study, while another study claimed a benefit in a quarter of osteoporotic women who were calcium deficient. *None of the women in John Howard's study of osteoporosis had low serum calcium levels.*[7] Whether the women were pre- or post-menopausal, whether or not they suffered from osteoporosis or were taking HRT, their serum calcium levels were the same and not altered by daily nutritional supplements, which included 500mg calcium.

Calcium supplements increase the risk of kidney stones especially in the presence of urinary infection. One to three grams of calcium each day causes abnormally high serum and urine calcium levels in a quarter of the women who take these high-dose calcium supplements. Such megadoses have not been shown to prevent the loss of the inner bone tissue which happens in the first decade after the menopause in some women. Because excessive-dose calcium supplements can cause unwanted calcification, Dr Guy Abrahams advises no more than 500mg calcium citrate each day and even that may not be necessary.[8]

Calcium supplements can interfere with iron and zinc absorption which can cause serious problems. In younger pre-menopausal women calcium supplements can cause infertility, upsetting the normal hormone production from the corpus luteum in the second half of a normal cycle. Calcium can block the binding of the luteal hormone to its receptors on the corpus luteum, resulting in the cyst dissolving prematurely. Although bones contain nearly all our body calcium, populations with the lowest calcium intake have the fewest hip fractures.

Magnesium

Bone magnesium tends to decrease sharply after the menopause while calcium levels remain normal. If a post-menopausal woman is short of magnesium an excessive parathyroid hormone production may be increasing her loss of bone minerals.[3, 8] Oestrogen can protect against this type of accelerating osteoporosis by preventing the release of the hormone. But it is magnesium which normally suppresses excessive release of parathyroid hormone. Clearly, the answer to menopausal osteoporosis is magnesium supplementation and not extra oestrogen and progestogens as they will exacerbate the magnesium deficiency.

Dr Guy Abrahams says most cases of osteoporosis are not caused by calcium deficiency and cannot be prevented by calcium megadosing. Instead he has found magnesium deficiency plays the key role.

Magnesium supplements are an efficient, safe and cost-effective way of preventing osteoporosis and helping those who already have problems. Dr Abrahams emphasises that important causes of osteoporosis are lack of exercise, stress, low weight, alcoholism and taking steroid hormones. To that list can be added contraceptive steroids, fertility stimulants and HRT.

Post-menopausal women taking more magnesium have denser bones. Osteoporotic women with low whole body and bone magnesium have abnormal crystal formation in their bones. This abnormality can be corrected by taking magnesium. Magnesium deficiency is common in both the UK and America where most women consume less than the recommended daily amount. A high unrefined cereal and potato diet can provide 1gm per day of magnesium but the recommended daily amount is only 280mg each day. Biolab patients often need about 500mg daily taken as magnesium amino acid chelate plus selenium 200 micrograms. This amount usually returns sweat and red cell magnesium levels to normal. Too much magnesium can cause diarrhoea and increase a deficiency!

We discovered in the 1960s that the enzyme alkaline phosphatase is increased by oestrogens and decreased by progestogens in the womb. As the bone enzyme is involved in forming new calcium crystals with the help of magnesium, its level of activity gives an indication of whether or not new bone is being made.

Women with osteoporosis have low levels of bone alkaline phosphatase but women with osteoporosis taking oestrogens as HRT had the lowest levels of bone alkaline phosphatase in Dr Howard's series. The women on HRT had abnormally high total serum alkaline phosphatase levels but low bone activity. When Dr Howard gave these women nutritional supplements, the bone alkaline phosphatase levels were normal after six weeks in the women with osteoporosis and at twelve weeks they were higher than normal. *In contrast, the women with osteoporosis taking HRT still had abnormally low bone enzyme levels after twelve weeks of adding nutritional supplements including extra boron. They were not making new bone.*

Red blood cell magnesium levels were low in the women with osteoporosis but reached the normal range after six weeks of supplements. Again *those taking HRT had the lowest levels and, although increased, were not yet in the normal range after twelve weeks of 250mg of magnesium per day.*

Dr Abrahams gave magnesium-rich nutritional supplements to nineteen women taking HRT. Most of these women had suffered from a premature menopause, their average ages being only forty and forty-one years old. After eight to nine months the bone mineral density in the women taking the supplements had increased by 11 per cent while there was no increase in the women taking HRT alone without nutritional supplements. At the start of treatment, 15 out of 19 of these very young women in HRT had a bone mineral density below the threshold for spinal fractures; after a year on nutritional supplements only 7 out of 19 still had excessively thin bones. The best results were obtained when magnesium-rich nutrients were given at the menopause and the bone minerals were still improving after two years of supplements. If nutritional screening tests were employed throughout life, most of these women might have avoided the early halt in their natural hormone production.

Zinc

Zinc is not only essential for brain development and function, it is critical for all tissues, and chronic long-term lack of zinc is also a main cause of osteoporosis. Zinc is essential for normal bone formation and is a co-factor for vitamin D.

It is disturbing that an increase in pill taking in the 1970s has been followed by a sharp fall in children's sweat zinc levels during the 1980s. The drop in sweat zinc from an average of 710 parts per billion to 530 among apparently healthy children, while those with dyslexia average 350, is highly significant statistically. As the pill steroids lower zinc levels, osteoporosis in mothers and their children is likely to become a long-term problem. Women giving up HRT because of side effects are likely to be more deficient than they were before.

The lower the sweat zinc levels, the higher is the concentration of toxic metals in both sweat and hair. Lead, cadmium and mercury are also significantly higher in the hair of zinc-deficient children. Hyperactive children and anorexic young women also usually have abnormally low zinc levels. Professor Derek Bryce-Smith and Dr Neil Ward found that the bones of still-born babies had high levels of lead and cadmium. These toxic metals concentrate in the bone, displacing calcium, especially when zinc is deficient.[9]

There is concern in the industrialised societies that toxic metals, lead from traffic fumes, cadmium from cigarettes, aluminium from the packaging in convenience foods and mercury from tooth fillings are interfering with bone metabolism. The highest mercury levels among my patients are in dentists. When both the husband and the wife are dentists, their combined high mercury levels often give them fertility problems. Maintaining adequate zinc status is our main protection against toxins. HRT with excessive oestrogen stimulation robs women of important safety mechanisms.

*Among Dr Howard's women with osteoporosis, all were
zinc deficient in their white blood cells. Once more, the
women on HRT had the lowest levels. Again, they failed
to achieve normal values after twelve weeks of supplementation.* All the women took 30mg of zinc each
night at bedtime and the zinc levels of the other group of
osteoporotic women *not taking HRT* were well into the
normal range by this time.

Copper

In Dr Howard's study all the serum copper levels were
normal in the post-menopausal women and in the women
with osteoporosis. *Only the osteoporotic women who also
took HRT had abnormal, above the range, copper levels.
Although zinc tends to lower copper, after weeks of supplements, the HRT women still had much higher serum
copper values than the other post-menopausal women.*
High serum copper levels do not rule out copper
deficiency. When copper is deficient functionally, for
example, as diagnosed by a special enzyme test, taking
extra zinc may result in both zinc levels and copper stores
falling further. It is my experience that long-term hormone
use, for example, a few years on oral contraceptives or
fertility hormones, or several years of undiagnosed infections, can induce abnormally high serum copper levels.
Copper stores become depleted and in spite of exogenous
hormone stimulation the serum copper starts to fall to
abnormally low levels. When the serum and sweat copper
are below the normal range, copper supplements are
needed – 3mg of copper taken on alternate nights with
30mg of zinc for three weeks is enough to replace copper
stores. Some multisupplements have up to 2mg of
copper and this is probably too much to take every day.
While copper is essential, too much copper is toxic and
interferes with brain and liver function. The typical American diet contains about 1mg of copper while the recommended daily amount is 2mg. In Dr Howard's

osteoporosis series, his supplements included zinc 30mg daily and 3mg of copper every third day only. The women on HRT (who already had high serum copper levels) were not given extra copper although their copper stores might be falling giving a low blood enzyme reading.

In animals fed a copper-deficient diet, the bone mineral content and bone strength is reduced. Copper is a cofactor for the enzyme lysyl oxidase which strengthens connective tissue by cross-linking the strands of collagen.

Manganese

Manganese is needed for bone mineralization and making bone and cartilage connective tissue. Genetic factors influence the susceptibility to manganese deficiency, which should always be looked for in anyone with a history of epilepsy especially when attacks started at the menarche for no obvious reason (such as a head injury). Individuals with so called idiopathic epilepsy are therefore susceptible to manganese deficiency osteoporosis.

Again, in the Biolab study, *serum manganese levels were lowest in those osteoporotic women who were taking HRT* but were increased after six weeks of daily 10mg manganese supplements.

Boron

Not only do boron supplements decrease urinary calcium excretion, but they actually markedly increase serum oestradiol levels. Women taking boron, 3mg each day, can have as high oestradiol levels as women taking small amounts of HRT. Boron helps the body make its own personal oestrogen and is involved in the conversion of cholesterol to steroid hormones and vitamin D3. Fruit, vegetables and nuts are the main dietary sources. In some parts of the world the diet contains as much as 41mg of boron daily with no harmful consequences. Prescribed oral conjugated oestrogens (like Premarin) are mostly converted to oestrone in the gut, and large amounts are given to achieve a small rise in serum oestradiol levels. In contrast, the amount of endogenously produced 17 ß oestradiol required to raise serum levels may be as little as 5 per cent of the prescribed oral dose. Dr Howard gives 5mg boron as sodium tetraborate daily to patients with osteoporosis.

Silicon

Silicon also strengthens connective tissue by cross-linking collagen strands and high concentrations of silicon are found at calcification sites in growing bone. Chicks fed a silicon-deficient diet had abnormal skulls and thin leg-bones with impaired calcification. Refined foods, especially for osteoporosis patients, may cause deficiencies.

Strontium

Large concentrations of this mineral accumulate in bone and teeth. Radioactive strontium from nuclear fallout therefore accumulates in bony tissues. Non-radioactive strontium in food has been given in large doses (1.7gm per day) to osteoporosis patients with most showing radiological improvements and reduction in bone pain. Again, chronic consumption of strontium-depleted, refined foods may adversely affect bone growth.

Vitamin C (ascorbic acid)

Osteoporosis occurs in scurvy. While overt scurvy is rare, mild vitamin C deficiency is common and can contribute to osteoporosis. *The average values for all the post-meno-pausal women in Dr Howard's study were below the lab-oratory normal range for white cell vitamin C levels. All reached the normal range after six weeks of supplements* with 1gm of vitamin C. Serum ascorbic acid levels were low in 20 per cent of elderly American women in one study, although they were taking more than the recommended 60mg per day.

Smoking lowers vitamin C levels and smokers are more likely to suffer from osteoporosis.

Vitamin K

Calcium crystallises on a bed of osteocalcin, a protein found only in bone. Vitamin K is needed to make osteocalcin. Recently, it has become possible to measure vitamin K levels in blood. Frequent use of antibiotics can destroy naturally occurring vitamin-K-producing bacteria in the intestines. Rats fed a vitamin-K-deficient diet have an increased calcium excretion. Vegetables contain vitamin K but in one series of sixteen osteoporotic patients, their serum levels were only a third of those of matched controls. Extra vitamin K reduced urinary calcium loss by 18 to 50 per cent. Vitamin K supplements may be needed when accelerated bone formation is desirable, as in treating osteoporosis and in aiding healing after a fracture.

Vitamin D

Vitamin D – the sunshine vitamin – is needed for calcium absorption. Elderly women often have reduced levels due to lack of sunlight, deficient intake, malabsorption or abnormal metabolism. Both magnesium and boron facilitate the conversions of vitamin D precursors to the more biologically active form calcitriol (D_3).

When medical students in the 1950s, we were told that so much extra vitamin D had been added to cereals and baby food that many children and adults were suffering from overdosage. Lumps of calcium form in soft tissues and calcium stones form in the kidneys and their tubes causing obstruction and excruciating pain. Fortified foods can give several thousand units of vitamin D when only 400 units is the recommended amount. This scare turned many doctors against nutritional supplements leading to a reluctance to take advantage of modern analytical screening tests.

Vitamin D is changed into its calcitriol with the help of magnesium. If calcium is low in the diet, calcitriol can be made from vitamin D in the diet and from cholesterol in the skin. It can also be made in the kidneys by a magnesium-dependent enzyme. A small amount of calcitriol improves calcium absorption in osteoporotic women. As these women are also usually magnesium deficient, vitamin D supplements are ineffective unless magnesium is also given.

Excess salt – sodium – intake increases calcium loss in the urine. In young people there is a compensatory increase in calcium absorption by increasing vitamin D_3 synthesis. In magnesium-deficient post-menopausal women, this mechanism is impaired.

Magnesium deficiency also impairs the potassium pump in the cell membranes so that the cells cannot retain potassium. Potassium deficiency may then prevent vitamin D_3 synthesis.

Folic Acid

One of the eight essential amino acids in dietary proteins, methionine, is converted in part to homocysteine which can be toxic. Another genetic disorder causes large amounts of homocysteine to accumulate and be excreted in the urine – homocysteinuria, which is looked for in infants. Untreated, these individuals develop severe osteoporosis at an early age.

Before the menopause, women can effectively convert homocysteine to less toxic compounds, but after the menopause women need extra folic acid to maintain this efficiency.

Tobacco smoking, drinking alcohol and using oral contraceptives and HRT all tend to promote folic acid deficiency. Most Western diets contain only half the recommended daily amount of folic acid and men and many older people are deficient.

Vitamin B6

Deficiency of this vitamin produces osteoporosis in rats and it is the commonest vitamin deficiency detected in Biolab's screening investigations whether in patients or in apparently healthy individuals. Vitamin B6 deficiency ranks with zinc and magnesium deficiencies in affecting many people for most of their lives unless they make considerable efforts to change their diets and take supplements. B6 deficiency is especially likely in women taking the contraceptive pill, using fertility drugs or taking HRT.

Again, B6 is a cofactor for the enzymatic cross-linking of collagen strands. Like folic acid, B6 helps to break down the harmful homocysteine product of methionine which promotes osteoporosis.

In America, the intake of B6 is usually less than the recommended amount and one survey found half of a group of supposedly healthy volunteers were deficient biochemically. One test involves checking enzyme function which is reduced when B6 is deficient and is restored when supplements are taken.

Efficient Absorption

Zinc deficiency, especially in women taking pancreas-damaging contraceptive or HRT hormones, interferes with absorption. The gut mucosa needs zinc for healthy active cells. Reduced pancreatic enzyme production causes impaired food digestion and a vicious circle is set up. Older people are more likely to have hypochlorhydria, lack of stomach acid, although this condition also can affect young people perhaps for genetic or hereditary reasons. Lack of stomach acid interferes with calcium absorption. Individuals with osteoporosis often have impaired calcium absorption and this can also be caused by vitamin D deficiencies.

Supplements of hydrochloric acid and pancreatic enzymes can restore flagging absorption to normal efficiency.

Jenny

Persuaded to take HRT at fifty-two because of a family history of osteoporosis, Jenny was getting dizzy three years later. A visit to Biolab showed she had the usual deficiencies. She was severely deficient in zinc, magnesium, chromium, selenium and B vitamins. The extra oestrogen had pushed up her blood, sweat and hair copper levels but an enzyme test signalled that her copper stores had become too low. Essential fatty acids were deficient while saturated fats were elevated. I suspected the family problem would show up on the gastrogram and, sure enough, Jenny's gastric acid production was low and she was only making a third of the usual amount of pancreatic digestive enzymes. When Jenny's sister was screened she also had an identical degree of pancreatic deficiency. Although a bone scan had shown some osteoporosis, after eighteen months supplements-taking but no more HRT Jenny's nutritional profile was excellent. A high bone alkaline phosphate result showed increased bone formation and Jenny now felt a hundred per cent fit.

Toxic Elements

Toxic minerals such as lead, cadmium, mercury and aluminium can accumulate in bones and replace essential minerals. Stillborn babies had higher bone lead and cadmium compared with live babies. John Howard writes that fluoride is one of the most toxic inorganic chemicals. It interferes with the release of carrier proteins and cytokinins (chemical immunity) causing immune suppression, auto-immune disease, reduced resistance to infection and increased cancer risk. Fluoride inhibits the migration of white blood cells at levels as low as 0.1 parts per million with only thirty minutes of exposure. He says fluoride is more toxic than mercury or paraquat, neither of which are added to the water supply, unlike fluoride. There is now evidence for an increase in bone cancer (osteosarcomas) among young males drinking water which has been fluoridated. Increased hip fractures occur with 1ppm fluoridation. There is an equal reduction in tooth decay in areas not adding fluoride to the water supply and a review article in the *Journal of the International Society for Fluoride Research* concludes that as fluoride is toxic to bone at all levels of exposure, that 'is reason enough to discontinue fluoration immediately'.[10] It is alarming to think how much fluoride-contaminated toothpaste children consume. Fluoride can exacerbate AIDS, ME or post viral syndrome and some types of allergy and cancer. A fluoride-sensitivity test is now available commercially which measures the effect of fluoride on white cell migration rates – a test of immune function.

Essential Fatty Acids

Deficiencies in essential fatty acids are more likely in women taking the pill, HRT and fertility hormones because of the pathway blocks caused by zinc, magnesium and vitamin B6 deficiencies. Raised copper levels also block the pathways, and infections, more likely, in hormone takers, will also further raise serum copper levels and eventually lower copper stores.

Lack of essential fatty acids will impair membrane function in bone cells and also make osteoporosis more likely in the long term.

Essential Amino Acids

Clearly protein deficiency, especially during early development and childhood, will result in reduced bone mass and an increased future risk of osteoporosis. Dancers and athletes on inadequate protein diets risk more fractures.

Bone is more than just a collection of calcium crystals. Bone is living, active, and needs a wide range of nutrients and healthy blood vessels. Dr Kitty Little explains how HRT, oral contraceptives and extra hormones can increase osteoporosis by causing minute thrombi in bone blood vessels especially in the presence of stress hormones.[3] Multiple deficiencies over a long period of time – before conception, in the womb, during lactation, childhood and adolescence, pregnancy and pill taking – all this prolonged lack of essential nutrients comes home to roost after the menopause or in old age. People, badly fed when young, are less likely to stay healthy and are more prone to osteoporosis.

The adverts for HRT continue to swamp doctors and women. The blurb for a new book proclaims 'HRT is life-transforming. It helps to maintain skin elasticity and bone density and to facilitate an active sex life.' Many women who cannot resist such pressure will indeed have their lives transformed – transformed by illness and death. The next chapter will describe the relentless increase in breast and cervical cancers. Conan Doyle predicted the effect of monkey glands in *The Creeping Man*, one of his Sherlock Holmes stories. The professor who took hormones went mad. The British HRT suicide results show he was right. One of my friends took HRT following an early hysterectomy. Her sex life, indeed her only life, was transformed when she committed suicide. She said, 'They don't believe you.' I hope readers of this book will be persuaded otherwise. Another friend, wary of HRT, only took nutritional supplements after her ovaries were prematurely removed and now, well into her sixties, she is a hot shot in golf tournaments.

KEY POINTS

- Hormone levels fall when no more egg follicles can be stimulated – natural age of menopause about fifty-two.
- Early age ovarian failures in 20–40-year-olds due to maternal or contraceptive hormone exposure, fertility drugs, smoking, alcohol zinc and magnesium deficiencies.
- Hormone takers more likely to have pelvic inflammatory disease (PID), fibroids, cancer and early removal of womb and ovaries.
- When magnesium is deficient, excess parathormone secretion increases bone loss.
- Osteoporosis is increased by smoking, alcohol, toxic chemicals and deficiencies in magnesium, zinc, boron and vitamins B, C and D, first-class protein and essential fats.

Chapter Seven

The Hormone-dependent Cancers –
Cutting Down the Risk

For the best part of two centuries we have known that
sex hormones cause cancer in hormone-dependent tissues
like the breast. How then has the fact that prescribed
hormones like the pill and HRT are causing a cancer
epidemic been so skilfully played down?

Very simply, epidemiologists only talk about an
increased cancer risk if the victims have taken hormones
for longer than usual. As the women most vulnerable to
side effects soon stop taking hormones the evidence
becomes muddled.

BENIGN BREAST DISEASE AND BREAST
CANCER

Mr Ian Burn said he'd never seen breast lumps disappear
so quickly before. The consultant surgeon running Charing Cross Hospital's Breast Clinic was talking about
patients he had referred over to the hospital's Migraine
Clinic because they also had headaches. Mr Burn knew
that if he prescribed an anti-oestrogen such as danazol,
which also has male-hormone-like actions, his patients'
headaches would become worse. Instead we tried the usual
migraine clinic routine. The women stopped smoking and
drinking alcohol, tea and coffee or taking hormones

including the pill and HRT, or any medication including tranquillisers like Valium and started the water, lamb and pears diet. Again the result was dramatic. After a day or two of more headaches, backache or other withdrawal symptoms, both the headaches and sore lumpy breasts got better. The foods causing reactions were bread (wheat and yeast), cheese (milk and yeast), alcohol, tea, coffee, corn, oranges and chocolate – the same common foods that precipitate migraine.[1]

Possibly foods with yeast or moulds were acting like oestrogens and overstimulating the breast tissue into hyperplastic overgrowth and cyst formation.

Recently, a journalist on HRT was told she must have a mammogram immediately and it was arranged for the following day. That night, because she had already interviewed me some weeks earlier, she decided to strip off her oestrogen patch. She awoke next morning to find her lumps, three, including a large one, had disappeared. She still went for the mammogram and the technician was amazed.

The same is happening for migraine. One woman had severe migraine appearing and disappearing as she stuck on or alternatively removed an oestrogen patch, probably because of the immediate and rapid absorption via the skin's blood vessels especially when they are dilated during exercise. Oestrogen from the patch enters the blood stream straight away, bypassing the liver. The woman, described in the *Lancet*, was aiding rapid absorption from her patch by doing aerobic exercises, a popular fashion among women trying to stay young and fit.[2] A silly piece of advice was for women to remove their patch each time they exercise!

Breast pain (mastalgia) is very common and affecting as many as two in every three women with one in five women having severe pain[3] Pain is usually a sign that the breasts are lumpy, especially in the upper and outer quarters, before a woman's periods. If a nodule persists, and doesn't improve with the hormone changes each month, it is biopsied to check that it is not malignant. Fortunately, nine out of ten times the breast lump is benign. Cyclical benign breast disease affects women who have not yet reached the menopause while most breast cancer is discovered later. Breast cancer is the commonest cancer in women. *Although it is the number one cause of death in women up to age fifty-five, the risk goes on increasing with age with 80–90-year-olds having the highest incidence.*[4] Only 28 per cent of breast cancers registered in 1984 were diagnosed in women under fifty-five.[5]

The same drugs tend to be used for both benign breast disease and endometriosis. They are designed to block a woman's own hormone production. A common prescription for lumpy or sore breasts is Danazol 200mg daily for at least two months. Danazol's side effects, which are menstrual irregularity, weight gain, headaches and nausea, 'can reduce compliance, although some patients are certainly willing to tolerate these side effects if their mastalgia is much improved' writes a general practitioner in *GP* magazine.[6] He goes on to say danazol should be stopped immediately if the voice deepens in pitch, otherwise this male-hormone-like effect may persist. Testosterone (Restandol) has also been given. Recently developed drugs which stimulate the release of luteinising hormone from the pituitary – releasing hormone agonists – inducing temporary medical castration by cutting off a woman's own hormones, are being given as monthly injections. Most GPs now tend to use a low-dose diuretic to increase fluid loss via the kidneys for a few days before a period. They may also prescribe bromocriptine which reduces the milk hormone prolactin concentrations in the blood. This drug may cause nausea, headaches, constipation, low blood pressure and worsening of Raynaud's disease (cold fingers) and Parkinson's disease. It is also now given to one in three new mothers to block their milk supply, instead of stilboestrol.

A hospital surgeon writes in the same *GP* review that he doubts the effectiveness of exclusion diets and vitamin supplements on breast disease but has experienced 'how *simple withdrawal of oral contraceptives or HRT can produce dramatic benefits'*.

Male doctors are unable to test for themselves how an exclusion diet diminishes breast pain but they would only need to try the effect of excluding most common allergens from their patients' diets to see what happens. Personally, my breasts know the difference between skimmed milk, butter and cheese in order of increasing severity of discomfort. *Countries with a high dairy fat consumption have a high and escalating breast cancer incidence, but they are the same countries which have been vigorously prescribing hormones.*

As for vitamins – their levels and activities can be measured in a laboratory. Most pill, HRT, alcohol and tobacco users tend to be deficient in vitamin B6, other B vitamins, zinc and magnesium. These deficiencies impair essential fatty acid pathways. For best results, evening primrose oil needs to be given with EPA fish oils, vitamins, minerals and a low-allergy rotation diet. As oestrogens become more powerful when linked with saturated fats, supplementation with unsaturated essential fatty acids can reduce this effect but need about six months to have the maximum beneficial result. In laboratory experiments essential fatty acids have anti-cancer actions. Large doses of gamma linolenic acid (GLA) 40mg per ml are extremely effective in killing three human malignant cell lines – breast, prostate and lung cancer cells. Evening primrose oil which contains GLA is a good form of treatment for benign breast disease and trials are underway to test if GLA prevents breast cancer by damping down the response of breast cells to oestrogens.[7]

Obviously, a low-animal-fat, low-allergy diet plus monitored essential nutrient supplements are devoid of side effects – apart from the initial food withdrawal symptoms – and clearly preferable to the array of unwelcome drug-induced changes.

Both the hospital doctor and the general practitioner

agreed that stopping oral contraceptives and HRT may improve breast symptoms dramatically.[6] It is now over twenty years since the medical establishment began to deceive itself. Ever since Professor Sir Bradford Hill and Sir Richard Doll published the link between lung cancer and smoking, epidemiologists have been given great prestige and influence. In 1971 Vessey and Doll published a paper about breast disease in women taking the pill.[8] As very few women under forty then developed breast cancer fairly small numbers were analysed but the results were clear. Breast cancer cases were more likely to have taken the pill for longer than two years compared with their controls – women who didn't have breast cancer. Half of these young breast cancer victims had used the pill for longer than two years before the cancer was first diagnosed (50 per cent of cases compared with 36 per cent of controls). The opposite was true for benign lumps. Sixty-two per cent developed lumps during their first year of pill taking and only 14 per cent of women with lumps went on taking the pill for more than two years compared with 33 per cent of controls. As fewer longer users had benign breast disease, it was concluded by the epidemiologists that longer use of the pill significantly *decreased the risk of breast disease*. The fact that it is the women with side effects, including sore breasts, who stop early – after a month or two, within the first year or before two or four years are up – was not mentioned, and has not been taken into account since.

Common sense and experience dictate that it is the women with faulty or over-sensitive immune systems, those who are otherwise at risk of developing cancer or other fatal illnesses, who are most likely to give up the pill within the first few months. The tougher women stay on, perhaps symptom-free for years, unaware that they are undermining their immunity and greatly increasing their cancer risk.

Mr Ian Burn says he never saw worrying types of breast disease in young women before the pill became available.

Aggressive precancerous breast diseases are known as atypical hyperplasia and carcinoma-in-situ. A young woman with atypical hyperplasia has a four to five times risk of developing breast cancer which increases to eleven times if she has a family history of breast cancer.[9]

Large pill studies can be misleading for many reasons. Younger, healthier, higher social class women are given the pill while women with known pill-related diseases, like thrombosis or breast disease, are advised to use other methods of contraception.

By 1979, the RCGP study had reported that 224 women taking pills with less than 3mg of progestogen and 57 taking higher dose pills had developed breast disease. It was calculated that breast lumps were twice as likely with pills containing lower doses of progestogen.[10] The authors claimed they had confirmed 'a reduced incidence of benign breast neoplasia becoming apparent after two years of Pill usage.' At this point in the report there was no reminder of the fact that of the 6,324 completely 'new' pill takers enrolled, only 799 (12.6 per cent) were known to have even begun a third year of pill taking ten years into the study.

Women who stopped the pill, ex-takers, had more breast disease than the larger number of control never-users. To claim that the pill prevented breast disease after two years when *nearly 90 per cent of new users had given up before the magic two years ended,* is ridiculous in my opinion. Nevertheless, my protests were ignored and a 'protective effect' of the pill on breast disease became establishment dogma.

I think this was an important mistake. Doctors no longer worried about the fact that both of these hormones could cause breast cancer in animals. As breast cancer in young women was very unusual they did not know that more and more were falling victims of the disease. Doctors no longer refused to prescribe hormone pills to women who already had lumpy breasts or to give renewed prescriptions to those who got lumps when they started the pill. Instead, doctors told their patients that the longer they stayed on the pill, the better would be their health.

This misconception coincided with the unfortunate switch in pill taking to younger age groups. From 1971 onwards, when women over thirty-five years old were warned off the pill because of the thrombosis risk, single women under twenty-five years old became the main pill starting and taking group. In the RCGP study only one in three women were enrolled so young and only one in ten single women in England and Wales had even tried the pill. Ten years later, by 1981, nine in every ten women had started the pill before they were twenty-five years old. This change has had enormous consequences including increasing the number of women likely to develop breast cancer any time up to forty years later. We are only beginning to understand the long-term damage to their children. Although in the 1970s there was massive publicity that the pill was causing thrombosis, strokes and heart attacks, little was said about cancer which kills twice as many women under fifty-five as vascular disease.

The number of women developing breast cancer has relentlessly increased since 1961 (see Appendix One).

Breast cancer in young women in the UK study was mostly diagnosed ten to fifteen years after they had used the pill. This means women who took the pill when they were under twenty-five get breast cancer in their thirties. Most by then have had one or two children.[11] Three out of four of them die within five years of being diagnosed. Breast cancer can be especially rapid in young women. It has long been known that breast cancer can spread with the speed of an abscess during pregnancy when the cells are overstimulated by high hormone levels.

Susie
Susie's father, a doctor, apparently did not object when his daughter started the pill at age seventeen or when she

175

continued on the pill after she had developed a breast lump at age eighteen which needed an operation to remove it. Susie's father believed that it was up to other doctors to take charge of his daughter's future. She came to consult me when she was twenty-seven. She had been on and off the pill for ten years with a six months' break. She had an occasional cigarette, disliked beer and drank very little. After a few years on the pill, Susie developed a rash – widespread, red, blotchy and itchy. Cheese made the rash worse. She mostly ate cereals, bread, yoghurt, coffee and snacks.

Biolab mineral analysis showed zinc, magnesium and manganese deficiencies. Selenium, known to protect against breast cancer, was deficient in her red cells. I prescribed a high-protein low-allergy diet and nutritional supplements. Two years later her zinc and magnesium levels were still low although her manganese and selenium levels were now normal. Her B vitamins were deficient and the 6-series essential fatty acid pathway was blocked with GLA deficiencies. She had a positive gut fermentation test and needed antifungal therapy. A gastrogram showed that Susie's pancreas was functioning at only 30 per cent of normal. This finding is common among long-term pill users. When pancreatic supplements were added to help digest her food, Susie's health improved rapidly and her friends noticed the difference. Uncorrected, these deficiencies and infections would have impaired Susie's future fertility and increased her risk of developing breast cancer in the future.

Diane

Diane was not so lucky. Having started taking the pill at age twenty-two, breast cancer was diagnosed at age twenty-five. Diane had tried three different pills: they all made her moody, irritable and bad tempered and she got vaginal thrush. She had thrush on and off until she gave up oral contraceptives after a few months.

Three years later a lump with only 'a few malignant cells,' was removed from Diane's right breast. She was told to wait three years before trying for a baby. Diane became pregnant when she was twenty-nine but the baby died. The missed abortion was removed by a D and C at eleven weeks. There was infection and more bleeding needing a second operation. One month later Diane and her husband tried again. This time, as soon as she was pregnant, a lump grew in her breast, a very small lump the size of a peanut. It was entirely composed of cancerous cells while the remaining breast tissue had changed into precancerous cells. The result came through when she was six weeks pregnant and Diane's second baby was taken away a week later. The termination was followed by a mastectomy at a famous cancer hospital. Before Diane and her husband had 'time to think', a silicone implant had been inserted. The implant became infected, her chest wall was 'all covered in pus' and after three months of torture the implant was removed. She had been given radiotherapy when the cancer was first diagnosed and since then she had been aware of food allergies. Cow's milk, oranges, pork and soya all made her sneeze. Diane's mother had had benign breast lumps and her father had always, including before Diane was conceived, smoked forty cigarettes a day.

When they came to see me, Diane and her husband were thankful she was alive. They were not worried about the missing breast, by now thinking an implant was neither needed nor desirable. But Diane still desperately wanted a baby and she contacted Foresight.

Biolab tests showed that Diane was very severely deficient in zinc and magnesium, and lowish in chromium and manganese. Her pancreatic function was 40 per cent of normal, while her stomach acid production was also low. Diane's essential fatty profile was normal and she had no sign of yeast in her gut test – she was not making alcohol when given sugar. Her blood chlamydia antibody test was negative but Diane had heavy infections with anaerobic bacteria and candida albicans in her cervix. Her husband had a heavy gardnerella infection in his prostate.

After treatment with antibiotics, nutritional supplements and a high-protein, low-allergy diet, Diane felt wonderful. Her energy had returned and so had her confidence.

John Howard had worked out, with help from Japanese research,[12] how to prevent zinc supplementation from encouraging tumour growth. Manganese stimulates the production of carrier protein which is then available to mop up any extra zinc. Diane was first given manganese for two weeks before switching to a daily supplement of zinc to help boost her health and immune system.

Hormone-dependent Cancer

As long ago as 1836, when AP Cooper observed that breast tumour cells grew faster at different times in the menstrual cycle, it has been recognised that breast cancer is influenced by ovarian hormones.[13] The Scottish surgeon Beatson removed the ovaries from women with advanced breast cancer and induced remission.[14] Since then numerous accounts show that the younger a woman is when her ovaries are removed, the less chance she has of developing breast cancer. By 1932, animal experiments defined the hormone-dependent cancers, showing *extra* oestrogens, progesterone and testosterone could cause cancer in the pituitary, breasts, ovaries or womb.[15] Oestrogen causes breast cancer in several animals, while pure progestogens, like those in the British pill, Volidan, were withdrawn from use as oral contraceptives because they caused breast lumps in beagle dogs.

While the role of endogenous ovarian steroid hormones in the natural history of the disease is well established, the fact that breast cancer becomes more likely each year of age, reaching a peak incidence in 80–90-year-old women, is a clear sign of increasingly incompetent cell growth control systems, which is likely because zinc deficiency tends to increase with age.

Women who have an early menarche (start having periods at younger than usual ages) have an increased risk of breast cancer. Dr Schoental thinks the increase in precocious development in Puerto Rico was due to perinatal exposure to the first contraceptive pills causing oversensitivity to natural oestrogens in food. Animal research has shown that before-birth exposure to hormones can cause future breast and ovarian tumours, and that, giving sex hormones after maturity can increase these effects.[16]

An early menarche, nowadays, may well mean that a girl is encouraged to start exogenous hormones (the contraceptive pill) before her sex organs are fully mature. In the 1990s it is said up to 40 per cent of school girls are engaged in active vaginal sex before they are sixteen years old. These unfortunate children, already damaged by media and peer pressure, are being further pressurised into taking oral contraceptives.

A late first full-term pregnancy is also a well-established risk factor for breast cancer. In 1970, MacMahon calculated that if a woman has a child before she is twenty she has half the usual risk of developing breast cancer. In contrast, delaying a first-time birth to over thirty-five years old means that a woman has doubled her risk of breast cancer.[17] But isn't it precisely the women who delay their first birth until later who are the women who are most likely to continue using the pill for longest? As I know from my Foresight patients, many of them have become infertile due to infections or mineral deficiencies but they continue on the pill for five or even ten years blissfully unaware of their underlying state of health.

There are differences between the breasts of women who had had a baby and those who had not yet had a full-term pregnancy.[17] After a baby is born, the mother's breasts respond to the rises in progesterone each month by increased DNA synthesis and increases in the immune protein immunoglobulin A. Nulliparous women, that is those who have not yet had a baby, do not have these cyclic responses nor do women who have had early

179

miscarriages or terminations unless they take the pill. Anderson found greater cell turnover (accelerated mitotic activity) only in the breast tissue of nulliparous pill takers.[18] It seems that pill hormones interact in an irregular way with the immature as yet unspecialised breast cells and make cancer more likely. Women who breast feed their babies are less likely to develop early breast cancer.

Breast Cancer Latent Period

Like other cancers, breast cancer can take up to forty years to develop from the time it is first initiated. Women who were given stilboestrol (DES) during pregnancy apparently had no obvious increased risk after twenty years, but only after forty years of follow-up.[19]

Many women who regard themselves as never having been on the pill were in fact given stilboestrol. Half of all new mothers from the 1950s to the 1970s were given stilboestrol to dry up their milk supply. More than a third are still given hormones or bromocriptine to block prolactin. Other mothers were injected with the long-acting progestogen, Depo Provera, before they left hospital or were given progestogen-only contraceptive pills. They were often not told what was in their jab or that the hormones would be excreted in their milk and could affect their baby's development.

Both groups of women would then have an increased risk of breast cancer but might be labelled as never-user controls in pill studies. In the large UK pill study young users developed breast cancer within fifteen years. This is sooner than exposure to radiation. A follow-up study of teenage survivors of the atom bombs in Hiroshima and Nagasaki found increases only fifteen years *or longer* after the events.[20] While the UK was not the first country to use the pill, it was the first country to give the pill en masse to the youngest women. Professor Klim McPherson estimates that *young women in the UK started using the pill five years earlier than young women in the USA.*[21]

In 1983, Malcolm Pike and his team published results from California, where women also started the pill when young.[22] The women who developed breast cancer before they were thirty-seven had used the pill for longer than control women (averaging 49.6 months compared with 39.2 months). This was a similar result to Doll and Vessey's 1971 paper – that women with breast cancer had taken combined oral contraceptives for longer than their controls. Pike concluded that *women who have taken the pill for six or more years before they are twenty-five years old have 4 to 5 times more risk of breast cancer.*

There was uproar, both in the medical world and in the lay press, although it was now sixteen years since similar information had been available about the increased risk of cervical cancer. The appalling and continuing increase in early cervical cancer had been efficiently blamed on sexual activity. But now, in the same issue of the *Lancet*, the Oxford/FPA study results showed that the pill was a main cause of cervical cancer to add to the breast cancer results.[23]

The pill should have been banned there and then but in the 1990s the 'fact' that 40 per cent of under-16-year-olds are already having sex is being trumpeted as a reason for even earlier age of pill use.

The Californian report was the third case-control study to find that young women, starting the pill before they were twenty-five or before their first full-term pregnancy, were more likely to develop breast cancer. The risk went up the longer the pill had been taken and higher dose progestogen pills were incriminated in particular.

In May 1989 breakfast television announced that the UK National Case-Control Study Group, with main authors Chilvers, McPherson, Peto, Pike and Vessey, also found that young women who had taken combined pills were more likely to get breast cancer before the age of thirty-six.[11] Confusingly, they postulated that 'there may be some protective effect of progestogen-only pills.'

Two groups of 755 women were compared. Nine out of ten women in both groups had used the pill. The 'cases' had developed breast cancer before they were thirty-six while the 'control' women had not yet developed breast cancer, although they might do so later and already suffer from other pill side effects. For both cases and controls women developing other malignancies or mental illnesses were excluded from the study.

Among the women with breast cancer, 2 per cent were diagnosed younger than age 25 while most of the rest were diagnosed between the ages of 32 and 35, by which time they were likely to have one or two children. One in twenty had had a biopsy for benign breast disease before the breast cancer was diagnosed and one in ten had a mother or sister with a history of breast cancer. The cases had taken the pill for an average of a year longer than the controls. Among 755 women developing breast cancer before age 35, those who used the pill for more than four years had a risk of 1.43. Women with eight years of pill-exposure had an immediate increased risk of 1.75 which further increased to 3.1 when they had given up the pill six years previously.

What I found fascinating about the UK data was that the younger a woman was when she was given the pill, the more likely she was to stay on it longer and, in doing so, increase her chances of developing cancer within the next fifteen to twenty years or longer.

Pill Starting Age	Percentage of women taking OCS for more than 4 years	
	Breast cancer cases	Controls
up to 18 years	80	70
19 to 21 years	71	61
22 to 24 years	57	48
25+ years	50	29

Dr James le Fanu wrote in *GP*, the magazine for general

practitioners, that the UK data meant pill prescriptions to under-21-year-olds should be discouraged. But the reality is that breast cancer increases rapidly with age.[4]

In the Oxford/FPA pill study breast cancer death rates doubled over ten years but doubled in only three years among older women followed in the British HRT trial.

Professor Julian Peto claimed the American CASH study showed that pill use increased the risk of breast cancer for all women up to age forty-four, increasing with length of use before a first pregnancy. Those who had taken the pill for less than four years also had an increased risk in his working of the data. He said the recent increase in breast cancer incidence and mortality in women aged under fifty is of concern.[24]

The authors of the UK pill study claimed that 'there may be some protective effect of progestogen-only pills'. What the data actually showed was that, of the small number of women who had taken these pills, 9 out of 10 developed breast cancer after using progestogen-only pills (POPs) for less than 24 months. Only 14 cases compared with 22 controls had stayed on POPs for more than two years. It seems logical to me that this means fewer women with a tendency to develop breast cancer can tolerate progestogen-only pills before discontinuing them earlier than their matched controls. This is quite the opposite of protection – only a very short time on a progestogen seems long enough to induce breast cancer. Progestogens are, in fact, highly immunosuppressive and this is what would be expected. The average progestogen use was only 13 months. *The majority,* 90 cases and 67 controls, had used them for one to 12 months and had an *increased breast cancer risk* (Relative Risk 1.35) but 'protection' continues to be claimed.

Clearly there are problems in using the blunt tool of epidemiology when the incidence of cancers keeps on rising and the epidemiologists come to falsely reassuring conclusions.

Rosie

A mother of twins who had never taken the pill, Rosie was thirty-nine when she went to her GP complaining of heavy bleeding. Over the next four years she was given Ponstan with no effect. Two D and Cs were carried out and she bled so much that on one occasion she needed 4 pints of blood. Her cervical smear was negative but when she was forty-three her doctor recommended a hysterectomy. Rosie was reluctant to have such drastic surgery. The doctor prescribed a progestogen – Primolut – to be taken daily for the third week of each cycle. He advised her that she would need to keep taking the hormone until her natural menopause.

After three months, she took a month off to see what would happen and her period was normal. One month later, a 2-centimetre lump was discovered in her right breast by her partner. She had a lumpectomy and radio-therapy for six weeks. Four years later, when forty-seven, a first-time mammogram revealed a 0.5 centimetre lump in the left breast. This was treated in the same fashion. At this point, Rosie was told that she must take the anti-oestrogen tamoxifen. As she believed an anti-oestrogen in the form of Primolut had caused her cancer, she refused the tamoxifen. She was still reluctant to have an early menopause. In her cancer support group, the other women given tamoxifen complained of abrupt menopausal symp-toms, flushing, rapid weight gain and headaches. None of them were alive two years later, perhaps because their cancers were more advanced or perhaps the tamoxifen had impaired their immunity. Rosie prefers a low-allergy diet, nutritional supplements, lots of rest and exercise. She looked and felt great as she danced at the party for her fifty-second birthday.

RCGP Pill Study

The world's largest pill study, begun in 1968, is by now mostly following past pill users and 'never' users. Little new on pill experience was added between the 1979 and 1987 reports (only 1.5 per cent of the total 406,836 on pill years).[25] Many women have left the study but if they die the cause of their death is known from the National Register.

In spite of the well-known fact that breast cancer can be exacerbated by pregnancy, 'all events reported during pregnancy were excluded.' There was no mention of the use of hormones for period problems, fertility drugs or as HRT for the older women, although it seems inconceivable that these were not used by ex-pill takers or controls. Nevertheless, the breast cancer increases among pill ever-users compared with their controls are alarming.

By 1985	Increase
Women aged 30 to 34 who stopped the pill 8–9 years before	15.8 ×
Women with one child stopping the pill 10 years before	13.19 ×
Women aged 30 to 34 when breast cancer diagnosed who took the pill for 10 years	10.17 ×
All women aged 30 to 34 when diagnosed	3.33 ×
All women aged 25 to 29 when diagnosed	2.53 ×
All women aged 45 to 54	1.77 ×

These results are standardised rates. Standardisation is a form of statistical manipulation which may or may not give a more accurate picture. For example, the actual number of pill ever-users diagnosed with breast cancer younger than thirty-five years old was 27 compared with 6 controls which looks like a 4.5 times increased risk. Standardisation reduces this to only 2.38.

Results are manipulated according to social class, which may depend on a husband's job, age at diagnosis, number of children when diagnosed and whether or not the women smoked when they joined the trial. It seems to me too many unwarranted assumptions are made. The effects of the hormones on the brain and immune system mean women are more likely to become addicted to nicotine and have more difficulty giving up. Any damage is multiplied with smoking plus the pill several times worse than smoking alone. But smoking alone is being blamed for the sharp increase in women's deaths. Many of these young women may not have died for another twenty years or more if they had only smoked and not also taken the pill.

Also by March 1985, three out of four known pill takers with breast cancer had died within five years from diagnosis (105 out of 143). In the control group two out of three had died in that time (63 out of 96). Survival was better for the under-35-year-olds who had not used oral contraceptives. Half were still alive.

The story of the Bristol Cancer Help Centre illustrates how confusion can result from an epidemiological study. The *Lancet* published a paper claiming poorer survival of patients with breast cancer attending the Help Centre.[5] There were detailed smoking histories but no mention of previous hormone use. The study was supervised by Chilvers and funded by the Cancer Research Campaign and the Imperial Cancer Research Fund. There was massive media coverage, panic among the many women with breast cancer who had attended the Bristol Centre which was brought to the brink of closure. Three of the women involved with the centre, Penny Brohn, Isla Bourke and Heather Goodare started a campaign to publicise the facts behind this unwelcome result. They eventually received an apology from Sir Walter Bodmer of the Imperial Cancer Research Fund accepting that 'women going to Bristol had more severe disease than control women.' He was good enough to apologise on camera for the distress caused, saying 'I am very sorry that a mistake was made.'[26]

In the country as a whole in 1984, only 29 per cent of women diagnosed with breast cancer were under the age of fifty-five, but the majority (85 per cent) of the Bristol patients were diagnosed at these younger ages. Young women are more likely to have been on the pill and the data from the RCGP study shows that women pill takers have a poor chance of surviving for more than five years after being diagnosed.

Heather Goodare said that the two cancer charities involved have an annual income of £90 million. 'They have the power to decide what research is done and they have control. They decide how much we are told.' She wanted an independent inquiry.

Breast Cancer and HRT

There has been only one large British study which was reported on by Hunt, Vessey and McPherson in 1987.[27] A total of 4,544 women attending twenty-one menopause clinics had taken oestrogens for *at least a year* between 1963 and 1983 as already described. This means up to 70 per cent of the women given HRT at these clinics were not followed up and only about 5 per cent lasted on the HRT for eight years. Most of the women were aged forty-five to fifty-four when recruited, a third had had a hysterectomy and one in five had already had her ovaries removed. They took 'over 175 different treatments'.

There is no matched control group: instead the disease incidence is compared with that of women in the general population. But the study group is not comparable – they are mostly of a higher social class and fewer are smokers. In spite of this, in 1987, roughly ten years after most of the HRT users were first given oestrogens, their breast cancer incidence had increased 1.59 times. At this point the HRT ever users death rate was 0.58, or half that expected in the general population. But, alarmingly, three years later, by 1990, death rates from breast cancer in this selected originally healthy group of women had doubled.[28] The breast cancer rates were rising as time lengthened since first use of HRT, according to Professor Vessey, speaking at an Anglo-American Conference held at the Royal Society of Medicine in September 1991.[29]

Other speakers also described increased risks which were statistically significant. Colditz from Boston found current users' increased risk was 1.3, Adami from Sweden quoted a risk of 1.7 after nine years of oestradiol. (More recent data shows Swedish women given progestogens with their HRT oestrogens are developing breast cancer more quickly than those taking only oestrogens.)[30] La Vecchia, from Italy, gave a 1.3 risk for ever users of oestrogens. Kaufman from Boston published a risk of 1.2 for any use of oestrogens. Hulka's North Carolina data for six months or more of oestrogen use in women with a natural menopause was 1.6 compared with community controls and 1.7 compared with hospital controls. Injectable hormones had produced a four-fold elevation in risk.

Professor Gambrell from Georgia showed the graphs of the national USA incidence of female cancers. Breast cancer rose to a peak of over 400 which means *one in nine women in the USA is developing breast cancer.*

Because of the huge HRT experience in the USA – half of all menopausal women prescribed at some time – the American national data also showed a peak of endometrial cancer in HRT users at the menopause. This had not yet happened to British women as, by then, only 5 per cent had taken HRT. Baber and Studd mistakenly used the American graph in an article in the *Journal of Hospital Medicine*.[31] They said that as there is a peak of cancer at the menopause more women should take HRT. I wrote to the *Journal* saying that the higher cancer rates in the American women had been caused by HRT.[4] Nevertheless, the advertising campaign for HRT has gone ahead relentlessly unchecked and our breast cancer and hysterectomy rates continue to rise. We have gone, in a few years, from one in sixteen to *one in twelve women in the UK developing breast cancer.* Professor McPherson has estimated that because of the latent period, this risk could increase to *one in four* among women who were long-term users of the pill in their early lives.[32] The risk is already more than this for women who have a near relation with the disease.[33]

A genetic susceptibility can be recognised by the presence of characteristic markers on the long arm of chromosome 17.[34] It is clearly of the greatest importance that women with this hereditary tendency to develop early-onset breast cancer are never given prescribed pill hormones, while taking menopausal oestrogens has already been shown to increase their risk by at least three and a half times.[35] If the present ill-considered prescribing of hormones continues unabated it is difficult to know how many women in the 'civilised' world will develop breast cancer. Japan has held out against the pill and still has a low breast cancer incidence.

CERVICAL CANCER

The commonest cancer in young women is cervical. Women who use a diaphragm as a contraceptive are taught to feel their cervix, a hard knob high in the back of the vagina. They are taught to make sure their cap fits properly, completely covering the entrance to the womb. A spermicidal cream is applied on both sides of the diaphragm to make sure no live sperm circumvent the obstacle. A cervical cap is sometimes fitted closely over the knob of the cervix. The male or newer female condom can be used. Condoms have the extra advantage of trying to prevent contact between the cervix or vagina with the semen, which may be carrying infection.

The pill was greeted with such enthusiasm in the 1960s because barrier methods of contraception were unpopular. The cap was mostly used by married women in stable relationships but the introduction of the pill has been accompanied by increasing sexual promiscuity. Not only has the age when men or women first have sexual intercourse fallen from twenties to early teens but the number of sexual partners has escalated.

Few of the hundreds of women I examined before the pill was first prescribed had either cervical or vaginal infections and none of the smears were positive. Now, *one in five* of my preconception patients, many of whom have taken the pill for over five years, have had a positive smear – a sign of very early cervical cancer – before they are forty years old. Most have had between five to ten different sexual partners. In fact, the last couple I saw exceeded this by a long way; the man had totalled over 500 and the women over thirty previous partners. Not surprisingly, the woman had been plagued with bouts of vaginal thrush while the man's sperm count had fallen to near zero. I find two out of three couples have usually unsuspected genital infections.

Cervical cancer is closely associated with sexually transmitted infections or venereal diseases. Many women who have had multiple partners have had viral infections in their cervix which may recur from time to time. Wart viruses are the most closely associated with future cervical cancer but any viral infection including herpes attracts other invading organisms. Viruses, mycoplasmas, bacteria and fungi thrive on a damaged cervix. When semen is deposited on an infected cervix, or into the rectum containing faecal bacteria as a result of anal intercourse, nitrosamines are formed. Nitrosamines are chemicals which by suppressing immunity increase the likelihood of the cells lining the cervix changing into uncontrolled cancerous growth. Gina Schoental believes this mechanism helps to spread the wart virus and cervical cancer. This is one reason why women with cervical infections are more susceptible to HIV infection and AIDS.[36]

The chances of smokers having wart viral lesions on their cervix increases with the number of cigarettes smoked.[37]

The cells of the cervix are perhaps the most hormone-sensitive of all the cells. When we tested progestogen-only pills in Yugoslavia in 1969, we found that doses too low to have any effect on the lining of the womb changed the cells lining the cervix. Cervical secretion dries up with the effect of a progestogen.[38] These are probably the reasons why combined oral contraceptives or progestogen-only pills quickly cause carcinoma-in-situ in the presence of cervical infections plus the fact that progesterone is highly immunosuppressive.

Sexual promiscuity and infection alone without the help of exogenous 'outside' hormones do not cause cervical cancer so quickly. Prostitutes starting sex after age eighteen previously had a low incidence of cervical disease and women infected with venereal diseases after the world wars tended to develop cervical cancer twenty years later.[39] The increase in early age cervical cancer is a new post-pill phenomenon or a sign of hormone exposure in the mother's womb. Sexual activity during the adolescent phase of active metaplasia of cervical cells seems to predispose to early age dysplasia and cancerous change.[40]

A positive smear means that some of the lining cells of the cervix have changed into cancer cells. This is called carcinoma-in-situ because the cells have not yet invaded deeper tissues. At this stage the early cancer is easily treated by laser or cone biopsy. Serious cancer is unlikely to develop if a woman avoids taking hormones – the pill, fertility drugs or HRT. It is also important she is checked regularly for hidden cervical infection with an endocervical swab, using a laboratory which tests for mycoplasma as well as bacterial infections. Mineral and vitamin deficiencies, especially deficiencies of folic acid, have been linked with cervical cancer and such deficiencies are prevalent among hormone takers and smokers.

Debby

Debby was referred to me by a gynaecologist. He had treated her abnormal smear grade CIN3 with laser eighteen months before. A repeat colposcopy, (looking at the cervix through a microscope with a powerful light), showed no abnormalities and her smear was clear. However, Debby, by now aged thirty-four, was plagued by a heavy, irritating vaginal discharge. The gynaecologist had cauterised her cervix using a double freezing technique which he usually found was very effective but, in Debby's case, her discharge returned.

I found she now had a heavy growth of anaerobes (bacteria which thrive without oxygen) and candida. There was no mycoplasma infection and her partner was not carrying infection in his urine or prostatic secretion.

Debby had started the pill aged eighteen and had taken four different pills for about seven years until she was twenty-eight. She first had sexual intercourse at eighteen and had 'about twenty partners.' While she took the pill her weight 'rocketed up two stone at first'. She also had repeated bouts of thrush – candida. Biolab screen now showed the usual severe zinc and magnesium deficiencies in her sweat and blood, although the hair pattern would have passed as normal. Her serum iron was low due to the heavy menstrual loss which often accompanies cervical infection. After years of the pill and infections she now had too-low copper stores as judged by the SODase enzyme test and needed extra copper. Like nearly all 'long-term' pill users tested, her pancreas was impaired and was secreting digestive enzymes at 34 per cent of normal. Her stomach acid was also low. Both may be due to long-term zinc deficiency and will probably improve with mineral, vitamin and essential fatty acid supplements together with pancreatic and stomach acid pills over the next year or two.

Already by 1968, two studies reported pill users were getting more early cervical cancer. Among 40,000 women screened by Professor Weid in America, only 500 had used the pill for more than five years and they had 6 times more cervical cancer.[41]

Twenty years after women were enrolled in the RCGP pill study the number of genital cancers were reported. Among 25–44-year-olds, early cervical cancers had increased 6 times (150 women compared with 26) and invasive types 3 times (49 women compared with 16) but after 'standardisation' the risk was reduced to 1.8. The results were 'standardised' or adjusted for age, parity, smoking, social class, number of previously normal cervical smears and a history of sexually transmitted diseases.[42] Invasive cancer was mostly diagnosed in women over fifty-five, in spite of more women having hysterectomies by that age.

Women with 'more than one primary cancer counted only one in the totals', meaning some women had developed more than one type of cancer. Patients treated by chemotherapy for breast cancer are also more likely to develop cervical cancer as are longer pill takers. Women who took the pill for more than ten years had a standardised increase of 4.4 times.

Few pill users continued the pill for more than five years but among those who did so there were 89 cervical carcinomas-in-situ and 28 invasive cancers, 3 ovarian cancers and one endometrial cancer. *For the majority of women, those who had taken the pill for less than five years, the incidence of ovarian cancer was nearly the same as in so-called 'never-users', standardised rates being 7 and 9 per 100,000 respectively.*

How many of the so called 'never-users' had been given at some time hormones for period pains, PMT, fertility drugs or HRT is not recorded but is clearly of the greatest importance: twelve ever-users developed ovarian cancer and eighteen controls. As more never-users had fertility problems before enrolment, they may have been prescribed hormones as infertility treatments. More pill users had difficulty becoming pregnant after stopping the pill.

There were only two cases of endometrial cancer among pill users and sixteen cases among 'never-users' who may have taken oestrogens. Pill takers are more likely to have early hysterectomies, obviously reducing their chance of developing either cervical or endometrial cancer.

There is no clear evidence that the pill takers are less likely to develop either ovarian or endometrial cancer. Case control studies merely show that the women who go on to develop these particular tumours are less likely to have taken the pill or, if they have done so, they give it up sooner than other women. (See also Chapter 2.)

Many studies worldwide have shown increases in both squamous carcinoma of the cervix and the rarer adenocarcinoma with prolonged pill use.[43] Women who have had a positive smear and continue to take hormones are more likely to develop more severe cancer.[44]

Early results from the Oxford/FPA and Walnut Creek studies illustrate once again that the pill is more toxic and more quickly carcinogenic than smoking. The studies had 36 non-smokers with cervical cancer compared with 35 smokers. Only 10 cases (including 7 IUD users) occurred in the non-pill group but there were 67 among pill takers including all the cases of invasive cancer in the Oxford study.[45] Invasive cervical cancer in young women is another reason for early age hysterectomy.

MELANOMAS

Girls used to have pink nipples. The skin around the nipples – the areola – used to darken for the first time when we became pregnant. Today, many topless, sunbathing teenagers already have darkened nipples if they are on the pill.

When the pill was first given in Mexico and Puerto Rico, unattractive dark patches known as chloasma appeared on the faces of some of the women. In the 1960s it was predicted that the pill would increase the chances of a woman developing the most lethal of all skin cancers – a melanoma. Since then the numbers of melanomas have increased sharply among young women in North America and Europe – in the pill-taking countries.

In animal tests, oestrogen stimulates the formation of the black pigment melanin, but the effect is greatly augmented by the addition of a progestogen – as in the pill. The hormones urge the pituitary to release a melanocyte-stimulating hormone. Pigment forms both outside and inside cells, increasing the numbers of melanocytes.[46]

Because hormones control pigmentation, Ellerbroek thought that oral contraceptives would predispose to the development of malignant melanomas.[47] The tumours, like breast cancer cells, have oestrogen receptors, and women on HRT are also more likely to develop melanomas. Hersey found that a previous pregnancy protected against death from melanomas but this finding could also reflect shorter pill use in women with children.

The American Walnut Creek study found pill and HRT users were more likely to develop melanomas, studying women from age eighteen to over fifty. Among pill takers under age forty, 37 developed cervical cancer, 10 breast cancer and 5 melanomas. The rare skin cancer was rare no longer. All the women who developed melanomas under age forty had taken the pill. By 1981, the overall increased risk for ever-users was statistically significant at 3 times.[48]

By 1990, in spite of no longer following up 31,000 women, the Royal College of General Practitioners found a 'standardised' increase of 1.77 times for women who had taken the pill for at least ten years.[49]

An Australian case-control study, led by Dr Valerie Beral, described how more than five years of pill use significantly increased the melanoma risk if the pill had been started ten years before the cancer was diagnosed. The increase remained significant even after adjustment for many factors including eye, hair and skin colour, level of outdoor activity and history of sunburning, chloasma and number of moles on the body. Dr Beral found increases among women who had been given hormones to regulate their periods, as HRT or to suppress lactation.[50]

Regular exposure to sunlight induces tanning, thickening of the skin and premature ageing. A tan gives some protection from the carcinogenic effects of solar radiation. Becoming red and blistered increases the risk of skin cancer. Pill users are getting more melanomas on their legs, possibly due to spasmodic sunbathing. Office workers, sitting in rooms lit by ultraviolet light and using VDU's, are increasingly being affected by melanomas on their bodies. The light seems able to penetrate thin clothing. Such superficial spreading melanomas on female legs and male trunks have increased three times in the past ten years with women having twice as many as men.

More thin lesions are diagnosed among recent OCS and HRT users. Professor Rona Mackie believes that her dual campaign in Glasgow, warning against the risks of unprotected sunbathing and urging earlier diagnosis, is responsible for a reduction in thick melanomas in women[51] but the fall in pill use among over-25-year-olds may be a more likely explanation.

The use of complete sun block creams is increasing and Australian children are now being protected from the sun by beach shirts and zinc-based face creams. Stress, zinc deficiency and lack of protective anti-oxidants increase the chance of too many moles, any of which can change for the worse when hormones are taken.

CANCER OF THE TESTIS

Testicular cancer is the commonest malignant disease in young men. Its incidence has doubled in the past fifty years with a life-time risk of the disease being one in 450. Denmark has the highest incidence at fifteen per 100,000 men per year. This is twice the incidence in the UK and five times more frequent than in Finland.[52]

While the quality and numbers of sperm have sharply deteriorated over this period in hormone-prescribing countries, the men in Finland still have normal sperm counts. It is only relatively recently that young women in Finland have started to take oral contraceptives. Testicular cancer appears to be initiated at a very early stage of development with an increased risk if the mother has been exposed to oestrogens, such as diethyl-stilboestrol. Abnormal cells may be produced as early as six weeks' gestation. Early carcinoma-in-situ is found in the other testes in 6 per cent of men with testicular cancer and half of these going on to develop a second bilateral tumour within five years.[53] Three out of four men with testicular cancer have reduced sperm counts and some have atrophy of the other testis. This probably reflects their poor zinc status, as normal sperm production needs plenty of zinc.

Both types of testicular cancer (seminoma and teratoma) are thirty times more likely to develop in a man with an undescended testicle at puberty. Undescended testicles are more likely if a mother has been given oestrogens during pregnancy and she is zinc deficient. In spite of pregnancy scans the incidence of sexual abnormalities in baby boys continues to increase with 5 in every 100 new-born infants affected. If a man has a brother with testicular cancer, he has a ten times increased risk of developing the disease before he is fifty. If his father was affected, a man's own risk is increased four times.[54]

Fortunately, the treatment of testicular cancer has dramatically improved survival in recent decades, especially when an early diagnosis is made.

PROSTATIC CANCER

Why, some men are beginning to say, is there so little publicity about male genital cancers? Women are urged to have regular smears and breast examinations but few doctors examine their male patients' prostates. And yet prostatic cancer is increasing and affects over 500 per 100,000 seventy- and eighty-year-olds each year – an incidence much higher for this age group than even American women's breast cancer incidence.

The prostate is a secretory gland and is basically similar to breast tissue. Histories of both types of cancer run in the same families. Secretory glands need a good supply of zinc, magnesium, selenium, anti-oxidants and essential fatty acids. The prostaglandins, derived from essential fatty acids, were so named because of the high concentrations in prostatic secretion. I have found that three out of four men are deficient in the 3-series fatty acids. Alcohol drains away zinc, magnesium and B vitamins, blocking essential fatty acid pathways. When men are zinc deficient, the zinc in their prostate is quickly replaced by the toxic metal cadmium if they smoke cigarettes. The body has difficulty getting rid of cadmium which then accumulates in the kidneys and prostate causing high blood pressure and prostatic disease. Like benign breast disease, benign overgrowth of the prostate gland affects younger people but may go on to cancer after some years. The body can only cope with a certain level of cadmium, and once that amount has been reached, toxic effects are certain.

Just as viral, mycoplasmal and bacterial infections of the cervix predispose to cancer, so infections of the prostate predispose to prostatic cancer. Regular bacteriological examinations of prostatic fluid are important in today's promiscuous society when as many as one in five men have hidden prostatic infections. They usually have no symptoms although they may have previously experienced frequent discomfort on passing urine. Squeezing the prostate through the rectum to burst any abscesses and obtain fluid seems a repulsive procedure to many doctors who are quite accustomed to taking cervical smears. This attitude should change if prostatic disease is to be prevented.

Once prostatic cancer develops either oestrogen or progestogens are prescribed to block the man's endogenous testosterone production. High-dose oestrogen therapy caused such distress including migraines, strokes and heart attacks that its use has been largely abandoned.

Donald

Donald had never been a heavy smoker – just two or three cigarettes a day in his thirties. He took very little alcohol. First sexual intercourse was at age twenty and he had ten different sexual partners over the years. At age sixty-five he was very concerned that hormone treatment was making him impotent. Six months before he had begun to have signs of prostatitis – urgency and discomfort, passing only a weak stream of urine. Prostatic cancer was diagnosed. There was already metastatic spread to his bones. It was decided to give him an anti-testosterone hormone – a progestogen. Oestrogens had been used for years to block natural testosterone production, but side effects included thrombosis, strokes, heart attacks, headaches, high blood pressure and even breast cancer. The effect of the progestogen was dramatic. His symptoms cleared within four days and his prostatic specific antigen levels were down to normal within two months. The secondary tumours in the bones vanished.

Donald contacted a self-help cancer group and collected supplies of nutritional supplements from a health food shop. He met a new younger partner and wondered if he could lower the dose of his progestogen. In spite of the rapid initial improvement on anti-testosterones the outlook is poor with only a 10 per cent five-year survival rate. I could not agree to a lower dose. Biolab analysis showed that Donald had a very low stomach acid production which may have caused long-term zinc deficiency by impairing food absorption. He was severely zinc deficient in his sweat, serum and hair. Magnesium, chromium and selenium were low, while B vitamins, vitamin E and n–3 fatty acids were deficient. Copper stores were low in the SODase enzyme test. With supplements, three months later, the blood and sweat levels were normal. The hair results were improving as they tend to lag behind. Against my advice, Donald, who was feeling somewhat manic, which is common in the first months of steroid treatment, persuaded his oncologist to lower the dose of the progestogen. A few months later Donald phoned me to say the cancer had recurred in his prostate and bones. He still felt well and would be taking the higher dose once more.

In 1982 in the USA, thanks to routine annual screening, 70 per cent of men diagnosed with early prostatic cancer survived for over five years. In the UK, where screening tests tend not to be used, only 35 per cent survive.[55] Prostatic cancer has doubled in incidence in the last thirty years. Since it became obvious during the 1960s that pill side effects limited its use, male sterilisation, via vasectomy, rapidly became a favourite method of contraception for older couples. Vasectomy may double a man's chance of developing cancer of the prostate and could be one of the reasons for the increase.[56]

LIVER TUMOURS

Both benign and malignant tumours can be caused by the sex steroid hormones. Liver cancers are very rare in the UK, affecting only a few people in every million, but their incidence is increased by taking oestrogen, progesterone or testosterone.[57] In 1986 it was calculated that women who had ever taken oral contraceptives are four times more likely to develop hepatocellular carcinoma. Women who have taken the pill for eight years or more have a 20 times greater risk of this cancer.[58] After five years of use the risk of having a benign adenoma is estimated to be 100 to 500 times.[59] Occasionally pill-induced adenomas become malignant. This is more likely to happen if the liver is also damaged from past exposure to hepatitis B infection, aflatoxins, alcohol or mycotoxin-contaminated alcoholic drinks. Oestrogens encourage viruses to proliferate. In the RCGP study pill takers were twice as likely to develop infectious hepatitis as ex-takers and much more likely than never-takers to complain of pruritus or itchy skin which is an early sign of liver disease.[60] Individuals with a past history of jaundice may become symptom-free carriers of the virus and are more liable to become jaundiced for a second time when given the pill or HRT. DNA from the hepatitis B virus has been found integrated into tumour tissue removed from a woman who had been taking HRT, although her blood no longer carried signs of her past infection. In countries where liver cancer is common, pill and HRT hormone prescriptions must be having a considerable impact on the number of women suffering from this lethal type of cancer.

Patricia

This lady is keen that her story should be told. Her mother is now eighty-six years old and in extremely good health. Why Patricia now wonders, has she herself taken hormones for the last seventeen years since she was thirty-five? The first sign of something wrong was when she was twenty-two when she had a miscarriage. Two other miscarriages followed. Although neither Pat nor her husband had had sexual intercourse with anyone else, Pat had infections leading to salpingitis and cervical erosions. Three years later Pat managed to conceive again and her son was born when she was twenty-six. Then mental problems started. Pat spent six months in hospital being treated for severe post-natal depression. Antidepressants never really helped, just made her feel doped, and she took two years to recover.

Suddenly, at thirty-eight, Pat's periods stopped. Her GP advised her to see a specialist who gave her progesterone suppositories for the next nine years. At the same time, she was taking a variety of drugs, including MAO inhibitors and, at one point, she became addicted to Ativan. While the anti-depressants did not really help, trying to come off was difficult – she tried seven times to stop Parstelin. Withdrawal symptoms included insomnia, anxiety, irrational fears and agoraphobia. She says she has what is now known as an addictive personality – 'thank goodness I never smoked or liked alcohol!'

Aged forty-nine, back problems made Pat more depressed and anxious. This time, her GP sent her to a gynaecologist who said her problems were due to lack of oestrogen. According to Pat she was implanted with 100mg of oestrogen. Then she began to bleed so heavily that she was sent to another gynaecologist who removed her womb and both ovaries. She was told that both ovaries were small and pitted and no longer functioning. Two further years of progesterone suppositories and injections were followed by more oestrogen implants. At first the implants were at nine-monthly intervals but Pat became ill with increasing frequency in between. She was a victim of tachyphylaxis – her oestrogen levels were getting higher and higher and when the high level dropped she had headaches, aches and pains, and extreme anxiety. This happened after nine months at first, then after six months and then after four months. She was also given the male hormone testosterone, which gave her acne.

At age fifty, Pat saw a clinical ecologist who tested for allergies and advised her to stop taking hormones and antidepressants. Pat felt well for six weeks on a low-allergy diet but she continued with the progesterone suppositories and oestrogen patches.

Eventually when she was fifty-four Pat consulted me. She was using patches with smaller and smaller amounts of oestrogen, as her levels were being gradually lowered. She had developed a liver tumour which was thought to be benign but very vascular. Biolab tests showed zinc, magnesium and chromium deficiencies. Copper was abnormally high in her serum which is typical of an oestrogen effect. Her 3-series fatty acids were deficient and her platelets were abnormally sticky in three tests, again typical of an oestrogen effect. She had been having severe migraine and was in danger of developing clots on a 15 microgram oestrogen patch twice weekly.

The clue to Pat's long-term problems was in her gastrogram result. She had abnormally low stomach acid production, interfering with her absorption of key nutrients. Pat now wants to take control of her own health and started a low-yeast diet and treatment for gut candida. She had tended to binge on bread and cottage cheese. Wheat and cow's milk are notorious brain allergens but, like many other long-term hormone users, Pat had become increasingly vegetarian as her abnormal zinc/copper balance impaired her liver's ability to deal with proteins. With the help of nutritional supplements and a higher protein, low-allergy rotation diet, Pat is now keen to manage without hormones or antidepressants.

TAMOXIFEN

As more women take the pill and HRT, so more develop breast cancer. This means more healthy women will have mothers or sisters with the disease and be labelled as at high risk themselves. Instead of the obvious solution, the withdrawal of hormone prescriptions, the latest fashion is to prescribe the anti-oestrogen, tamoxifen, to women who have not yet developed breast cancer.

The American National Cancer Institute launched a trial, recruiting 16,000 healthy women at 'high risk' of breast cancer which included all women over sixty. Other trials involve women in the UK, Italy and Australia. In the UK the Medical Research Council restricted its support for the trial because of adverse results in animal studies, in particular the induction of liver tumours and highly malignant liver cancers. The half-life (time taken to clear a drug through the liver) is five days in humans and five hours in rats. The *Lancet* commented that few healthy women have been taking tamoxifen for over five years.[61]

An overview of 133 cancer trials claims any use (or strangely 'intended' use) prolongs the survival of post-menopausal women with breast cancer over ten years. In eight randomised control trials, tamoxifen apparently reduced by a third the development of cancer in the second breast but only in post-menopausal women.[62] Avrum Bluming pointed out that 2 per cent (184 out of 9135) of women not given tamoxifen developed a contralateral tumour, while 1.3 per cent (122 out of 9128) in the tamoxifen group did, so the reduction overall was merely 0.7 per cent.[63]

Adriane Fugh-Berman and Samuel Epstein wrote that

this result was no reason for giving tamoxifen to healthy women.[64] They said that, in spite of the claims of prolonged survival, few breast cancer patients had taken tamoxifen for more than five years. In tamoxifen-treated subjects, new tumours that do appear tend to be highly malignant with an increased mortality. As many breast cancers spread to the liver, in the absence of routine liver biopsies or post-mortems, it is impossible to find out if a liver tumour is a secondary from the breast or a tamoxifen-induced liver cancer.

A daily dose of 20mg increases the risk of endometrial cancer 5 times which is similar to the increase with oestrogen HRT. Ovarian cancer may also be increased.

Thromboembolic disease is 7 times more frequent. Eye damage, retinopathy, has been reported in 7 per cent of women in one study, while menopausal symptoms are the most common side effects. Fugh-Berman and Epstein go on to say that hot flushes, vaginal discharge or dryness, irregular menses, nausea and depression may be acceptable as part of cancer therapy but with healthy premenopausal women 'one can anticipate difficulties with compliance.' They conclude that 'tamoxifen although less toxic than conventional chemotherapy fails the more stringent standard of safety that is imperative for a primary prevention measure.'

In contrast Dr Trevor Powles of the Royal Marsden Hospital has recruited over 1,700 healthy women since 1986 for his tamoxifen trial.[65] Massive television advertising raised money to replace the missing Medical Research Council support. He says he has had the misfortune to look after thousands of women who have died of breast cancer, many in the prime of life. A double-spread picture in the Radio Times showed a cancer expert with one of his patients. She was a woman doctor whose breast cancer was being treated with tamoxifen but, surprisingly, she was also taking HRT. She had begun a premature menopause and extra oestrogen was prescribed to mask her symptoms.

Although tamoxifen blocks oestrogen receptors it can also stimulate them causing endometrial hyperplasia and cancer.[66] A rise in serum copper may give an early warning of this change but copper will rise if HRT is also given. Scientists are looking for safer and more long-term oestrogen blockers.

There clearly is no good reasons for giving healthy or menopausal women either HRT or tamoxifen and many good reasons why these practices should be condemned especially for women who already have a higher risk of cancer.

KEY POINTS

- Sex hormones cause cancer of target organs – breast, cervix, endometrium, ovaries, prostate and testes; also of the skin and liver.
- Any time from weeks to up to 40 years after exposure to sex hormones.
- Benign breast lumps reason for giving up pill or HRT after a short exposure.
- Youngest women have longer exposures and breast cancer may affect one in four starting early.
- British pill and HRT studies show increases in breast cancer which is the main cause of death at hormone-taking ages.
- Breast cancer death rates doubled in ten years in pill trial but doubled in only three years in older women attending British HRT clinics.
- Early cervical cancer in 20–40-year-olds is epidemic.
- Up to a few years on the pill cervical cancer increases 5 to 6 times.
- Up to a few years on the pill or HRT increases skin melanomas 2 to 3 times.
- Maternal exposure to oestrogens – incidence of testicular cancer double over last fifty years.

- Prostatic cancer doubles over the last thirty years in older men possibly due to increase in vasectomies.
- Rare liver tumour increases with hormone exposure: benign but vascular – 100 to 500 times after five years; cancer – 4 times increase or 20 times after eight years.
- Anti-oestrogen tamoxifen is prescribed to treat or to possibly prevent breast cancer but it is carcinogenic and can cause early menopause, osteoporosis, endometrial and liver cancer and clotting diseases.

Chapter Eight

Immunity and the Sex Infections

THE SILENT EPIDEMICS

When I was a medical student in the 1950s we had a patient in the ward suffering from general paralysis of the insane – a long-term consequence of syphilis. Venereal diseases were terrible, discussed in whispers and warning notices lined every public toilet. During the two world wars there had been sharp increases in VD. The taboos and customs of family life were temporarily swept aside. By the 1950s stability had returned.

It is hard for young people today to believe how differently my generation behaved. Most of my school friends lived with their parents until they got married. The sexes were segregated in university residences. An invitation to a formal ball was accompanied by a flowery corsage and no expectation of sexual intimacy other than a goodnight kiss. Some of my contemporaries were recently discussing their experiences and saying – and it is true – that none of us slept with our boyfriends. We avoided the risk of unplanned pregnancies, venereal diseases and future infertility with great ease, merely going along to a family planning clinic for a cap and spermicides in time for our wedding day. One of our professors called us semi-virgins. Petting, mutual masturbation and orgasms happened in genuine long-term relationships, but vaginal penetration was unusual before marriage as were multiple partners.

Then there was the pill. Gradually, during the 1960s, the attendance levels at VD clinics increased, and their numbers rocketed upwards especially from 1970 onwards. Dr Catterall, from the Middlesex Hospital in London, published his seminal paper in the *Lancet* in 1981. It was called '*Biological Effects of Sexual Freedom*'.[1] Early infectious syphilis and gonorrhoea were increasing in spite of their easy treatment with antibiotics. In men, the incidence of NSU – non-specific urethritis – soared ever upwards. Dr Catterall wrote of this second generation of STDs which were becoming commoner than the old venereal diseases. These included bacterial, chlamydial, mycoplasmal and viral diseases. The doctor said one reason why STDs are so difficult to control is because they are frequently symptomless, especially in women. They may lead to local discomfort, chronic debility, infertility, ectopic pregnancy, recurrent miscarriages, stillbirth and neonatal death. Dr Catterall lamented that public health education about sexual matters in general and STDs in particular is inadequate and tends to be left to chance. In the 1990s sex education telling the real facts is almost non-existent. How many sexually active young women know that they have a one in three chance of being contaminated with the wart virus which can eventually lead to cervical cancer? So much government-sponsored sex education is verging on irresponsible sex promotion. Films and television reinforce these views while young children are automatically indoctrinated. It seems that the right of men to use women as if they were merely public conveniences must be protected! The implication is neither males nor females must be put off sex. When individuals belatedly discover the real facts of life it is often too late. Never in all history has so much been known and so little communicated effectively.

Dr Catterall says that an active satisfying sexual life has now become an essential human right. Modern life gives increased opportunities for casual sex and change of partners. An important consequence of the so-called sexual revolution has been the diminution of guilt feelings about sex. Who had guilt feelings? I'm sure I would feel much more guilty about promiscuous sex than I ever would about saying 'No'. How guilty does a man or woman feel if they have damaged their own health and fertility, or that of their partners and their children if they can still have any? The 'sins of the fathers' are not always circumvented by antibiotics.

As a *sex life* became fashionable, reproductive health rapidly deteriorated. Dr Catterall gave the example of Sheila, put on the pill at seventeen. Her second partner infected her with gonorrhoea. He began to avoid sex and within three weeks Sheila had colicky lower abdominal pain, slight vaginal discharge and fever. She was admitted to hospital with acute gonococcal PID (pelvic inflammatory disease). Her partner was by now very concerned about her illness and admits he became infected when he got drunk at a party and had a one-night stand. A urethral discharge and burning pain on passing urine sent him to a clinic where gonorrhoea was diagnosed. He was told to make sure his partners were examined, but he could not bring himself to tell Sheila in time before her PID developed. She now had moderately severe inflammation of her Fallopian tubes and chlamydia on her cervix. She then had a 50 per cent chance of a relapse, a 1 in 3 chance of being sterile, a 25 per cent chance of dyspareunia – pain on vaginal intercourse – and a 10 per cent chance of an ectopic pregnancy. What has happened to Sheila's right to an active and satisfying sex life?

During the 1980s I examined several hundred couples to find out if they were physically fit to have children. At first, Foresight, the Association for the Promotion of Preconception Care, concentrated on screening for nutritional deficiencies. Mrs Belinda Barnes had started Foresight in 1978 with the help of Dr Elizabeth Lodge Rees, the paediatrician who ran a mineral analysis laboratory in California. Both were extremely aware of the key importance of nutrition. By the mid 1980s, we were using Dr John Howard's analysis at Biolab and finding most of the couples tested had essential nutrient deficiencies.[2] Many had a past history of genital infection but, surprisingly, when routinely screened more than half the couples still had active, usually symptomless infections urgently needing treatment before they started a baby. We had uncovered the silent epidemics.

I had met the wife of a GP, Dr Graham Sutton, at a meeting about autistic children. She told me that her husband used a colposcope to inspect the ulcers, known as erosions, on the cervices of his patients and said, 'He is finding that most of the girls on the pill have infections.' I visited Dr Sutton who kindly demonstrated his procedures. He was very interested in mycoplasmas, the smallest organisms capable of independent life outside cells. In contrast, viruses must live inside cells. Mycoplasmas die within thirty minutes after being removed from the cervix so Graham was freezing the specimens before sending them to the local Medical Research Council laboratory. He said mycoplasmal infection was greatly underestimated, both in the severity of the disability caused including premenstrual tension, infertility and miscarriages, and in its incidence. My own GP said she rarely was told which infections her patients had – just that their smear showed chronic inflammation or their swab showed vaginal vaginosis – whatever that was. NSU – non specific urethritis – was no better a diagnosis, simply meaning we haven't a clue what's causing the inflammation in a man's urethra.

I started screening for infections at the London Clinic and presented the results from 114 Foresight couples at a Clinical Ecology conference in Buxton in 1990.[2]

Ninety per cent of the women had been pill takers. No one was positive for syphilis, gonorrhoea or trichomonas vaginalis, but other infections were common.

Infections	Females (%)	Males (%)
Mycoplasmas	21	5
Bacterial infections	46	18
Chlamydia – cervix	5	2
– blood antibodies	45	
Candida	8	2

The commonest bacterial infections were:

ß haemolytic streptococci	16	4
Staphlococci	9	1
Anaerobes	14	1
Gardnerella	6	0
E coli	6	4

Another Foresight doctor, gathered her results of 77 women and 32 men finding that 22 of the men she had selected had low sperm counts. Half of the men had infection including most of those with normal sperm quality. Long-term infection can cause absence of sperm (aspermia). Several of my male infertility patients with histories of infection on and off over the past twenty years could produce only sterile pus. There was no longer any sign of either sperm or of the organisms which had done the damage. The count of one man dropped from 110 million to only 3 million after two bouts of infection with different bacteria.

The London Clinic reports say which antibiotics will work. Men with urethritis and prostatitis need two weeks of the appropriate antibiotic. They are tested six to eight weeks later when the infection has usually gone. Non specific urethritis (NSU) is diagnosed at some clinics merely because of the presence of pus cells, and two weeks of tetracycline is given on spec. This would be correct treatment for mycoplasmal and chlamydial infections but would not necessarily deal with all the other organisms such as streptococci and staphylococci. Anaerobes need a course of Flagyl which is notoriously well known for exaggerating the effect of alcohol. The male screen at the London Clinic consists of three urine specimens and a semen culture or prostatic massage secretion obtained after the first urine specimen. Sometimes the first urine specimen is clear for pathogens (organisms which cause disease) and pus cells, but the massage can burst an abscess in the prostate so that the subsequent specimens give the diagnosis.

Obviously, both partners should be investigated on the same day and they should avoid unprotected sex until any infections have been shown to be adequately treated. This seldom happens, with women only being screened regularly but not men. An endocervical swab is taken from deep inside a woman's cervix. Just as the male prostate can harbour chronic infection, the deep glands lining the entrance to the womb can be the seat of long-term infection. Dr Sutton says that the treatment is like peeling off layers of an onion. Ulcers from viral infections (wart or herpes) can attract mycoplasmas, then bacteria and then the larger fungi, like candida. Each has its own treatment. A follow-up smear two months later might show mycoplasmas although bacteria and candida may have been treated by antibiotics and antifungal suppositories.

Women with erosions, cervicitis or long-term recurrent infections often need double cryocautery, when the endocervical canal is frozen twice, in addition to systemic treatments. Women need what a Danish professor has called 'tender loving care' – avoiding penetrative sex until the cervix is well healed.

Most Foresight couples are in monogamous relationships. Few have active chlamydia trachomatis or trichomonas vaginalis in their cervical swabs. These infections are more common among the young who have multiple or changing partners. The typical Foresight mother-to-be is in her late twenties or thirties, took the pill for between a few months to more than five years and is now complaining of infertility or recurrent miscarriages. Couples are surprised to have infections as they tend not to have had other sexual partners for several years but, before that, previous partners numbered between five or ten or even more in some cases.

Chlamydia

Although few women attending preconception clinics have chlamydial cervicitis, many, particularly those infertile with damaged Fallopian tubes, still have chlamydial organisms inside these tubes. This type of infection damages tubes progressively and silently, increasing the chance of an ectopic pregnancy, which, in turn, often leads to loss of the tube. In ectopic pregnancies an egg can implant outside the uterus, in the tube or in the pelvis. Ectopic pregnancies increased in the US from 6.5 to 21.7 per 1,000 conceptions over ten years matching increases in STDs and especially the increases in chlamydial infections. The increase in ectopic pregnancies is also linked with increasing maternal age, IUD use and induced abortions. An acute attack of PID due to chlamydia or gonorrhoea increases the risk of an ectopic pregnancy 6 times.[3]

Blood antibody tests are invaluable in showing latent chlamydial infection which may flare up during infertility investigations such as salpingography, when dye is injected into the tubes, or during pregnancy. Such flare-ups can be prevented by two weeks of tetracycline before fertility investigations or before conception.[4]

Both men and women are often prescribed tetracyclines for years if they have severe acne. Bad skin conditions, acne, psoriasis or eczema are usually due to food allergies and nutritional deficiencies especially deficiencies in zinc, B vitamins and essential fatty acids. Long-term antibiotics add to the problems by causing candida or thrush in the gut and also may increase the permeability of the gut. Both conditions can be diagnosed by tests at Biolab and need treatment before a baby is conceived. Both increase the underlying nutritional deficiencies, especially causing zinc deficiency.

Tetracyclines are teratogenic. If a couple conceive while either are taking tetracyclines there is a high risk that the mother will abort or her baby will be abnormal.

Mr and Mrs F

Mr and Mrs F complained of infertility for the past eight years. Mrs F had been given the pill at seventeen because she had acne. Her skin improved at first but she began to have continuous headaches and gave up the pill at twenty-five. She was then given tetracyclines for five years and complained of premenstrual tension for three to four days before each period. Mrs F had had a raised prolactin level but it had fallen to normal although a scan suggested her pituitary gland might be slightly enlarged. She stopped drinking cow's milk and her sinus headaches disappeared. Biolab analysis showed a severe magnesium deficiency. Zinc was also low and an intestinal permeability test using polyethylene glycol showed a leaky gut. She had had cytomegaloviral and toxoplasmal infections in the past. Blood chlamydial antibodies were negative and there was no cervicitis.

Mr F was age forty-three. He had a marked zinc deficiency and the common male-type block in his fish oil 3-series fatty acid pathways and 40 per cent of his sperm were abnormal possibly because of his deficiencies or his daily alcohol intake. After correction of the deficiencies the couple should be able to conceive but Mr F finds it difficult to follow the advice to stop drinking alcohol.

Mr and Mrs E

Mrs E was French, had taken several oral contraceptive pills on and off between age twenty and twenty-seven, in spite of weight gain, fluid retention, sore breasts, distended leg veins and developing Raynaud's disease. She was now twenty-nine and keen to have a baby. She had had vaginal thrush and gardnerella infections in the past. The immuno-fluorescence test for antibody to chlamydia species antigen was very high. A complement fixation test was negative which indicated no evidence of pelvic spread but she was given tetracycline followed by antifungal pessaries to prevent thrush as precautions. Mr E had no pathogens (disease-causing organisms) in his urine or prostatic secretions but he had recurrent penile sores – possible due to herpes and thrush. He had a very low hair zinc reading, high sweat but low serum copper. Mrs E was short of zinc and magnesium.

When both had taken supplements for four months Mrs E became pregnant. She felt well but at six weeks an ectopic pregnancy ruptured and she lost her left tube. It was discovered she had a bicornuate uterus. One brother had a hydrocoele (an abnormal collection of fluid in the testicle) and hernia and another brother developed testicular cancer at two years old. Mrs E did not know if her mother had taken hormones in her pregnancies or even if she had fancied foods high in natural oestrogens such as mushrooms or cheese. Mrs E became pregnant again. This time at fifteen weeks her zinc was low and her copper had not risen. A copper response test showed no rise in sweat zinc or copper after a doze of oral zinc. After three weeks of alternating 30mg of zinc and 3mg of copper each evening, Dr Howard found Mrs E's copper response returned and the pregnancy proceeded uneventfully. Mrs E was able to breast feed her daughter who had top Agpar scores at birth.

Mycoplasmas

There is no argument that both chlamydia and gonorrhoea are the main causes of infected Fallopian tubes (salpingitis) leading to ectopic pregnancies and blocked tubes. The role played by mycoplasmas in infertility and recurrent miscarriages is more subtle and less well known. In 1986, the journal *Paediatric Infectious Diseases* reviewed these infections.[5] The organisms are three times more likely to be found in spontaneous abortions than in therapeutic abortions and they were cultivated in 60 per cent of still births in one study.[6] Women and men with more than three sexual partners and other genital infections are more likely to be infected. Infertile couples have a high incidence of infection in the cervix, endometrium and semen.

Some couples have as many as six different infections at the same time including mycoplasmas.

Mr and Mrs J

Mrs J had taken the pill from age twenty-two to thirty-five when she had developed a precancerous smear. A pregnancy was terminated when she was forty because the baby was abnormal. A preconception screen showed Mrs J was severely zinc deficient and her cervix was infected with mycoplasma hominis, streptococci and anaerobes. A blood test indicated previous chlamydial infection. Mr J had a heavy urinary infection with haemophilus influenzae and a prostatic infection with a different mycoplasma from his wife.

Mycoplasmas are associated with preterm birth, chorioamnionitis (inflammation of the membranes surrounding the baby), fever during and after childbirth and bacterial vaginosis. Infection is more likely in pregnant women under twenty-five, in those with pre-eclampsia and kidney disease. They can be found in sexually abused children and in patients with immunodeficiency causing polyarthritis and respiratory infections including pneumonia. Mycoplasmas require sterols for their metabolism which means their proliferation can be encouraged by the pill and HRT. Mycoplasmas produce chemicals (phospholipases) which can increase prostaglandin synthesis causing uterine contractions, painful period pains and irregular bleeding. The infection may alter lung lubrication – thought to be a factor in cot deaths and asthma. In some studies one in three newly born babies were affected. And yet mycoplasmas, discovered by Dr Maurice Shepard in 1951, are not usually looked for even in hospital fertility clinics. A new type of mycoplasma, known as mycoplasma penetrans, has been found in many HIV and AIDS patients.

Large-scale Trials

The world's three main pill studies showed immediate increase in many infections including STDs.

The RCGP report listed statistically significant increases of both viral and bacterial infections among pill users.[7] These included colds, respiratory infections, influenza, rhinitis, sinusitis and pleurisy. Urinary infections, cervicitis, cervical erosions, vaginitis, monilia, trichomoniasis, leukorrhoea (white discharge), and pruritus (itch) of the genital organs were also increased. There were 1,115 cases of vaginal thrush among pill users (rate 31.46) and only 661 cases among the controls (rate 15.89). Only 15 cases (rate 0.42) of PID were recorded among pill takers and 36 (rate 0.89) among never-takers. The often repeated publicity, that the pill reduced the risk of PID by half, ignored the fact that ex-pill-takers had a higher rate (1.02) than those who had never taken it.

In the Oxford/FPA study 17,000 married women, aged 25 to 39, were using either oral contraceptive steroids (56 per cent), diaphragms (25 per cent) or intrauterine devices (19 per cent) when enrolled in 1968.

By 1979 the IUD users had an unplanned pregnancy rate of up to 4.3 per 100 women years.[8] The IUD users were more likely to be referred to hospital for anaemia and salpingitis. Women who used the diaphragm were less likely to be referred for carcinoma-in-situ (CIN) and dysplasia of the cervix. Women who used OCS at the start of the study had more referrals for vaginitis, cervicitis, cervical erosions and cervical cancer, amenorrhoea and sterility.

By 1987, among parous women referred to the hospital for pelvic inflammatory disease, 99 were current IUD users compared with 18 pill users and only 12 diaphragm users. This is in spite of the fact that only 9 per cent of IUD users and 12 per cent of the OCS users continued their method for more than five years compared with 52 per cent of the diaphragm users. Diaphragm users had an unplanned pregnancy rate of 2.4 per cent and more cystitis and haemorrhoids presumably due to localised pelvic pressure. Users of the now banned Dalkon shield had 5 times more PID referrals than users of other IUDs, with copper IUD users having half the risk compared with users of inert IUDs.[9]

Clearly, the pill gives no protection against infection, and pill users have an increased incidence of those infections which later lead to a diagnosis of PID which is often only made when fertility problems are being investigated. PID is difficult to diagnose and may be confused with appendicitis, endometriosis or ectopic pregnancy. As many STDs are asymptomatic in women, gonorrhoea or chlamydia are commonly only diagnosed when female contacts of men suffering from sexual diseases are routinely investigated and yet their long-term consequences are far greater for women and their children.

Viral Infections and Damage to Children

The pill has increased a mother's risk of having viral infections which can damage her children. A pregnant woman has some immunosuppression due to high progesterone levels. Her chances of developing infection during pregnancy are especially high if her essential nutrient levels are already deficient or imbalanced due to years of pill taking. Antibiotics have had a spectacular impact on the long-term effects of syphilis and congenital syphilis has become very rare, but the new generation of STDs including the viral infections are now affecting thousands of mothers and their babies every year.

Genital Wart Virus

Genital warts are becoming more common. A third of all women tested by a polymerase chain reaction (PCR) test have evidence of a human papilloma virus (HPV) lesion. Nearly all cervical premalignant lesions are infected with the virus. There is evidence that the pill, smoking and herpes act together with the HPV wart virus to increase the development of early in-situ cervical cancers.[10] Both oestrogen and progesterone increase small DNA tumour virus polyomas in mouse tissue culture. Vulvar warts tend to increase in pregnancy but the alarming increase in early cervical cancer in young women began when the pill was introduced.

Herpes

Herpes is another common cause of genital ulceration. The infections cause recurrent painful ulcers, interfere with the sufferer's sex life and are highly infectious, readily transferring from person to person. If a mother has an active attack during delivery, the baby is likely to be infected. In 1978 in the UK it was estimated that 740 babies died of herpes and 180 suffered permanent neurological damage.[3] There may be damage to the baby's eyes, skin or liver. Treatment is unsatisfactory and infection with herpes may be a life-long sentence. Several studies have linked antenatal viral infection with subsequent malignant disease.

Cytomegalovirus
If the first infection with this virus happens during pregnancy, the baby can have brain damage, blindness, deafness, microcephaly (small head), mental retardation, cerebral palsy or even die. The virus, a member of the herpes family, is mainly sexually transmitted but is also found in saliva. Prenatal infections affect thousands of babies and 1 or 2 per cent will have a severe disease. In the UK it is estimated that about 2,800 babies are infected annually, and at least 500 have severe brain damage.

Two per cent of the women we tested before conception had evidence of active CMV infection in their blood and they were advised to avoid becoming pregnant. Screening during pregnancy is second best.[11]

Hepatitis B

Another common sexually transmitted virus is the hepatitis B virus which is an important cause of liver damage resulting in an increase in food and chemical allergies in a mother. If a woman has allergic reactions to common foods, these can affect her baby and cause infantile colic when she is breast feeding.

Toxoplasmosis

One woman in a hundred tested before they conceived had active infection with toxoplasmosis. Pregnancy is contraindicated for these women because of their high chance of having a damaged baby and, in the case of toxoplasmosis, a child who becomes blind. Women with past infections no longer have an IgM response in their blood to these infections and it is safe for them to conceive.

Multiple Infections

A study of 115 pregnant inner-city adolescents aged thirteen to seventeen in Baltimore, found most had multiple STDs, including chlamydia, gonorrhoea and mycoplasmas. Cervical infection with trichomonas vaginalis was associated with lower gestational age and weight at birth. Mothers infected with both chlamydia trachomatis and trichomonas had the smallest babies. Some mothers, delivered by Caesarean section, had inflammation of the lining of the womb after delivery. Among 90 infants 11 had conjunctivitis, 27 upper respiratory infections and 4 had pneumonia in the first four months of life. There was one stillbirth.[12]

Chlamydia is an important cause of conjunctivitis in the new-born. In San Francisco over 5 per cent of new-born babies are infected during delivery. Erythromycin or tetracycline eye ointments cure the eye disease but they do not prevent chlamydial pneumonia, which accounts for 30 per cent of all cases of pneumonia in infants under six months of age.[13]

AIDS

The advent of AIDS in 1981 focused the attention of the world's scientists on immunity. Why were the HIV viruses destroying defensive white blood cells? How do essential nutrients protect immunity? What part do the sex hormones play in the regulation of the immune system?

In the *Biological Effects of Sexual Freedom*, Dr Catterall said that gonorrhoea was increasing among young male homosexuals. Or was it the case that there was an increasing number of homosexuals being born forty years after the manufacture of stilboestrol? The first cases of AIDS were described in California. Acquired Immune Deficiency syndrome is now, along with suicide, a main cause of death in young men in the USA and is devastating sub Saharan Africa and parts of Asia. The disease has spread at an alarming rate with over half dying within a year of diagnosis from a wide range of viral, mycoplasmal and bacterial infections or from vascular tumours (Kaposi's sarcoma). At first the cause of this fatal illness was a mystery and then it was shown to be caused by HIV – the human immuno-deficiency viruses. The latent period between infection and full blown AIDS averages ten years which means victims are being infected as teenagers. Clinical deterioration is accompanied by falls in the number of circulating T-cells. The viruses enter these protective white cells and destroy them. This direct assault on cellular immunity leads to difficulties in finding an effective vaccine.

Early cases were described in young men with a history of over 1,000 different sexual partners. Especially vulnerable are male prostitutes needing money to buy drugs for their addictions. AIDS is more common in passive homosexual partners, many of whom take oestrogens to be more receptive and feminine.

Dr Schoental has drawn attention to the evidence that in history the partners of famous homosexual men were more likely to die at much younger ages than their famous friends. She thinks that nitrosamines, formed in the rectum after anal intercourse due to the effect of faecal bacteria on semen, are highly immunosuppressive, resulting in infections and early death. Amyl nitrite poppers are used to produce nitric oxide (NO) which also increases nitrosamine production. Poppers have the dual purpose for male relationships of both aiding penile erections and dilating the anal sphincters. This also increases nitrosamine production.[14]

When I gave a lecture in 1989 on the nutritional and infection screening of AIDS patients, a handsome, stylish HIV positive young journalist said he was delighted with this approach. He thought there was too great a concentration of resources on drug therapy and not enough interest in the details of immunity-boosting nutritional supplements. He did not understand why so many homosexual men were so promiscuous as he himself enjoyed a stable long-term relationship.

Is the promiscuous behaviour and tendency to become addicted to drugs merely a continuation of the hyperactive restless, unsatisfied and insatiable behaviour of zinc-deficient children?

A study of young men whose mothers took oestrogen and progesterone during pregnancy revealed that less than half were likely to be married and that they had a higher than normal incidence of sex organ abnormalities. Such men are also more likely to develop testicular cancer which is increasingly common as is a reduced sperm count. Before the current AIDS epidemic, the violet Kaposi's sarcoma mostly affected the skin of old men in Africa and was rarely fatal. Testosterone levels fall in older men and, if their liver has been impaired by alcohol and mouldy grains containing oestrogenic mycotoxins, they would become more sensitive to their natural oestrogen production. The sarcoma is a tumour of blood vessels which spreads rapidly to the skin and lymphatic system. Post-mortems of pill victims have occasionally shown vascular tumours, especially in the liver. Dr Kitty Little describes a vascular tumour removed from a 21-year-old girl which stretched the whole length of her largest artery.

In May 1991, letters to the *Lancet* reported a dramatic increase over the past two years in the number of pregnant women who were infected with HIV in London.[15] About one in 500 women (one in 200 in some areas) attending antenatal clinics were infected. There had been a ninefold increase in a year. The incidence in G U clinics was much higher, with one in 100 heterosexual men and one in five homosexual men being positive for HIV. Among 196 cases, 86 per cent were homosexual or bisexual males, 9 per cent heterosexual males, 2 per cent heterosexual females and 3 per cent were drug users of either sex.[16]

In view of the ease of HIV transmission to the newborn, affecting one in five children, and the lethal prognosis for AIDS, couples should take up the option of HIV testing which is available as part of the preconception hidden-infection screen. As subfertile couples may become highly fertile during treatment of their nutritional deficiencies, negative HIV test results for each partner are clearly desirable before treatments are started.

Women with HIV infection have an increased prevalence of wart infection and cervical erosions and early cancer relating to the degree of immunodeficiency. Women being treated in a New York colposcopy clinic were five times more likely to be HIV positive than those attending the antenatal clinic.[17] Heterosexual spread accounts for more than nine in ten new infections worldwide. A single exposure to an HIV positive woman with genital infection increases a man's risk of becoming HIV positive by as much as thirty times.[18] Transmission in a single exposure can be as high as 8 per cent. In one study of married couples in which one partner was infected the sero-conversion rate for the other partner was 17 per cent within a year and a half even when condoms had been used.[19]

	Total cases	AIDS in the UK Total deaths
1985	206	114
1992	6929	4291

The number of deaths is questioned in a letter to the *British Medical Journal* in July 1992. In one London district HIV or AIDS had become the commonest cause of death in young men but was rarely reported or recorded on their death certificates.

Thirty-four out of 213 deaths of men aged 16 to 65 were attributed to HIV infection but only six were recorded in the official office of Population Censuses and Surveys (OPCS) data – an under-reporting of 5–6 times.[20]

Dr Valerie Beral and her colleagues reported that Kaposi's sarcoma tended to be associated with faecal-oral contact especially insertive oral-anal contact (rimming) among homosexual or bisexual men.[21]

While there has been strong pressure for men to use condoms to prevent the spread of HIV, in 1992, three out of four women attending an STD clinic said they could do nothing to protect themselves against infection as they lacked the power to negotiate 'safer' sex with their partners. Some men refuse to wear condoms and object to women using barrier methods.[22]

The sheath or condom has a failure rate for pregnancies of up to 18 per 100 people using it for one year. If condom use cannot even prevent pregnancies, how can it prevent the spread of lethal viruses?

Multiple partners are a recipe for disaster. At first, from the mid 1980s to 1988, changing sexual practice plus condom use among homosexuals reduced gonorrhoea. But complacency set in, perhaps due to the long incubation period from the time of infection to full-blown AIDS. Younger men doubted the need for safer sex and gonorrhoea increased in 1989 and 1990.[23]

IMMUNITY

It is clear that both infections like AIDS and hormone-dependent cancers have increased since hormones have been prescribed. Normally our immune systems should be protecting us from invading organisms or from chemicals which can cause DNA changes and cancer (mitogens), but sex hormones can interfere with our natural immunity.

The single-celled amoeba can engulf bacteria or viruses and secrete chemicals to digest them. We have developed special cells with the same actions as part of our immune defence system. White cells in our blood attack invading bacteria and secrete immune proteins (antibodies) to kill the invaders (antigens). If we produce too many antibodies and there are too many antigens, they stick together in a lattice called an immune complex. This gives off complement, a chemical which makes platelets clot. The platelets then secrete other chemicals, such as prostaglandins, which dilate or constrict blood vessels, damage their walls and make even more platelets clot. When out of control, these mechanisms can cause headaches or thrombosis, while too few antibodies can also lead to tissue damage.

When a women has sexual intercourse, the sperm are foreign to her body like invading bacteria but she does not usually destroy them. Her body does not usually reject the foreign protein of the father in the fertilised egg. As the baby grows in her womb, her progesterone levels rise and stop white cells attacking the developing embryo. Some women do reject the foetus and antisperm antibodies can be a cause of habitual abortion. Reaction to the father's tissue may also be a reason for early pregnancy sickness. Oestrogens can increase antibody levels and this means that pregnant women are more likely to have allergic reactions to food in the first three months. Progesterone has the opposite effect and lowers antibody formation. The high levels of both steroid hormones during the last six months of pregnancy tend to suppress allergic reactions and give a feeling of well-being but a pregnant woman is more susceptible to infections and if she has a tumour it can grow more rapidly.

When the levels of hormones suddenly fall after the child is born, the mother may become more allergic once more. She may get thrombosis or postpartum depression. In auto-immune conditions where the body reacts to its own tissues, diseases like multiple sclerosis (MS) are likely to flare up. It is precisely at this critical time that long-acting injections of progestogen-only contraceptives are being given. Experimentally, oestrogens suppress MS in animals but progestogens intensify and prolong the disease. Progestogens are also more likely to intensify depression besides interfering with immune function.

In 1969, an editorial in the *Journal of the American Medical Association* warned doctors to be on the alert for signs of oral contraceptive steroids interfering with immune responses. Progestogens, especially, were likely to cause auto-immune disease.[24] Since then, multiple sclerosis has increased twice as much in women as in men.

In 1971, Joshi and others found that some women taking the pill were less able to form antibodies.[25] In 1972, Hagen and Froland described how white cells from pill-taking women reacted abnormally to testing with a mitogen.[26] The consultant physician, Dr Ronald Finn, who later proved that headaches could be caused by coffee addiction, looked at those lymphocytes down the microscope and asked himself what chaos it was going to cause. His reaction was quite different from that of the Royal College of General Practitioners. In their 1974 oral contraceptive study report they found significant increases in traditional allergic conditions and bacterial and viral infections. They quoted papers demonstrating that the pill steroids decreased antibody formation in rats, rabbits, mice and women. They concluded that the pill might suppress immunity but said, 'the effect of such a suppression, if it exists, is unlikely to be of clinical importance'.

In the same year a French allergist, Dr Falliers, wrote to the *Lancet* to report several cases of severe pill-induced allergies which disappeared when the pill was discontinued. 'But', he wrote 'it must be remembered that in clinical medicine, once the fire is lit, removal of the match does not necessarily extinguish the flame'.

In 1979, another French doctor, Dr J L Beaumont, and his team discovered a possible immunological basis for this view. They found that one in three women taking the pill had immune complexes containing antibodies to ethinyloestradiol (the oestrogen in all combined pills). The women who had developed thrombosis or phlebitis had the highest oestrogen antibody levels. The antibodies could be found two months after the pill was started and they persisted for years after the pill was discontinued as an 'immunological scar'.[27]

In the 1960s the introduction of long-acting progestogen injections struck me as an example of a particularly cynical and ruthless method of contraception. A woman can stop taking a daily pill if she feels ill. One injection is enough to alter her periods for the next nine months and what about the immunological scar?

Yvonne

Yvonne was prescribed the pill when she was twenty-five to see if it would help her menstrual migraine. After the second pill, she collapsed and lost consciousness for about four hours. When she came to, her whole body hurt and she had pins and needles all over. Although she did not take any more pills she had a *continuous headache for the next two years*. She also felt depressed and sometimes suicidal.

Later Yvonne had two pregnancies and suffered migraine throughout both. When her first son was born she was suddenly covered in a rash and after the second she bled from her breasts. By the time I saw Yvonne she had been given a variety of drugs which were either useless or made her feel worse.

One of her sons constantly needed antibiotics for very worrying upper respiratory infections. His blood was completely lacking in immunoglobin A (IgA), a hereditary defect affecting about one in a hundred people. Yvonne's blood also lacked IgA.

The four main groups of antibodies circulating in the blood are IgM, IgA, IgG and IgE. Newly born infants have hardly any immunoglobins in their blood and they rely heavily on their mother's antibodies transferred in the milk. By the time children are seven years old, they usually have nearly the same immunoglobin levels as adults. One or two individuals in every hundred have a hereditary IgA deficiency and are particularly susceptible to infection. IgA is normally plentiful in the gut where food is broken down and absorbed but when there is a shortage, as in Yvonne's case, reactions to food and prescribed hormones are more likely.

Besides hereditary defects, nutritional deficiencies can cause severe and prolonged reactions to small amounts of prescribed hormones.

Pauline
None of the many doctors Pauline had consulted believed her story that one month on the pill made her depressed for the next twenty years. Given the oral contraceptive pill at seventeen, Pauline had become very ill with a severe attack of blinding migraine. She thought her head would explode and she felt sick and depressed. She had never been depressed before. When she came to see me aged thirty-seven she said her depression had never lifted although she had no psychological reasons to be depressed. Psychiatrists had given her a variety of anti-depressants which either made no difference or made her

put on weight and feel even more depressed. Tests showed Pauline was severely deficient in zinc, magnesium, manganese and iron. Her stomach acid production was low, interfering with her absorption of these essential nutrients. Presumably these long-term nutritional deficiencies had resulted in this long-lasting illness precipitated by pill hormones.

Hormone Regulators

Sex hormones are key regulators of the immune system. The two main types of specialised white cells are T lymphocytes, made in the thymus, and B lymphocytes, made in the bone marrow. They usually circulate in our body fluids releasing antibodies and other chemicals to prevent tissue damage but in severe immune deficiency diseases such as AIDS there is increasing depletion of circulating T-cells.

When stilboestrol (DES) was given to mice, the oestrogen caused defects in the development of T-cells and decreased the number of T-helper cells. The ability of white cells to engulf invaders and to secrete antibodies was also impaired. In contrast the oestrogen stimulated immune suppression cells.[28] Oestrogens stimulate the proliferation of viruses and, in mice, viruses cause breast cancer.

Schoental has emphasised that prenatal exposure to oestrogens increases the tumour susceptibility in the target organs. She says a few large doses plus continuous small doses cause immunosuppression. Her findings are of great importance in view of the increase in STDs, AIDS and hormone-dependent cancers.[29]

Pregnancy would not be possible without immunosuppression. Both the incoming sperm and the implanting embryo would be destroyed without the primitive steroid progesterone which is essential to prevent the rejection of pregnancy. Progesterone can stimulate its own production. The cells lining the pregnant womb secrete a protein which increases progesterone concentration in the uterus. It acts directly on cells and, unlike the stress steroid cortisol, does not need special receptors. Progesterone prolongs skin graft survival and is anti-flammatory. It can block T-cells and other white cells and decrease the number of helper T-cells. Progesterone acts by temporarily blocking membrane transport and decreasing DNA synthesis. Cell membranes become more rigid. It acts as a powerful co-carcinogen. In experiments when known chemical carcinogens were given with progesterone, the cancers developed more quickly.[30] The type of cancer depends on the other carcinogen – for example cervical cancer plus the wart virus, tobacco smoke and lung cancer and melanomas with sun exposure. The pill and HRT have contributed to increases in these cancers. Now more women are dying of lung cancer than breast cancer in some cities such as Glasgow where women are heavy smokers and HRT is vigorously and freely prescribed.

ME

Where does the mysterious new illness, ME (myalgic encephalomyelitis) fit into the story? First known as Royal Free Disease in the early 1970s because it was diagnosed in some nurses working at the hospital, the illness, characterised by extreme mental exhaustion and muscle fatigue, was thought to follow viral infections (such as the Epstein-Barr virus which causes glandular fever or entero-viruses) and nick-named Yuppy Flu or post-viral fatigue syndrome.[31] Generally available biochemical tests gave little clue to what was going on and sufferers tended to be labelled as malingerers, much to the annoyance of famous campaigners like round-the-world yachtswoman Claire Francis. Although the disease mostly affects women, sometimes couples become ill.

Jill and Mac
This couple were in a sorry state when they came for a consultation. Brought by their parents, they were unable

to work or even drive a car. Both were severely deficient in zinc which is needed for the brain and the nerves (encephalomyelitis) and magnesium which is needed for muscles (myalgic). Mac's blood tests showed he had previously had glandular fever and toxoplasmosis. He was now also short of copper, a common finding in post-viral illness. Extra zinc would have made this worse, so he was given a zinc and copper pill on alternative days for three weeks. He was also short of fish oil (EPO). Mac, now aged thirty, first had sexual intercourse when he was twenty-one, and developed glandular fever aged twenty-eight just after meeting Jill. Post-viral ME had made him increasingly debilitated. Now that his main deficiencies had been demonstrated, he soon recovered with the help of the appropriate supplements and a low-allergy rotation diet and was even able to go back to work as a builder.

Jill was also severely deficient in zinc and magnesium but her story is more complicated and her recovery much more protracted. She had fallen into the hands of hormone enthusiasts, and when I first saw her she was barely able to move a muscle. Jill's mother had had a nervous breakdown when she had been given the pill and took seven years to recover. At sixteen Jill had sexual intercourse for the first time and had nine different partners by the time she was twenty-nine. Age twenty, she was given the pill to curb heavy menstrual bleeding. Within days she became severely depressed. Next month she was given progesterone which made her feel even worse with rages, crying, sleeping for days, headaches, breast pains and leg cramps and irregular bleeding. She was then implanted with oestrogen. Over the next ten years she was prescribed mixtures of oestrogen, testosterone and progestogens and continued to have heavy irregular bleeding. At twenty-seven, she developed glandular fever and three years later was diagnosed by a neurologist as suffering from ME – post-viral syndrome. When I advised her to stop the hormone, Jill thought she would need a hysterectomy to stop the heavy bleeding. A cervical swab showed mycoplasmal infection which was treated with tetracyclines. Clearing the infection helped to control the irregular bleeding which eventually stopped after the effect of the hormones wore off. Very gradually, with the aid of nutritional supplements and a low-allergy rotation diet, her health began to improve. Two years later, Jill said she felt a hundred times stronger and she and Mac were happily settled in a new flat and looking forward to starting a family. Once more essential nutrients had come to the rescue.

Helpful Nutrients

Professor Ranjit Chandra, who had spoken at the 1989 AIDS and nutrition meeting, studied the nutrition of elderly men and women in Newfoundland.[32] He managed to reduce from 48 to 23 the average number of days during a year that a group of over-65-year-olds were ill from infections. He gave them supplements in doses similar to those recommended as daily requirements in both Canada and the USA. The group taking minerals and vitamins were less likely to be deficient in zinc, iron, vitamins A, B6, C and beta carotene over the twelve months compared with a similar but unsupplemented group. (These findings could be one of the reasons that older migraine patients reacted to more foods when tested than younger sufferers. Allergic reactions increased with age.[33]) Professor Chandra found that nutritional supplements increased the number of certain T-cells and the numbers and activity of natural-killer cells (matching improvements in blood levels of zinc and ferritin). There was a higher antibody response, increased interleukin–2 production (zinc and beta carotene) and enhanced response to mitogen or more protection against cancer (vitamin B6). Professor Chandra emphasised that too high doses of fat-soluble vitamins could suppress immunity, e.g. too much vitamin E and D decreased interleukin–2 activity.

Zinc deficiency is so common among the elderly that some investigators think this is a normal state of affairs.[34]

Professor Chandra, by measuring only the blood levels in those who had remained healthy for the following one to three years, discovered that healthy old people had the same range of serum zinc values as healthy young adults.

The secret of staying young without extra hormones for both sexes is making sure that our nutritional status is adequate throughout our lifetime.

KEY POINTS

- Pill sex hormones promote huge increases in sexually transmitted (or venereal) diseases including AIDS.
- Nutritional deficiencies and silent undiagnosed genital infections have become endemic and are the main cause of infertility and recurrent miscarriages.
- Parental STDs make babies ill.
- Sex hormones upset immunity, increasing infections, cancer and auto-immune diseases like MS and ME.
- Immunity declines with ageing and is boosted by essential nutrient supplementation.

Chapter Nine

The Next Generation

PREVENTING INFERTILITY, MISCARRIAGES, CONGENITAL ABNORMALITIES, COT DEATHS, DYSLEXIA, ALLERGIES AND HYPERACTIVITY IN CHILDREN

Sexual chemistry is designed to arrange that the genes in an egg meet and mingle with the different genes in a spermatozoa. The mother's hormones should then ensure that the developing offspring is well nourished. We know that it isn't always so simple. A preoccupation with preventing conception has succeeded in encouraging habitual sexual intercourse with many different partners from young ages, rather than with one bonded lifetime's mate and companion, helping to cause many of the problems already discussed.

Disordered sexual chemistry can victimise children. The Foresight book, *Planning for a Healthy Baby*, ends with the sentence: 'For tomorrow's child is everyman's eternity'.[1] Foresight, virtually alone among the charities, has the dream that tomorrow's child can be born undamaged, naturally healthy, naturally able and naturally loving. Belinda Barnes has been indefatigable in her promotion of preconception care based on the work of Elizabeth

Lodge Rees, Weston Price, Carl Pfeiffer, Answar Prasad, Lucille Hurley, Linus Pauling and Isobel Jennings – pioneers in the fields of nutrition and orthomolecular medicine.[2] It seems to me that so much research and charity money is dedicated to shutting the stable door after the horse has bolted. Foresight, in an age of greedy instant self-gratification, stands out like a beacon of light showing future parents how they and their children can still live in harmony with nature.

There are five possible reproductive outcomes.
1. Infertility affecting either or both parents.
2. Miscarriage or stillbirth of a normal or abnormal baby.
3. A baby born with congenital abnormalities.
4. The baby seems healthy but soon shows sign of being allergic with colic and infantile eczema. Later he or she may have a reduced ability to cope with stress, suffer from learning difficulties, become hyperactive or develop behavioural or sexual problems.
5. The baby is healthy and well balanced.

Infertility

Infertility surveys estimate that one in six couples have difficulty in conceiving a first or subsequent child. Now 'sexual activity' has come to mean both the number of years since age of first sexual intercourse and the number of partners. As this type of sexual activity has increased, the fertility of both men and women has decreased. A young couple having first sex with each other are likely to be highly fertile. The post-pill tendency to delay child bearing for ten to twenty years after the onset of adult fertility is also a good method of population control. Older women are less fertile with a rapid decline after the age of forty. *Women who have spent years on ovulation-blocking hormones are then given ovulation stimulants. This often*

happens even when they can still ovulate spontaneously.
The excuse is that progesterone levels are too low, but
natural hormone and hormone receptor production are
usually impaired because of pill-induced zinc and magnesium deficiencies. Ovulating women with normal progesterone rises are given Clomid-type drugs or IVF when
their partner has poor sperm as a consequence of
nutritional deficiencies, toxic minerals, infections or intake
of alcohol or tobacco or because of his exposure to oestrogens early in development.

Stimulating multiple egg follicles to develop cycle after
cycle causes a low zinc and high copper imbalance, ovarian
cysts, and increased risks of ectopic pregnancy or ovarian cancer. Previously fertile women will have become less
fertile or even infertile because of the induced deficiencies
and ovarian or tubal damage.

About one in 200 women have amenorrhoea (no
periods) after coming off the pill. It has been calculated
that for most of them fertility returns after about two
years. Over this time they may be subjected to extensive
investigations, including, for those with high prolactin
levels, brain scans to see if they have developed a pituitary
tumour.

Infertile women are given postcoital tests, scans, laparo-
scopies, injections of dye, X-rays and repeated courses of
stimulating hormones while their nutritional deficiencies
are ignored. Past or current genital infections, probably
the commonest cause of infertility, are under-investigated.

Women who once gloried in the freedoms of the pill are
angry or resigned as they face a childless old age. They
join with mothers and grandmothers in working for a
better deal for future generations. Australian doctor
Robyn Rowlands, in her book *Living Laboratories* says
there is still time to stop the 'dehumanisation and com-
modification of living beings'.[3] She founded the Feminist
International Network of Resistance to Reproductive and
Genetic Engineering (FINRRAGE) to counter the current
'thoughtless pursuit of scientific control and greed for

profit'. The famous Australian author Germaine Greer says with brilliant cynicism that women make perfect laboratory animals; they feed themselves and keep their cages clean. Women have been inviting this sort of exploitation because of their worries about whether they can or cannot conceive, while their doctors say they are only trying to help.

In Vitro Fertilisation (IVF)

Women who have absent, blocked or irreparable tubes or a partner with very low sperm count can go to an IVF clinic. Many of these clinics are private in the UK and, in spite of my attempts to demonstrate the need, are reluctant to add essential nutrient analysis and more detailed infection screening to the heavy financial costs of a single pregnancy attempt. Even women with unblocked tubes are treated by IVF when a fertilised egg or eggs are inserted into the womb. GIFT or ZIFT (gamete or zygote intrafallopian transfer) is often used when at least one of the Fallopian tubes seem patent. Gametes (eggs and sperm) or zygotes (fertilised eggs) are placed in one of the Fallopian tubes. Tubal transfers are twice as likely to result in a confirmed pregnancy as intrauterine transfers. Frozen embryos are half as likely to implant as fresh transfers.[4]

Jill and James

Jill had been infertile for five and a half years. Now thirty-nine, she had been given hormones in some shape or form since she was twenty when first married. To please her husband who didn't want children, she took three different contraceptives over the next eleven years. During this time she had changed to the IUD but bled so heavily that it was removed after only two weeks. Jill's marriage failed after nine years and Jill said she became quite promiscuous, having about ten different partners in rapid succession. When she married James she used a diaphragm but 'not very carefully'. Realising there was a problem they both sought infertility investigations.

Jill was given Clomid for six months to 'boost ovulation' even though her temperature charts showed normal post-ovulatory rises. After this a laparoscopy revealed apparently normal-looking tubes. The second IVF attempt was successful but she miscarried a blighted ovum at twelve weeks. Then AIH (artificial insemination from husband) was tried, but with no better luck. Jill bled at eleven weeks expelling another blighted ovum. Next time it was the turn of GIFT. Jill religiously sniffed human chorionic gonadotrophins to prevent her ovulating at the 'wrong' time and was then injected with follicle-stimulating hormone at the 'right' time. Four attempts failed. In despair and utterly exhausted Jill contacted Foresight.

Screening showed deficiencies in zinc, iron, manganese, chromium, selenium and B vitamins. Magnesium in particular was drastically low in her sweat and red cells. Consequently, her muscle contraction and relaxation patterns were very abnormal with signs of muscle damage with low exercise activity. Jill was not fit enough for a pregnancy and, alarmingly, she had moles all over her back which she thought were growing. Biolab tests showed she had very low red cell selenium levels, low glutathione peroxidase enzyme values, and increased fragility of both red and white cells. Jill had reduced anti-oxidant protection (see Appendix two), which could be improved if she took selenium, vitamin E and vitamin C supplements. This treatment should help in preventing a mole change into a melanoma which would be more likely if she became pregnant. Jill's infection screen uncovered a Group C streptococcal cervicitis. She was treated with Penicillin tablets. They were both given Flagyl because James had an anaerobic gardnerella prostatitis which was uncovered when secretions collected during a prostatic massage were tested. This was the first time during their long-running infertility saga that he had been thoroughly checked. Both were warned to avoid alcohol, given a range of supplements and a low-allergy rotation diet. James had also been zinc deficient when first tested.

Jill's next IVF attempt was successful. Against my advice, she took progesterone for the first three months of the pregnancy and her nutrients levels fell needing extra boosting. Both parents were delighted when their son was born. Later on, Jill, preoccupied with the baby, was very surprised when she became pregnant naturally. Unfortunately she had stopped taking the supplements and she had another miscarriage. Both zinc and magnesium were again deficient. Only time will tell if their IVF son has escaped the long-term consequences of extra hormone stimulation.

No one reading *Living Laboratories* would want to have a test-tube baby unless they were desperate, and many women are, especially if both of their tubes are blocked or missing and a growing number of men have low sperm counts. As more women suffer from premature ovarian failure they are being offered embryo transfer (ET). Early onset ovarian failure is classified as atrophy before the age of forty due to 'genetic' causes (which might mean their mother had taken hormones) or 'auto-immune' disease (possibly really meaning they themselves had taken hormones) or because of infections, surgery, chemotherapy or irradiation – all more likely among pill takers. Their only chance of a pregnancy is to be donated an egg from someone else. The prospective mother must take 2–8mg per day of oestradiol for several weeks before the transfer. Then progesterone is added in doses of 25–100mg per day (intramuscular) or 75–300mg per day (per vaginum) and both are taken for several months.

Among the first 100 donated cycles in one London clinic 27 women became pregnant, two of these pregnancies (7.4 per cent) were ectopic and six miscarried (22 per cent). The chance of success declined from 50 per cent for 25–29-year-old recipients to 9 per cent for the 45–49 age group. Fresh tubal transfers of three or four zygotes obtained from parous donors and given to young women with primary ovarian failure gives the best chance of a pregnancy.[4]

Drugs and hormones used to synchronise cycles include:

Group 1 *Anti-oestrogens*
   Clomiphene is sold as Clomid or Serophene
   Cyclofenil is sold as Rehibin
   Tamoxifen is sold as Tamofen or Nolvadex

These drugs act by blocking oestrogen receptors (although this effect can wear off and the receptors are stimulated). They prevent the normal feedback of oestrogen on the pituitary. This results in an increased FSH output and one or more follicles are stimulated to develop and release eggs.

   Common side effects are hot flushes, headaches, abdominal discomfort, ovarian enlargement, ovarian cysts and visual blurring. If the latter occurs the drugs should be stopped immediately. Increase in hormone-dependent cancers and liver cancer have been recorded although tamoxifen is given for suppression of breast cancer.

Group 2 *Gonadotrophins*
Both pituitary hormones, follicular stimulating hormone (FSH) and luteinising hormone (LH) are used to stimulate ovulation and mature follicles.

Human menopausal gonadotrophin or menotrophin is obtained from the urine of menopausal women and sold as Pergonal, Humegon or Metrodin.

Human chorionic gonadotrophin (hCG) is obtained from the urine of pregnant women and is sold as Pregnyl, Profasi or Gonadotrophon LH.

Gonadotrophins are given by nasal spray or by intramuscular injection.

Group 3 *LHRH (Luteinising hormone-releasing hormone)*
The natural hypothalamic hormones stimulates the release of both FSH and LH gonadotrophins from the pituitary. Very powerful forms known as *gonadorelins* have been developed.

Buserelin is sold as Ferital, Supercur or Superfact
Nafarelin is sold as Synarel
Goserelin is sold as Zoladex
Leuprolin is sold as Prostap

Gonadorelins can be used to suppress normal cycles when given continuously by injection, subcutaneous long-acting depot or by nasal spray. When injected intravenously in bursts to mimic the body's own pulsatile hormone release, they stimulate ovulation.

Side effects of both gonadotrophins and gonadorelins include abdominal pain, nausea, headache, hot flushes, loss of libido and mood upsets, painful breast changes, heavy bleeding and ovarian cysts. Possible complications with all of these drugs are induction of a premature menopause, osteoporosis and hormone-dependent cancers.

One in five women becoming pregnant when taking follicle stimulants or gonadotrophins have multiple births. These babies are more likely to be born prematurely, be small for dates and have later health problems.

Multiple births following assisted conception, are less likely when pulses of LHRH are given during a continuous intravenous infusion, compared with intamuscular hCG stimulation.[5] Extra eggs increase the chances of implantation and if too many succeed some embryos are culled by a potassium injection which kills the extra foetuses usually leaving two behind. Professor Robert Winston of Hammersmith Hospital says this should not be necessary and IVF should be fairly inexpensive and successful.

Worldwide the results of assisted conception are poor. The live birth rate is up to 10 per cent with only half of these pregnancies being uncomplicated. Apart from couples who have known problems which make it impossible for them to conceive naturally, the chances of unaided conception over time are as high as 70 per cent in two to three years. But, as fertility decreases sharply with age, women who have delayed childbearing until they are well in to their thirties are told they do not have any more time and they must keep taking ovulatory stimulants. If women suffering from anorexia and bulimia already have polycystic disease, as many do, their infertility does not benefit from forced stimulation which will increase their zinc deficiency.[6]

If a man has no sperm, after congenital problems, surgery or long-term infections, AID – artificial insemination from a donor or donors, can be performed on his wife. AID can infect her with AIDS if HIV viruses are transferred. Other infections known to have been passed on via contaminated sperm include chlamydia, hepatitis B and the other causes of pelvic inflammatory disease which may not have been excluded. The woman's immunity can be affected as is shown by the appearance of anti-sperm antibodies in her blood.

Miscarriages

Estimations of miscarriage rates range from one in ten to one in two pregnancies. Risks increase with numbers of previous miscarriages and exposure to hormones in early pregnancies. In the case of 'DES daughters', hormones given to the pregnant woman's own mother during her pregnancy doubles her daughter's chance of miscarriage, often because of malformed sexual organs.[7, 8] Children born to women firstly given the pill to block ovulation and then given FSH stimulants, were subject themselves to progesterone during their early development and are now reaching reproductive age. Abnormalities in male children are obvious at birth and recorded numbers have gone on increasing each year while sperm counts keep falling. Tubal abnormalities are only discovered later during investigations for infertility or following an ectopic pregnancy which, like miscarriage, is more common among these women.

Moles and Choriocarcinomas

There is a sinister type of hidden miscarriage which is more likely with the less effective progestogen-only or low-dose combined pills. Pill takers are told they may become accidentally pregnant if they have a bout of vomiting or diarrhoea or if they need a course of antibiotics. Then they should take the morning after or post-coital pill which is a bigger-than-usual pill dose to induce an early miscarriage. In the 1960s pill takers had less than a 1 per cent chance of an accidental pregnancy each year on the generally available pills; now their risk of pregnancy can be as much as 7 per cent because too low doses are being used. Some of the products of conception are occasionally left behind if the baby dies and form a hydatidiform mole. This can be diagnosed from raised chorionic gonadotrophin (hCG) levels in the mother's urine and sometimes happens without the mother realising she has been pregnant, especially if she had been taking a weak-dose pill which makes her bleed erratically. A mole can become malignant – a choriocarcinoma. Professors Bagshawe and Newlands at Charing Cross Hospital found that one in three women (103 out of 335) who were given pill hormones while hCG was still appearing in their urine after an incomplete abortion developed choriocarcinomas and were treated by chemotherapy.[9]

But this is precisely what is still happening. Couples are told following the discovery of a missed abortion or a mole that a further pregnancy must be avoided. While the wife is tested regularly to make sure no foetal tissues remain in her womb, she is told to go back on the pill as it is still the best bet for contraception!

The incidence of molar pregnancies is higher in Japan and the Far East. The incidence in Hawaii between 1968 and 1981 was one in 600 for Oriental and one in a 1,256 for Caucasian women. The risk of having a molar pregnancy increases sharply with age which coincides with falling serum zinc levels in both husband and wife. One in three of all pregnancies are molar in women over fifty; this is the group now perversely being offered embryo transfers from younger donors.

Foresight screening has shown that women with a history of recurrent miscarriages, like many infertility patients, have hidden essential nutrient deficiencies, hidden infections and masked reactions to foods and chemicals. Foresight claims dramatic results in treating recurrent miscarriages and infertility. In the October 1991 newsletter, among 648 couples having 780 babies only twelve women known to be following the programme miscarried.[10] Often the programme consists only of a hair test for mineral levels, nutritional supplements and advice on eating a low-allergy rotation diet and avoiding tobacco, alcohol and unnecessary medication.

Full nutrition and infection screening is expensive to a generation brought up on free hormone pills. The result is that many couples follow the 'preconception on a shoestring' procedure.[11] Until all the necessary costs are met it is hard to know how much better the results could be. Any new Foresight doctor quickly sees the benefit among couples with a history of recurrent miscarriages: 173 couples, previously losing 320 babies, went on to have 207 Foresight babies. Even couples who have already lost as many as three babies, which means that without help they would have a 50 per cent chance of losing the next one, have gone on to have full normal pregnancies and healthy babies when fully investigated and treated. A typical Foresight baby is about 200 grams heavier than usual (possibly due to the extra zinc and fish oil), is born and breast fed without problems and has top Agpar scores.

Sally and Paul

Six years ago Sally telephoned. She had lost a baby at thirty-seven weeks of pregnancy the year before – stillborn due to placental insufficiency. This year she lost another baby at twenty-three weeks and had an early miscarriage. Sally was desperate – no one could give her a reason but she had been 'on the pill' for seven years from nineteen to twenty-six. Headaches on a 30mcg oestradiol combined pill were swapped for swelling and fluid retention with another so-called low-dose pill. She had conceived the first baby she lost three months after giving up the pill.

Blood tests showed she had had both toxoplasmosis and cytomegaloviral infections at some time in the past but neither infection was now active. A deep endocervical swab showed a heavy group B streptococcal infection and candida. Sally's husband Paul had also had toxoplasmosis in the past. They thought they may have been infected from eating undercooked beef in France. Paul was deficient in zinc, magnesium and lowish in chromium and manganese. Three months later, these deficiencies had been corrected. The deficiencies tended to recur when he forgot to take the supplements. Sally was more severely zinc deficient with a particularly low serum zinc. Three months later her zinc was nearly normal but this time her magnesium was much more deficient. A gastrogram showed decreased pancreatic enzyme secretion. Taking extra pancreatic enzymes helped to stabilise the nutrient levels.

Over the next few years Sally and Paul managed to have two healthy children. Sally had been very careful to follow a low-allergy diet especially in early pregnancy to avoid morning-sickness, and to have her zinc and magnesium levels monitored throughout. They are thrilled to have their lively and bright sons. The elder could recognise written words when he was two years old.

Prematurity

It is usually possible to avoid prematurity with good pre-conception and pregnancy care. Maternal nutritional deficiencies, especially lack of zinc and magnesium, parental smoking or parental genital infections cause prematurity. Smoking is the main cause because of damage to placental blood vessels. Exposure to tobacco smoke during development increases the risk of childhood cancer. The Department of Health in the UK is concerned that six out of ten unskilled women (i.e. belonging to Social class V) are smoking at the start of their pregnancies and less than one in ten give up during pregnancy.

Premature babies are given vitamin K to prevent haemorrhages. A small study suggested that injections of the vitamin might be causing leukaemia but this possibility has been discounted by a much larger study. Premature small-for-date babies are more likely to suffer from congenital abnormalities.

Congenital Abnormalities

Not all children are born normal. Some are aborted at such an early stage of pregnancy that the mother didn't know she was pregnant. Known as a chemical pregnancy, diagnostic tests may be briefly positive. A recent fashion is to scan the developing baby frequently merely to reassure the mother. Ultrasound can be used to destroy tissue and routine scanning was introduced without the long-term effects being known as Dr Ian Chalmers of the UK National Epidemiology Unit has pointed out. It may damage a woman's ovaries and affect her baby's growth, development and immunity. Possible increased leukaemia incidence in children is being monitored. No one knows if the doses used are safe but an increase in left-handedness has been recorded among children given a single short exposure between 16 and 22 weeks in-utero. This is when cells are migrating to different areas in a baby's brain and may be a first sign of minimal brain damage.[12] Women with a history of recurrent miscarriage are invited to view their baby each week or even every day during its earliest development. Their obstetricians seem to me to resemble bakers giving into the impulse to open the oven door to see if their cakes are rising. But beforehand they did they check out all the necessary ingredients and make sure they were uncontaminated? At the first sign of a visible abnormality the pregnancy is terminated. Reasons for this excessive vigilance are the increase in ectopic or molar pregnancies, both more likely due to hormone taking during pregnancy or worry about litigation in the case of assisted conceptions. Several women have told Foresight that they had a miscarriage a day or two after a scan and our advice is to delay scanning until as late as possible to allow the baby peace to develop. A mother can be reassured, without risk to her baby, by confirming that she is well nourished with a monthly serum and red cell mineral check. Worry and stress can lower serum zinc, while magnesium deficiency induces anxiety. Even a woman who has had several miscarriages can face the next attempt quite happily when the couple's preconception care has been thorough.

Congenital abnormalities began to be registered in the UK in 1964. The rate per 10,000 total births (including stillbirths) increased each year from 163 to 220.8 in 1983 but reaching 240 for males in 1984. By 1989 there were 46 per cent more notifications for live males than females, mostly due to abnormal external genitalia, although the overall rate had fallen to 180.3 due to patchy registration. As some areas were no longer recording 'minor abnormalities such as undescended testes', from 1990 onwards minor abnormalities were excluded. This led to spurious claims of improvement when the revised rate for 1990 was only 115.7. In reality, *even more males are being born with heart and genital abnormalities* while numbers of babies born with cleft lip, cleft palate and Down's syndrome have also increased.[13] One in a hundred baby boys, or one in ten if they were premature, are born with undescended testicles. It is now accepted that these boys should be referred to a surgeon for orchidopexy (bringing the testicle from the abdomen down into the scrotum) or the removal of a poorly developed testicle, in order to diminish their increased cancer risk. Clearly the official figures are misleading.

Central Nervous System Abnormalities

These include anencephalus, spina bifida and hydrocephalus. Rates have fallen since the 1970s with at least 30 per cent of the decrease is known to be due to the increasing use of diagnostic ultrasound and alphafetoprotein screening followed by abortion. In general, before screening became available, the incidence of malformations was three times higher among social terminations and ten times higher among spontaneous abortions than among total births.[14] The RCGP 1974 report recorded that women who stopped the pill because of side effects had a 30.6 per cent abortion rate compared with 12.3 in controls. Both types of abortion have become more common since the pill was introduced and many happen before a diagnosis of CNS abnormality can be made. Although the fall may also be due to a greater awareness of the importance of nutrition and avoiding tobacco and alcohol during pregnancy, I find that in some couples with a history of a grossly abnormal foetus, it is the husband who smokes and drinks.

Dr Isobel Gal showed that much of the very high spina bifida incidence between 1964 and 1972 was due to hormone pregnancy tests when as much as a nine months' dose of oral contraceptive was given during early pregnancy.[15] The success of her campaign, which succeeded in banning this practice, is the main reason for the improvement but, she says, the morning-after pill is along similar lines.

Part of the problem is that on the pill or during pregnancy, the levels of zinc, magnesium and B vitamins including folic acid tend to fall but vitamin A rises. Isobel Gal discovered that women pill takers had high vitamin A levels which didn't always return to normal when the pill was stopped. Mothers of spina bifida children had particularly high levels and their babies had high vitamin A concentrations in their livers.[16] In animals, vitamin A accumulates in the liver when zinc is deficient. If a mother has either too high or too low levels of vitamin A, her baby could be abnormal, but blood levels are usually well regulated. Like vitamins D and E, vitamin A is fat-soluble and excess gathers in fat tissues. Vitamin E helps to regulate vitamin A metabolism and prevents the oxidation of fats. We have already seen how the pill hormones interfere with fat metabolism.

In the UK the Chief Medical Officer has warned against vitamin A supplements in the form of retinoids during pregnancy, instead recommending the safer vegetable form which is mostly carotene. Although a wide range of oral contraceptives raise vitamin A levels, especially retinol and its transporting protein, carotenoid levels may be lowered. Zinc fingers bind retinol to its transporting protein, releasing it from storage and preventing a toxic build up in the liver.

It has long been known that zinc deficiency in both animals and humans can affect brain development and cause a range of abnormalities including spina bifida. Recent Foresight research led by Dr Neil Ward of Surrey and Professor Derek Bryce-Smith of Reading Universities measured minerals in placental tissue obtained from three parts of the UK, South Wales, North-West England and South Yorkshire.[17] South Wales has the highest incidence of spina bifida in the country and placental tissue from women living there had the lowest zinc levels. Non-malformed live birth tissue averaged 53.3 micrograms per gram in South Yorkshire compared with 29.7 in South Wales. Zinc values decreased among social terminations, fell further for hydrocephalus and dropped to only 9.9 for those born with spina bifida who also had low iron and selenium levels. Stillbirths had the highest lead and cadmium concentrations due to the links with pollution and smoking and hydrocephalus the highest copper, probably because of the link with infection.

There has been much publicity that lack of folic acid is the main cause of spina bifida. Medical Research Council studies report a 75 per cent improvement in preventing a recurrence.[18] All women contemplating pregnancy are now advised to take 400mcg each day or 4mg if they have already had a spina bifida child. The government advisers do not mention that taking a large dose of one B vitamin can cause deficiencies of the others, as I found recently in a patient whose abnormal foetus had probably been damaged by her recent toxoplasmosis infection. She had been taking 4mg of folic acid for two years but was short of vitamins B1, 2 and 6. Suddenly stopping a large dose of folic acid can cause a functional deficiency. It is always important to check what is actually going on. There is accelerated folic acid breakdown in pregnancy.[19]

Hormones given to women are now causing abnormalities in fish. The recirculation of treated sewage waste as tap water has always seemed bizarre. For the past ten years deformed, hermaphrodite trout have been found near water outlets. Ethinyloestradiol and mestranol, given to millions of women on the pill or on HRT, is highly active at one part per billion on the reproductive system of animals and fish. Oestrogens are contaminating our water supply.[20]

The first report that the pill increases the risk of chromosome abnormalities in women's blood cells appeared in 1967.[21] Women taking 'low-dose pills' had higher rates of sister-chromatid exchanges (more DNA divisions) than pregnant or non-pregnant controls, said a 1979 publication.[22] As women get older they have increased risk of chromosome abnormalities. Professor Lejeune in Paris questioned mothers of 730 children with Down's syndrome and found that those over thirty were significantly more likely to have used the pill for longer than one year and/or to have become pregnant within six months of stopping it.[23]

The Oxford/FPA study reported the results of 5,700 pregnancies and found 'a surprisingly low incidence' of congenital abnormalities among live infants born to women having their first baby who had never taken the pill compared with pill ever-users. The figures in 1976 were 0.4 per cent compared with 3.8 per cent and in 1979 were 0.9 per cent compared with 4.3 per cent for the pill ever-user group.[24,25]

Birth Marks

A large study of 16,000 women in Jerusalem in 1978 found that children were more likely to be born with birth marks (vascular skin abnormalities) if their mothers got pregnant as soon as they came off the pill.[26] These women, along with mothers who were underweight or over thirty-five, were also more likely to have a miscarriage or an abnormal baby. Since then women are advised to wait for at least three months before conceiving. Previous pill users have more risk of miscarriage, stillbirth, twinning and having babies with cardiovascular abnormalities. Foresight results show that women can be unfit for pregnancy for years until they start taking nutritional supplements.

The evidence is so strong against taking hormones during pregnancy that it is unbelievable that this practice is growing yet again, as reliance is placed on rejection of abnormal embryos during IVF programmes or later termination of pregnancy following ultrasound scans. Once more it is clear that extra hormones are more toxic and more teratogenic than smoking. Although a wide range of abnormalities can be caused by smoking, this was not very obvious at first, as tobacco smoke causes placental insufficiency by damaging blood vessels which tends to lead to the abortion of a normal foetus or birth of a small premature baby. Prescribing hormones to pregnant smokers is absurd.[27, 28, 29]

Hormone exposure in early pregnancy increases the risk of limb defects in the foetus by 23 times.[30] The pill can cause riboflavin and vitamin B2 deficiency within seven months of taking low-dose pills. It was one of the underlying causes of limb defects in the thalidomide tragedies. A study by Nora and Nora discovered that of 30 babies born with multiple abnormalities, 15 had been exposed to oestrogen/progesterone preparations, 3 to alcohol, 2 to X-rays, 1 anaesthetics and the rest various drugs or severe infections.[31]

Cot Deaths

Registrations of neonatal deaths have been steadily declining for decades. There are many reasons, including improved premature baby units with high-tech equipment and, also, smaller sized families as more women become permanently infertile in their thirties due to blocked tubes or early hysterectomies. An exception was the increase in registration of cot deaths (sudden unexplained deaths during sleep). Started in 1971, registration reached a peak of 2.3 (2.79 males and 1.78 females) per thousand live births by 1988. A quarter had underlying respiratory conditions mentioned on the death certificate. Since then registrations have fallen and success is being claimed for the publicity campaign informing parents to stop smoking and to lay babies on their backs. Cot deaths happen in all social classes, suggesting a cause more important than nutrition, housing, hygiene or even smoking. It seems not unreasonable to think of the residual effects of maternal hormone exposure, especially as 60 per cent more boys than girls were dying by 1988. It was discovered that the babies had breathing problems due to lung surfactant defects (perhaps related to abnormal essential fatty acid metabolism or undiagnosed mycoplasma infection?) and/or poor kidney development. Then it was discovered that babies were less likely to become cot death victims if they were laid down on their backs in a well-ventilated room, away from cigarette smoke and not wrapped up with too many covers. Publicity campaigns, such as *Back to Sleep*, successful spread this knowledge and cot deaths fell to 1.44 by 1991.[32]

The odd thing is that babies have been laid down the wrong way for decades; perhaps cot deaths were not being recorded or perhaps babies have become more likely to suffocate, rebreathe their carbon dioxide or simply stop breathing. We have evidence of a sharp fall in children's zinc status from the 1970s to the end of the 1980s. Cot deaths are more common when a mother suffers from post-natal depression and we now know depressives are usually short of zinc and magnesium. Low zinc can impair development at the microscopic level in brain and other tissues in a baby who looks normal, while low magnesium will impair nerve and muscle function. Another possible contributory cause might have been the unhygienic fashion for lying babies on sheepskins, possibly still contaminated by the potentially neurotoxic organo-phosphates used in sheep dip.

Premature babies are more likely to develop lung disease after they are born. Women in premature labour are being given steroids, which seems a bad idea as it could cause many problems including further zinc deficiency in both mother and child who would then have more risk of developmental problems or late hypertension than if its parents were smokers. The basic Foresight approach before and during pregnancy should prevent premature deliveries and underdeveloped newborns. A baby can have a sweat test to make sure the nutrients in the mothers milk are being absorbed effectively. This is especially important for boys as they have a higher requirement of zinc than girls.

Preventing Dyslexia, Allergies, Hyperactivity and Behavioural Problems in Children

Your baby can seem perfect at birth but within a few years it may become clear that there is a problem. Other children are learning letters and words but your bright lively son is still reading pictures. And he goes on reading pictures for years and years, the smallest word remains unrecognised. Severe word blindness in an intelligent child is a very distressing condition. Do we know enough to be able to prevent it even when the gene carrying the dyslexia-related chromosome has been inherited? We now know a basic problem for brain development is lack of zinc; lack of zinc in the sperm or the egg, during pregnancy, during lactation and during growth. Hopefully, this may give a way of bypassing the hereditary tendency by ensuring adequate preconception care.

Fifty-one separate studies analysing hair minerals, including my study of children attending the Dyslexia Institute and Grenville College, found that children with both learning and/or behaviour problems tended to have higher lead and cadmium in their hair compared with controls. Unfortunately hair zinc levels ranged from low to high, giving an average normal range result.[33, 34]

Meanwhile animal tests were clearly demonstrating the importance of zinc status for brain development and function. When Oberleas and Caldwell tested the effects of iron, manganese, magnesium or zinc deficiency, they showed that only lack of zinc adversely affected the animals' behaviour and learning. The animals became lethargic to a measurable degree and they exhibited inferior learning performance and an increased level of emotionality.[35]

Then the investigators gave young animals a zinc-deficient diet and the animals couldn't find their food at the end of a maze. Adding zinc to their diet restored their ability to pass the test. When pregnant rats were kept short of zinc, supplementation did not always help. This time their offspring were permanently unable to perform the tests. These experiments testify to the overwhelming importance of nutrition during pregnancy, but if zinc is so important why were the hair tests misleading?

The problem was solved by using Dr John Howard's sweat test. This time all the dyslexic children tested were zinc deficient. Hair and sweat results matched for copper, lead, cadmium (higher) and chromium (lower) in dyslexics compared with their controls, but not zinc.[36] Hair zinc can be low, high or normal range when zinc is deficient. As zinc is needed for hair growth, when there is a shortage the hair growth slows down and all the mineral levels tend to rise including zinc and the toxic metals. Blood or serum zinc isn't always helpful either as young people have good control mechanisms and are more capable of holding up their circulating zinc. The opposite happens with advancing age; very low serum zinc is so common among old people that Dr Helen Goode thinks this is a normal sequelae of ageing.[37]

An interesting study from Neil Ward showed how hyperactive children, who already had a poorer zinc status than their controls, suffered a sharp fall in their serum zinc and an increase in their urinary zinc excretion when they ingested tartrazine. The dye had no effect on the zinc levels of the control children who had better zinc status at the start of the experiment.[38]

This result probably partly explains why even children who suffered from zinc deficiency in the womb were still zinc deficient at any age. We had already discovered, at the migraine clinic, that the lower the zinc and the higher the copper the greater was the number of foods causing a pulse test reaction. Both dyslexic and hyperactive children are more likely to overreact to food, stress, tobacco smoke, infections and so on by losing more zinc. But the over-reactivity is also likely to be due to brain changes during development increasing the excitability of the amine pathways.

Lack of magnesium and B vitamins causes irritability,

while individuals with idiopathic epilepsy are always, in my experience, also short of manganese. Often epilepsy is familial, with girls often having their first fit at puberty. Perhaps this happens because oestrogen increases copper levels and over-reaction to foods, chemicals, flashing lights or video games. Girls with epilepsy are given one or two anti-epileptic drugs indefinitely such as phenytoin or barbiturates which can be teratogenic. These can further elevate and eventually lower copper. When such a girl wants to become pregnant her baby has an increased risk of being malformed due to the additional effects of each of her drugs adding to her underlying deficiencies. The risk is estimated to be at least 15 per cent for mothers being prescribed two drugs. On the other hand, if women with a previous history of idiopathic epilepsy are treated safely with diet and nutritional supplements before conception, not only should they no longer be at risk of an attack but, hopefully they will no longer pass the tendency to have the same nutritional deficiencies onto their children and following generations. This also applies to prevention of inherited dyslexia due to parental zinc deficiency which is both strongly familial and very common.

Mineral deficiencies can be caused by familial tendencies to decreased stomach acid or poor pancreatic secretions. Both need early diagnosis. Hypochlorhydria is common in children suffering from asthma.[39] Both asthma and eczema have increased sharply in the last decades in pill-taking countries.

As zinc is necessary for absorption and metabolism of nutrients, zinc-deficient children may suffer from other deficiencies. Iron deficiency, sometimes severe enough to cause anaemia, affects about one in five zinc-deficient children. In some studies only iron is measured and iron deficiency is related to learning problems. If iron supplements alone are prescribed the children's zinc status can deteriorate further because ingested iron interferes with zinc absorption. A common cause of dyslexia may be giving large supplements of iron to pregnant women while ignoring their falling zinc status. As zinc supplements can lower copper, manganese and iron levels it is important to monitor the effects of supplementation. Zinc is taken separately from other supplements on an empty stomach. It is also important to check essential fatty acid levels. Fish oil type fatty acids are also crucial for brain development and function and are commonly deficient in sperm, eggs, pregnant women and breast milk.[40] Breast-fed children tend to have higher IQs than cow's milk fed babies due to the better balance and availability of these key nutrients in breast milk.[41]

Ideally all children should be screened regularly, especially if they have learning or behaviour problems or if they are allergic or unduly susceptible to infection. For each child it is impossible to predict how much better he or she will be until tests prove that their biochemical upsets have been and continue to be corrected, but numerous studies have shown improvement in IQ test scores after nutritional supplements.[42] It is cruel to subject a sick child to lengthy psychological tests and specialised education, often away from school or home, as is common practice, before first finding out if these expediencies will still be needed when a child's upset body chemistry has been restored to normal.[43, 44] The costs of tests and nutritional supplements, especially at key times of development, are negligible compared with the emotional, physical and financial costs of the alternative measures which often are the consequence of doing nothing.

Even worse than doing nothing is prescribing drugs to hyperactive children. Central nervous system stimulants have been widely used in the USA but rarely in the UK. They are controlled drugs as they can cause dependence, substance abuse and they induce withdrawal symptoms.

Dan
Eight-year-old Dan was the most badly behaved child that I ever met. He was on Ritalin, a CNS stimulant which

was withdrawn from use in the UK a few years ago. The drug is creeping back from the USA, to the concern of dyslexia teachers here. It is fashionable once more because modern brain pictures show improved blood flow in some of these children. Dan's mother had been told to take him off the Ritalin at the weekends but he was so much worse she had to keep giving him the drug. It was difficult to believe he could be much worse. He was swearing, fell onto the plate glass patio door, took his clothes off and urinated on the flowers. His minder just managed to catch the heavy plastic tennis racquet which he threw above his head while waiting underneath to be hit as it fell down again.

Biolab tests showed the expected deficiences – very severe shortages of zinc, magnesium and a 6-series fatty acid pathway block. Manganese was also deficient and, although Dan was not yet epileptic, his mother had noticed he stared into space from time to time. Supplements, a low-allergy rotation diet and the avoidance of junk food soon made a big improvement. If he had continued to take stimulants his deficiencies and inability to cope with food or stress would have got worse. Stimulant side effects include disturbed appetite, anorexia, growth retardation, mood upsets including euphoria, irritability, insomnia and vascular effects such as headaches, dizziness and even raised blood pressure.

There is a danger that children with learning and behaviour problems will become antisocial adults. Many studies conducted by Shoenthaller and Slauss with the inmates of prisons and drug addicts in the USA have shown dramatic changes in behaviour in response to improved nutrition.[44, 45] Violence among convicted offenders is such a problem that government support was given. Very small changes in prison diet such as fruit juice instead of cow's milk, fruit instead of sweets, soon decreased the level of violence. Now many studies have shown that the addition of nutritional supplements improve brain performance, concentration and behaviour. Unbelievably this approach continues to be met with apathy, hostility and even active resistance; perhaps this is a reflection of the poor zinc status in our society as a whole, or merely the protection of vested interests.

Allergic or intolerant reactions to common foods can persist in spite of normalisation of nutrients; there will then be fewer offending foods but reactions may still be troublesome especially in girls and women premenstrually. For children and adults unwilling or unable to avoid their main allergens, clinical ecologists use two desensitising techniques. One, the Miller method, uses regular doses of minute amounts of food or chemicals to neutralise unwanted reactions.[46] The other method, devised by Dr Len McEwan, makes use of an enzyme to make allergens in a long-acting injection more powerful (enzyme potentitation).[47] Several trials have shown the benefits of these treatments for many conditions including hyperactivity. Allergen avoidance in infancy helps to prevent allergic disorders.[48]

Another important cause of brain allergy is candida. Thrush or candida albicans grows and penetrates into the gut wall, especially after courses of antibiotics or steroids including sex hormones.[49, 50] Children and adults with low zinc status are more likely to have recurrent infections and repeated courses of antibiotics, leaving them with disabling candida symptoms. These are tiredness, irritability, depression, inability to concentrate, bingeing sweet foods, intolerance of common foods, alcohol and chemical pollution, abdominal distention, constipation or diarrhoea, vaginal or anal itching and irregular or heavy menstrual bleeding. The fungal overgrowth may be excessive enough to turn ingested sugar into alcohol in the gut fermentation test. Treatment is a low-allergy diet of meat, fish and vegetables and several weeks of antifungal medication.

Slowly the connections between learning and behaviour problems in childhood and adolescent and adult vandalism, drug addiction and crime are being recognised. As up to half the children play truant from some schools, their teachers are recognising that children with learning problems soon become bored or distressed at school, taking out their frustrations against the society which expects too much of them. It has been known for a long time that prison inmates have a high incidence of learning difficulties. More teachers are being trained in special needs but the underlying causes are still mostly ignored.

As the level of violence, including assaults and rapes, keeps on rising, concern has been expressed about the effect of anabolic steroids on young men. As some athletes strive for muscle development, their doctors are told to look out for signs of steroid abuse; thrombosis, jaundice, testicular atrophy with falling sperm counts and eventually impotence. Seven per cent of athletes or gym users are injecting themselves with anabolic steroids, mostly taking two or more different steroids in excessive high doses.[51] More exercise increases the steroid-induced nutrient imbalance which may explain this stacking and loss of effect. Both anabolic steroids and alcohol can cause mental upsets. Male hormones exaggerate an intolerance to the effect of alcohol, the combination of both being more likely to lead to violence and abuse of women and children. Tobacco addiction also adds to the damaging effects of alcohol. Young men are more likely to become violent if their mothers have been given hormones during pregnancy, more likely to have sexual problems and more likely to want extra hormones. It is time to think again.

KEY POINTS

- Ex-pill-takers have more risk of infertility or recurrent miscarriages.
- Risks of drug side effects and poor over-all success rates of hormone-assisted pregnancies.

- Reasons for frequent scans during early pregnancy. Hormone exposure can:
  - increase risk of abortion or baby's death.
  - increase risk of molar pregnancies changing into choriocarcinomas.
  - cause abnormalities in foetus including abnormal sexual development.

- Forsight nutritional approach is often successful and benefits babies.
- Reasons for previous sharp increases and recent declines in spina bifida and cot deaths.
- Increases in undescended testicles, dyslexia and hyperactivity, especially in boys and allergies in girls over last thirty years.
- Violence linked to abuse of anabolic steroid hormones, drug addiction and alcohol.
- Success of nutritional and allergy treatment for offenders.

Chapter Ten

The Way Forward – the Need for Knowledge

The message in this book is that recent discoveries reinforce the importance of living in harmony with nature. The good news is that much unnecessary illness can be avoided. The bad news is that too many of our doctors and experts are giving the wrong advice. How can they continue to prescribe powerful steroid sex hormones with such complete disregard for their wide-ranging effects? Steroids inevitably cause a deterioration of health and nutritional status. Zinc is the anchor of three-dimensional life. Zinc forms a rigid knuckle in the protein 'zinc fingers' which curl round and activate our DNA. Daniela Rhodes, one of the discoverers of the precise chemical structure of the oestrogen receptor, says that nature continues to surprise and amuse with the ingenuity of the designs it has evolved to enable protein receptors to recognise specific base sequences in DNA. But she adds that neither oestrogen nor androgen receptors can fold properly in the absence of zinc. The structure of the hormone receptors themselves are so alike that taking one hormone can stimulate the other receptors with unwanted results. Even in the unlikely event of essential nutrient status remaining normal, prescribed hormones have far too many potentially dangerous actions for unnecessary use. Hopefully in the future doctors will resist the temptation offered by a quick steroid-hormone-fix and instead give molecular biology the attention it deserves.

The two main social problems are our failure to cope with sexual activity and fertility in a civilised fashion and a natural desire to stay young, healthy and beautiful. Lust, vanity and greed are powerful emotions. Our young are not warned that we lack a perfect method of contraception. Instead sex education mostly consists of demonstrations of pulling a condom over a carrot and a highly inaccurate pro-pill eulogy which even claims, against all reasonable evidence, that the pill prevents cancer. The opposite is true. Three times more men than women develop smoking-related cancers especially at older ages, but the picture is different for the under-fifties.[1] *Women are twice as likely to be younger cancer victims than men even when the huge increase in pre-cancer of the cervix is left out of the calculation. This is another demonstration that the pill and HRT hormones are more quickly lethal than smoking.*

Women are paying a high price for ignorance, lust or vanity, but how much is their fault? World population experts and manufacturers have been influential in minimising the real impact of steroid hormone side effects and in keeping law suits at bay. Some women whose careers in films or politics depend on their looks, promote eternal youth through oestrogen. If one of them suddenly dies of a stroke or if they develop cancer the connection is never made public. But what do women really want? It is a male fantasy that women should be always available for full vaginal intercourse, while most women rank having healthy children and grandchildren as their greatest achievement, their strongest sexual instinct over a lifetime. Promoting early sex is a direct consequence of the promotion of the pill. Cashing in on budding sexual awareness, while great for business tycoons, has backfired on society.

The official teenage pregnancy rate in the UK in the 1990s is 69 per 1,000 for 15–19-year-olds, seven times higher than in Holland. Birth control 'experts' give this as a reason for the promotion of yet more indoctrination of ever-younger children in their brand of sex education. They demand instant abortions induced by a post-coitally inserted IUD or the morning-after pill. Pill hormones are prescribed up to seventy-two hours after unprotected sex but failure means that another embryo has been overexposed to hormones at a crucial phase in development.

Dr Glen Griffin, Editor of *Postgraduate Medicine*, gives a graphic account of how gynaecological clinics are being set up in American schools. Their doctors do on-the-spot testing for veneral diseases and prescribe steroid contraceptives without the parents' knowledge but do not take throat swabs. Sore throats must be treated by the family doctor who, like the parents, could be kept in ignorance about what is really happening.[2]

The RCGP pill study found that pill users were twice as likely to divorce, but now any figures are meaningless as the number of different partners both inside and outside marriage goes on increasing. Although in pre-pill days pregnancy before marriage was common, it was usually the spur to the start of stable married life and proof that the couple were fertile. At last, in the 1990s, as society cringes under the multi-billion-pound burden of caring for one-parent families whose numbers have doubled over the past ten years, the fathers are to be named. DNA testing can prove parental identity beyond doubt. This should be an opportunity to think about the issues behind the chaos. Do young couples want to engage in sexual activity before they are physically and emotionally mature and able to cope with our often unfair, demanding and increasingly complicated society? For the young, the very simple and only safe method of birth control is saying 'No', provided that society helps them follow their instincts to wait for 'the real thing', as we used to say, which meant a relationship which had a realistic chance of developing into a future family life.

Disc jockeys and agony aunts gleefully stretching condoms leave out the facts – a worldwide failure rate of 18 per cent per year and a method so disliked that the pill was hailed as the medical breakthrough of the century. While an 'r' gets tagged on to safe to make safer sex, HIV infection is still increasing year by year among homosexuals who are apparently largely unaffected by national publicity campaigns. Among 503 men followed, the number becoming HIV positive increased year by year from 16 in 1985 to 139 in 1992, which is *one in four*.[3] While predictions have overestimated the speed of the spread into the general population, the virus still threatens us all. Youngsters are coming off the pill and using condoms, mostly without spermicides, but when the condoms split or fail, the advice is to use both the pill and condoms at the same time. If condoms or sheaths are so poor at preventing pregnancy, how can they halt the onset of lethal HIV and AIDS, especially when immunosuppressive steroids are prescribed at the same time?

We can be reassured from history which has seen recovery again and again from decadence into civilisation and it should now be so easy to prove and spread the truth if the medical press stopped relying on income from drug companies. Banning the pill and HRT would soon lead to social discouragement of under-age sex, a halt in the cancer increases and an improvement in child health. Already, although the AIDS publicity campaigns may have temporarily increased accidental pregnancies, teenage females have benefited in another way. Although suicides have increased four-fold among under-35-year-olds over the last thirty years, between 1989/90 and 1991/92 attempted suicides rates fell from 825 to 600 per 100,000 among 15–19-year-old girls, the main pill-starting age group. The comparable rates for young men, 300 to 350, are only half the rates in girls, but men are more likely to succeed in killing themselves and usually do so following the break-up of a relationship.[4]

Unfortunately women and mothers who have spent years on the pill don't shout from the roof tops or even on the television chat shows the real reasons for their divorce, depression, headaches, miscarriages or infertility or why their son is homosexual or mentally ill. They probably don't know themselves whether or not they had or still have deficiencies or infections. If they do not warn their young, the scam is perpetuated. Instead they worry about eating meat, first-class protein, which they say is 'full of hormones'. It has become fashionable to eat mushrooms, cheese and soya beans (tofu) which really are high in oestrogenic moulds and yeasts, while using automatic refrigerators which may be harbouring moulds. In the UK hormones have not been generally given to animals since 1985, but that is not the case in other countries, and our water supply is contaminated by prescribed hormones and oestrogenic industrial detergents.

In truth, are not unwanted pregnancies leading to overpopulation, and limitless availability of women for sex merely two sides of the same coin? Neither are freedoms, but both can be assaults on women's basic rights. In a cold, hard world are the only warm relationships sexual or is sex too often used to dominate? Love surely includes not harming someone else. The problem of abortion and social termination of pregnancy, which continue to trouble young women more than men, would not arise if a perfect method of contraception did exist. The next best thing for a committed and caring couple is a diaphragm or sheath used with spermicides, and natural family planning which can be effective among the committed.[5] The woman is taught to recognise when she ovulates by changes in her cervix, mucus secretion and temperature and unprotected intercourse is avoided during the fertile days. But any method may be scorned by the lager lout at a teenage rave. Society needs to condemn the rape of its young as the crime against the future that it really is.

We have seen that the major claims for HRT don't stand the test of time. Osteoporosis and vascular reactions can be treated more fundamentally and there is no arguing with breast or ovarian cancer. To say that women must take fertility-blocking hormones like the pill, and then fertility-inducing hormones, followed by oestrogen HRT, followed by anti-oestrogens like tamoxifen, or even both together, is verging on the insane. Older women should not be pressurised into thinking they need to use friction-proof vaginal creams or must be medically oestrogenised to please their husband or partners no matter what cost to their own health. Younger women should be reassured that they have the right to avoid early cancer, infertility, or medical castration. It is to their advantage to refuse to be abused by numerous partners and they should guard their right to reject the tyranny of the pill and the other prescribed steroid sex hormones. Moralising is out of date but not, I hope, plain common sense. It has been said we are awash in a sea of oestrogens in the dark age of steroids. What are we going to do about it?

Appendix One

ORAL CONTRACEPTIVE TRIALS

Cohort Trials	Enrolment Dates	Total Women	at enrolment	% on OCS added later
1 RCGP	1968–69	47,174	49.6	+26
2 Oxford/ FPA	1968–69	17,032	56	+10
3 Walnut Creek	1968–72	16,638	61	+14.6 on HRT

1) RCGP PILL STUDY

In the Royal College of General Practitioners study, only one in five women was a new pill taker; the others were the tough remnant of a much larger number of women who had started the pill years before 1968. During the study 26 per cent of the control women switched over into the pill-taking group. The 1974 report listed an enormous increase in migraine, vaginal discharge, depression, infections and loss of libido among pill users and labelled these conditions 'subject to substantial bias'. The 'probable' benefits were reduction in menstrual bleeding and irregularities, and in iron deficiency anaemia – signs of taking progestogen-dominant pills. There were significant increases in over sixty conditions. Arthritis, pelvic inflammatory disease (PID) and benign breast disease were more common in ex-users than in never-users and yet were claimed as pill benefits – not reasons for giving up the pill as they may have been. PID is often diagnosed later when women discover they are unable to become pregnant and are being investigated for infertility. Higher doses of progestogen and longer pill use were claimed to be especially protective against breast disease but very few women used these pills for very long. The authors expected some health benefits would be common while adverse effects would be rare, which is not what these results actually show.

Fibroids

Five times more controls than takers had a history of fibroids before recruitment to the study. Since fibroids are associated with infertility, fibroid sufferers are less likely to need contraception. In spite of this, women using a 1mg dose of progestogen had 2.5 times more fibroids than those using pills with higher doses. In the RCGP study more ex-pill-takers than controls had heavy and irregular bleeding, which are common signs of infection or fibroids.

Mental Illness

The commonest single illness leading to stopping the pill was depression in 36 per cent. The doctor in charge, Dr Kay, calls this 'neurotic depression'. At the ten-year follow-up, twice as many ever-users had had accidental or violent deaths – 34 compared with 17. Ever-users made 283 suicide attempts compared with 106 in the control group. Suicide attempts were fatal in 10 current users, 5 former users and 7 controls. Former users who 'ceased to cohabit' were more likely to attempt suicide but pill users were twice as likely to divorce. Suicide attempts were 1.42 times more likely for current users and 2.12 times for former users compared with never-users. The incidence of 'neurotic' depression declined over the ten years as vulnerable women stop taking the pill.

Dr Kay found an increase in 'neurotic' depression with increasing oestrogen dose. The rate was nearly double for 100 or 150 micrograms of oestrogen compared with 30 or 35 microgram doses. These figures are 'standardised for age' but the fact is that far more younger women were started on low-dose oestrogen pills than older women. As I had already found depression increased as the dose of progestogen increased, it is clear that increasing both steroids increases the chance of a woman becoming both 'neurotic' and depressed.

Dr Kay said that most experienced clinicians were impressed by their patients commonly complaining the pill made them depressed. Frequently, the women recovered when they stopped the pill, only to relapse when another course was started. But such a history could be consistent with a 'psychological effect' and he hoped that reassurance and appropriate treatment would allow them to continue to choose the pill for contraception. I wonder what the 'appropriate treatment' would be – tranquillisers, MAOIs, tricyclics or a good talking to?

---

2) OXFORD/FPA PILL STUDY

The Oxford/FPA study is the main UK study of the intrauterine device (IUD) which attempts to follow up 17,000 married women who were aged 25 to 39 in 1968. Of these 56 per cent were using oral contraceptive steroids, 25 per cent diaphragms and 19 per cent intrauterine devices when enrolled.

In fact only women aged 25 to 39 who had already taken the pill for at least five months were enrolled and many later changed to use a cap or an IUD. Significantly fewer women with breast lumps were enrolled as pill users and the pill takers were eight times less likely to have had a history of previous thrombosis than women using other methods. By 1975, women enrolled when using the pill had been referred to hospital more often than the women enrolled as diaphragm or IUD users for migraine, venous thrombosis and embolism, thrombosis (x2), cerebro-vascular disease (x7), self-poisoning (x4), hay fever (x2), skin disorders, gallbladder disease, amenorrhoea (x2) and sterility. One in ten of the women admitted to hospital with vascular disease during the trial had become pill users, but their hospital admission was recorded under their original status; that is, as diaphragm or IUD users.

By 1979 the IUD users had an unplanned pregnancy rate of 1.1 to 4.3 per 100 women years. In these accidental pregnancies the ectopic pregnancy rate was 7 per cent and 13.6 per cent of the live babies were small-for-dates. The IUD users were more likely to be referred to hospital for anaemia, varicose veins and salpingitis. Women who used the diaphragm were less likely to be referred for carcinoma-in-situ (CIN) and dysplasia of the cervix. Women who used OCS at the start of the study had more referrals for vaginitis, cervicitis, cervical erosions (x2), CIN and invasive cervical cancer.

By 1987, among parous women referred to the hospital for pelvic inflammatory disease, 99 were current IUD users compared with only 12 diaphragm users and 18 pill users. This is in spite of the fact that only 9 per cent of IUD users and 12 per cent of the OCS users continued their method for more than five years compared with 52 per cent of the diaphragm users. Diaphragm users had an unplanned pregnancy rate of 2.4 per cent and more cystitis and haemorrhoids presumably due to localised pelvic pressure. Users of the now banned Dalkon shield had five times more PID referrals than users of other IUDs, with copper-IUD users having half the risk compared with users of inert IUDs.

Fibroids

In the Oxford/FPA study women enrolled as pill takers had had fewer fibroids than diaphragm users. The authors of the study claimed that for each five years women stayed on the pill their risk of fibroids was reduced by 17 per cent. By ten years of use the risk was down to a third but only a very small percentage of women had taken the pill for so long. 'In many cases the use of oral contraceptives had been abandoned between initial clinical diagnosis of fibroids and final pathological diagnosis.' A third of the women with fibroids had stopped the pill in the six months before the final diagnosis. If fibroids and an ensuing hysterectomy were the reason for stopping, it is fatuous to claim that longer use prevents fibroids.

Mental Illness

In the opinion of the authors of the Oxford/FPA Pill study there was 'no suggestion that oral contraceptives increased the risk of any type of mental disorder of sufficient severity to require a specialist opinion.' Again, as in the HRT study, there were only half the expected deaths compared with women in England and Wales at both the ten-year and twenty-year follow-ups. Only a quarter as many women died from accidents or violence as in the whole country, or as women pill users in the RCGP study, or as women in the Walnut Creek study.

Once more, the low Oxford death rates point to pre-selection of younger, mostly non-smoking, higher social class women as pill takers and the exclusion of the most sensitive women who gave up the pill within the first six months because of mood changes. Nevertheless, four times more pill users were admitted to hospital for attempting suicide than were women using a diaphragm for contraception. Is attempted suicide not serious?

The ages of women in this American study ranged from eighteen to fifty-four with most of the 10,135 pill takers starting during the previous six or more years. Less than half were still taking the pill when enrolled. One in ten of these 'pill users', were also taking or had taken oestrogens and one in five of the 6,503 'never-pill-users' were taking or had taken oestrogens. The ever-users of the pill were significantly more likely to be taking tranquillisers or other medication and they already had a higher incidence of thirty-four ailments including vascular disease.

With this predominantly older group of women, after ten years, the ever-hormone-users had more cervical, breast, endometrial, skin, lung, urinary tract and thyroid cancers. Cancer accounted for three times more deaths than vascular disease.

Mental Illness

Deaths from accidents or violence were more common than vascular disease in contrast to the British studies (see Table on page 276).

The American Walnut Creek Pill study found pill users were more likely to be taking tranquillisers, diuretics (to lose excess fluid), weight reducing and thyroid medicines, compared with women who had never used the pill. Women aged fifty to sixty-four had three times more accidents and suicides if they had used the pill.

BRITISH HRT STUDY

Mental Illness

In the British HRT study, among the mostly higher social class women given oestrogens, eleven women out of 4,544 died from suicide. The overall expected number from the England and Wales registrations from 1966 to 1983 was four. This was an increase of 2.53 times in a group of women with only half the expected death rate. Obviously, if women in the general population were given oestrogens, the increase in suicides would be much higher. By 1990, the death rate from breast cancer had doubled among oestrogen takers. The suicide rate had not increased further but the women most affected by mental symptoms would be the most likely to stop taking the hormones thereby reducing their risk. After discontinuing hormones, copper levels fall to normal within a few months.

In spite of this clear increase in suicides, oestrogen-induced mental changes were dismissed as happening to women with a previous 'psychiatric history'. Most of the eleven deaths occurred in women aged fifty-five to sixty-four years who had first started HRT five to nine years previously and seven were known to have had previous psychiatric illness. Clearly extra oestrogen did not help them. The report makes no mention of the many underlying changes in neurotransmitter metabolism, known since the 1960s, to be exaggerated by either oestrogens or oestrogens with progestogens added.

HORMONES

Percentage Increases in Cervical Cancer-in-situ (CIN) and Breast Cancer**

CIN

Age	15–19	20–24	25–29	30–34	35–39	40–44	45–49	50–54
1965–87	1344	9220	1591	1940	724	452	496	237

Breast					All
Age	20–24	25–34	35–44	45–54	ages
1962–87	217*	27	20.3	38.6	50.7

* small numbers only
** OPCS cancer registrations lag 7–8 years behind current year.

Cancer registrations per 100 000 women [men]

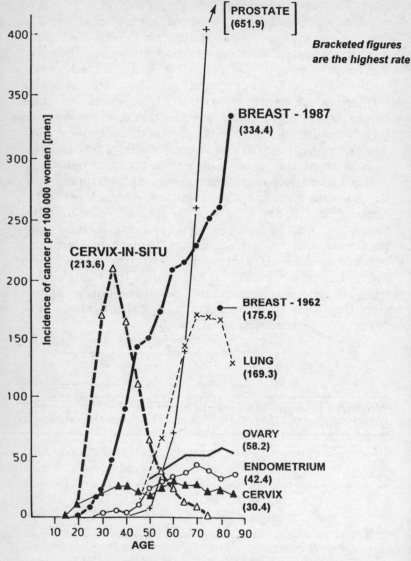

Figure 1

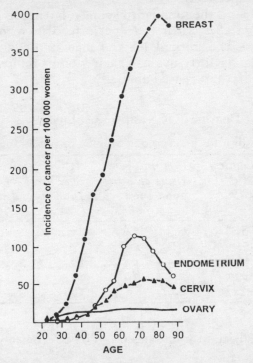

Figure 2

Frequent checking of cervical smears at yearly intervals allows early treatment to prevent the development of invasive cervical cancer.

Early diagnosis and treatment of breast cancer may also reduce the annual death rate for breast cancer which increased yearly from 389 in 1962 to 510 per million women in 1990, an increase of 31 per cent. Breast cancer remains the commonest single cause of cancer deaths in women.

In 1991 the annual death rate for breast cancer was 204 per million population among 35–44-year-old women and 572 for 45–54-year-olds. The incidence of cervical cancer deaths in the same age groups were 64 and 83 per million respectively.

In 1989–90 the number of women having hysterectomies was 73,280. Most were performed in women under fifty-two – the normal for the menopause age; 38,025 women under forty-five had their wombs removed. These numbers have increased annually.

Causes of Death in OCS and HRT Trials

Yearly death rates per 100,000 women in pill-taking ages

	Total population of England & Wales 1975	Oxford/FPA Users at entry 1968 –79	Oxford/FPA Users at entry 1968 –88	RCGP Ever users 1968–79	Walnut Creek % of all deaths 1968–77
All causes	108.5	52.9	84	87.2	100
Cancer	44.3	25.3	50	30	45
Vascular	21.9	12.3	16	29.9	15
Violence	17.7	4.6	8.4	18.2	19

British HRT study death rates per 100,000 women-years*

	1963–84 Expected	1963–84 HRT	1963–88 Expected	1963–88 HRT
All deaths	212.5	124 (58%)	419	236 (56%)
[OR as	1	0.58	1	0.56]
Main causes as percentage of all deaths				
Cancer	40	45	40	49
Vascular	37	32	38	30
Violence	4	11	3.4	9

Death rates in both OCS and HRT trails can be half the

278

expected national rates because of exclusions and selective enrolment in the beginning, and early discontinuation of hormones by the majority of current takers because of side effects. As many as 70 per cent of women give up HRT in the first year leaving only 5 per cent still taking it for eight years. This data is often erroneously interpreted as showing disease prevention although the main causes of death increased even with this relatively short-term use.

For example, in the British HRT study:

	Disease Incidence 1963–84	Mortality Causes 1963–84	Mortality Causes 1984–88
All causes	–	0.58	0.54
Breast Cancer	1.59	0.55	1.00 (doubled)
Endometrial Cancer	2.84*	0	0
Ovarian Cancer	1.15	1.43*	0.63
Vascular Disease	–	0.51	0.37
Suicide/Suspected Suicide	–	2.53*	2.21*

* Statistically significant increases compared with expected numbers.

Cancer deaths increase with longer use and longer time from first use. Vascular death rates are in keeping with, and not statistically different from, the biased low overall-death rates due to original exclusions and high drop-out rate for the majority of women because of early warning symptoms.

A 1992 analysis of the results of up to thirty-nine international studies found the risks for breast cancer ranged from 0.2 to 3.1 with oestrogen-only HRT and from 0.2 to 4.4 for more recent oestrogen-plus-progestogen HRT. With oestrogens the risks for endometrial cancer ranged from 0.4 to 20 and plus progestogens from 0.2 to 1.3. Coronary artery disease risk on oestrogens ranged from 0.3 to 4.2 and plus progestogens to 1.2, while cerebrovascular disease HRT risk ranged from 0.2 to 2.3. In eleven studies current oestrogen use equivalent to 0.625mg of conjugated oestrogen daily reduced the risk of hip fracture by 0.25 but this rose to unity six or more years after cessation of hormone taking. The authors conclude that for most women 'the best course of action is unclear' which belies the title of their review. (Ref. Grady D, Rubin S, Pettiti D et al. 'Hormone therapy to prevent disease and prolong life in postmenopausal women', *Annals of Internal Medicine* 1992; 117, 12: 1016–37.) While there is no evidence that HRT has any prolonged overall benefit, more women are being exposed to prescribed hormones and it is an irrefutable fact that more of them will develop cancer because of this exposure.

Appendix Two

FAT METABOLISM

Effects of the sex hormones summarised from Chapter Five

Lipoproteins	Oestrogen HRT	Testosterone/ progesterone	OCS
VLDL triglycerides	↑		↑
LDL cholesterol	↑		↑
HDL2 (protective) (protein)		↓	↓

ESSENTIAL FATTY ACIDS (EFAs)

The two essential fatty acids in flax, linoleic acid (LA) and alpha linolenic acid (ALA), both have 18 carbons on their fatty acid chains.

Linoleic acid has two double bonds on its sixth and ninth carbons and is written 18:2n6 in chemistry shorthand. It is the precursor of the 6-series essential fatty acids and the first and second series of prostaglandins.

6-series EFAs

LA (18:2n6) is given an extra double bond by a slow-acting enzyme known as delta desaturase. Gammalinolenic acid (GLA) is formed from 18 carbon atoms with three double bonds (18:3n6). This crucial enzyme is easily blocked by stress and common nutritional deficiencies. This means many people have 6-series deficiencies in spite of having enough LA from their food.

GLA is given two extra carbon atoms with the help of a fast-acting elongase enzyme to make DGLA (20:3n6). DGLA is important because it makes the first series of prostaglandins.

DGLA receives another double bond to become arachidonic acid (AA) which now has four double bonds (20:4n6) and makes the second series of prostaglandins.

3-series EFAs

Similar enzymes (desaturase and elongase enzymes) change the 3-series. ALA (18:3n–3) is converted into EPA (eicosapentanoic acid). EPA is important as it, in turn, makes the third series of prostaglandins and the leukotrines. Again, blocks in this pathway are common in spite of adequate amounts of ALA in the diet.

The short-lived local hormones made by the EFAs in our cell membranes help to regulate many cell activities including cell division. In all cell membranes EFAs are combined with phospholipids and before they become active they need to be set free by enzymes. EFA deficiency, whether due to dietary deficiencies or blocked enzymes, leads to abnormalities in all our cells and tissues. In animals deliberately deprived of both 6-series and 3-series EFAs, most readily observed abnormalities are rapidly reversed by 6-series EFAs alone. Deficits in the 3-series EFAs have been shown to cause abnormalities in brain and eye growth and development. If only 3-series EFAs are added, some abnormalities, such as those in small blood vessels and skin, may become worse.

PROSTAGLANDINS

About thirty prostaglandins have been discovered. They are like short-lived hormones and they regulate cellular activities moment by moment. Prostaglandins control blood vessel reactivity and thrombosis. They have 20 carbon atoms and belong to three groups having either one, two or three double bonds.

1-series prostaglandins

PGE1 – Platelets make prostaglandin E1 (PGE1) which stops them sticking together. PGE1 dilates blood vessels and helps to remove fluid from the body via the kidneys, and lowers blood pressure.

PGE1 prevents insulin resistance. It slows down cholesterol formation, regulates calcium metabolism, improves nerve function and gives a sense of well-being. It regulates immune responses such as instructing the immune system T-cells to destroy foreign cell invasions. PGE1 regulates cell division which is important for sperm production and preventing cancer. PGE1 also prevents inflammation and arthritis.

2-series prostaglandins

PGI2 – Healthy blood vessels release from their inner lining cells a 2-series prostaglandin (PGI2) called prostacyclin. It stops platelets gathering together and forming clumps.

PGE2 – When a blood vessel is damaged, the PGE1 production falls. Arachidonic acid (AA), stored in the cell membranes of the platelets, makes PGE2 (thromboxane) which encourages them to stick together. PGE2 also constricts the blood vessels to prevent bleeding while the clot seals any gap. The kidney's blood vessels also constrict, causing fluid retention and high blood pressure.

3-series prostaglandins

PGE3 – The 3-series prostaglandins are made from EPA and have powerful anti-stickiness effects and for this reason fish oils are very effective in preventing degenerative changes in the cardiovascular system.

REASONS FOR BLOCKS IN THE ESSENTIAL FATTY ACID PATHWAYS AND PROSTAGLANDIN IMBALANCE

When we have enough LA and ALA we can make the fatty acids which make the prostaglandins. In the membranes of our cells, phospholipids are converted into arachidonic acid (AA) which then makes small amounts of various locally acting prostaglandins including PGE2. The stress hormone cortisol blocks these local tissue reactions by blocking AA production. (See Chapter Five) Aspirin and other non-steroid anti-inflammatory (NSAI) drugs block prostaglandin production.

Aspirin

Drugs like aspirin are known as non-steroidal anti-inflammatory drugs (NSAIDs). They block the different kinds of prostaglandins. Long-term use can cause bleeding in the brain or in the stomach due to gastric irritation. Women taking aspirin for period pains are more likely to have heavy menstrual bleeding.

The use of these drugs by such large numbers of people shows how desirable it is to lower inflammatory PGE2 production. Very rapid relief from all sorts of aches and pains is the reason. We only need 1mg per day of arachidonic acid but a high meat diet produces 100–190mg per day. Avoiding meat and changing to fish and vegetables can also bring rapid relief to arthritis victims.

Minerals and Vitamins

Deficiencies

The pathway enzymes need enough zinc, magnesium, biotin, vitamin B6, B3, vitamin C and calcium. When any of these are short blocks can result.

Excesses

In contrast, high levels of copper (due to pregnancy, exogenous hormones, OCS, HRT, IUD or infections) block release of inflammatory PGE2, hence the popularity of copper bracelets with arthritis sufferers. But too much copper blocks both fatty acids' pathways.

Too much vitamin A acts in the same way as excess copper. Vitamin A accumulates when zinc is deficient. This happens with high doses of OCS. Hormone pregnancy tests caused spina bifida due to high vitamin A before their use was banned.

Infections

Viral infections reduce levels of linoleic acid and impair the desaturase enzymes. David Horrobin says that as both DGLA and arachidonic acid are needed to enable Interferon to exert its anti-viral effects, the reduction in DGLA and arachadonic acid formation may be part of the viral strategy to limit the efficacy of its host's defences. EFAs may also kill viruses by penetrating their fatty envelopes.

Patients with post-viral fatigue syndrome or myalgic encephalomyelitis (ME) have reduced EFAs and higher levels of saturated fats in their red cell membranes. Most improve when given both EPO and EPA supplements. I find such patients usually also have nutritional deficiencies, decreased pancreatic function and bacterial infections and severe food allergies, all needing treatment. Patients with atopic eczema, who also have low DGLA and AA formation, are known to fail to respond normally to viral infections.

Diet

Excess fat and sugar in the diet block EFA pathways through raising cortisol levels. High sugar consumption also leads to a pre-diabetic condition, usually associated with low zinc, chromium, magnesium and B vitamins. Fat metabolism and EFA pathways are interfered with.

Too much animal fat and processed vegetable oils can cause blocks. Processed fats like margarine may have double bonds but their shape has been altered in such a way that they partly fit into the enzyme and membrane structures with the result that the space is taken up but they cannot do the work of the essential fatty acids and they are unhealthy.

AGEING AND ANTI-OXIDANT PROTECTION

A long-chain unsaturated fatty acid is so unstable that it can be changed by a single photon of light. Chemical bonds are made up of pairs of electrons, which 'hate' to be alone. When an electron next to a double-bond carbon in a fatty acid is excited or agitated by light it takes off, leaving its partner electron behind. The partner will break up other pairs to find a mate. Essential fatty acids, with up to six double bonds, are prime candidates for this sort of interference says Udo Erasmus in his book *Fats and Oils*. A chain reaction from a single ray of sunlight may set up 30,000 cycles before it is stopped. It is easy to see how sunlight can destroy the protective waterproofing fatty acids in our skin and cause wrinkling. This type of sun damage probably causes the circular halo which commonly surrounds moles on our faces.

Some of the normal changes in our cells make oxygen with an unpaired electron which will can grab an electron from our fatty acids, so hastening ageing. When an element like oxygen or a larger molecule has an unpaired electron it is known as a free radical. In natural oils vitamin E traps loose electrons, while vitamin A – carotene from carrots – can mop up electrons from oxygen. Iron and copper encourage free radical reactions. In a way we rust as we age. We tend to limit prescriptions of iron and copper to a few weeks only when laboratory tests show extra supplements are needed. Unfortunately pregnant women are commonly given large amounts of iron even when they are not anaemic. This threatens their own and their babies' zinc status. Both pregnant women and pill and HRT takers have high copper levels. Some doctors prescribing HRT caution women that these hormones will not necessarily make them look younger.

In the human body, B complex vitamins (B1, B5 and B6), vitamin C, the sulphur-containing amino acid cysteine and sulphur-rich proteins, zinc, selenium and vitamin C's bioflavinoid co-factors all help to guard against free-radical damage and consequent vascular and neoplastic disease.

A close look at how our bodies function shows that, in general, taking essential nutrient supplements is beneficial. In contrast taking any type of steroid for any reason other than in a life-threatening emergency, is fraught with difficulties and dangers. With a wider availability of essential-nutrient screening, a great deal of unnecessary illness could be prevented.

EFA Pathways

Enzymes	n-6EFAs	Prostaglandins	n-3EFAs
	18:2n-6 LA		18:3n-3 ALA
6-desaturase	↓		↓
	18:3n-6 GLA		18:4n-3
elongase	↓		↓
		— steroids	
	20:3n-6 DGLA →	PGE1	20:4n-3
		— aspirin	
5-desaturase	↓	— steroids	↓ — steroids
	20:4n-6 AA →	PGE2	20:5n-3 EPA
		— aspirin	
elongase	↓	PGE3 ←	↓
	22:4n-6		22:5n-3
desaturase	↓		↓
	22:5n-6		22:6n-3 DHA

Desaturates	+ Zinc, + Magnesium, + Biotin,	
	+ Calcium — Aspirin(NSAIDs)	
Elongases	+B6	
Phospholipids	→ free DGLA release	+ Zinc, — Steroids
Phospholipids	→ free AA release	— Steroids
DGLA	→ PGE1	+ VitC, — Steroids,
		— Aspirin(NSAIDs)
5 desaturase		
DGLA	→ AA	— Copper, — VitA,
		— Steroids
AA	→ PGE2	— GLA, — Aspirin(NSAIDs)

Appendix Three

STEROID SEX HORMONE PREPARATIONS

A. Oral Contraceptive Steroids (doses in micrograms)
1. Combined pills

Trade Name	Progestogen		Oestrogen	
Conova 30	ethynodioldiacetate	2000	ethinyloestradiol	30
Loestrin 30	northisterone	1500		30
Norinyl-1		1000	mestranol	50
Ortho-Novin 1/50		1000		50
Neocon 1/35		1000	ethinyloestradiol	35
Norimin		1000		35
Loestrin 20		1000		20
Brevinor		500		35
Ovysmen		500		35
Ovran	levonorgestrel	250		50
Ovran 30		250		30
Eugynon 30		250		30
Microgynon 30		150		30
Ovranette		150		30
Marvelon	desogestrel	150		30
Mercilon		150		20
Femodene	gestodene	75		30
Minulet		75		30
Cilest	norgestimate	25		35

2. Sequential regimes

Trade Name	Progestogen		Oestrogen	
BiNovum	northisterone	500(7)	ethinyloestradiol	35
		1000(14)		35
Synphase		500(7)		35
		1000(9)		35
		500(5)		35
TriNovum	northisterone	500(7)	ethinyloestradiol	35
		750(7)		35
		1000(7)		35
Logynon	levonorgestrel	50(6)		30
		75(5)		40
		125(10)		30
Trinordiol		50(6)		30
		75(5)		40
		125(10)		30
Tri-Minulet	gestodene	50(6)		30
		70(5)		40
		100(10)		30
Triadene		50(6)		30
		70(5)		40
		100(10)		30

3. Progestogen-only pills (POPs)

Femulen	ethynodiol diacetate	500
Micronor	norethisterone	350
Noriday		350
Neogest	norgestrel	75
Microval	levonorgestrel	30
Norgeston		30

4. Long-acting progestogens
Depo Provera medoxyprogesterone acetate IM injection
Norplant levonorgestrel 6x38,000mcg rods implanted
under the skin to release 80–50mcg daily over five years
(removable).

B. Menopausel Preparations ('HRT' – doses in micrograms)

1. Sequential pills

Trade Name	Progestogen		Oestrogen		
Menophase			mestranol	12.5	(5)
				25	(8)
				50	(2)
	norethisterone	1000(3)		25	(3)
		1500(6)		30	(6)
		750(4)		20	(4)
Trisequens			oestradiol	4000	(12)
forte		1000(10)		4000	(10)
				1000	(6)
(or		1000(10)	with 2000, 2000, 500)		
Trisequens				2000	(12)
		1000(10)		2000	(10)
				1000	(6)
(or		1000(10)	with 1000, 1000, 500)		
Climagest				1000	(16)
		1000(12)		1000	(12)
Nuvelle				2000	(16)
	norgestrel	75(12)		2000	(10)
Cyclo-				2000	(11)
Progynova 2mg		500(10)		2000	(10)
Cyclo-				1000	(11)
Progynova 1mg	norgestrel	250(10)		1000	(10)
PrempakC 1.25			conjugated	1250	(16)
	norgestrel	150(12)	oestrogens	1250	(12)
0.625			conjugated	625	(16)
		150(12)	oestrogens	625	(12)

2. Oestrogen-only Pills (OOPs)

Trade Name	Oestrogen	
Zumenon 2mg	oestradiol	2000
Climaval 2mg	oestradiol	2000
1mg	oestradiol	1000
Prognova 2mg	oestradiol	2000
1mg	oestradiol	1000
Harmogen	oestrone	1500
Harmonin oestriol 270, oestrone 1400 and oestradiol		600
Premarin 1.25mg	conjugated oestrogens	1250
0.625mg		625

3. Combined Skin Patches

Trade Name	Progestogen	Oestrogen
Estrapack		oestradiol 50/24hrs (4)
	norethisterone 1000(12tabs)	50/24hrs (4)
Estracombi		50/24hrs (4)
	250/24hrs	50/24hrs (4)

4. Oestrogen-only Skin Patches

Trade Name	Oestrogen	
Estraderm 100mcg	oestradiol	100/24hrs (8)
50mcg		50/24hrs (8)
25mcg		25/24hrs (8)
Evorel		50/24hrs (8)

Hormones Used in OCS and HRT Preparations

	microgram doses
norethisterone	350–2000
norgestrel	30–500
mestranol	12.5–50
oestradiol	
ethinyloestradiol (OCS)	20–50
oestradiol from bile or soya (HRT)	1000–4000

Identical progestogens are used in both OCS or HRT. *More powerful progestogens, such as norgestrel, are given in lower doses. This means the doses on the packets do not necessarily match the biological power of marketed hormones.* Also blood levels of women taking an identical dose of an identical progestogen can vary ten times.

Natural oestradiol is derived from animal bile or plants such as soya and conjugated oestrogens from pregnant mares' urine are given in large doses as HRT. Oestriol, oestrone and conjugated oestrogens are also given. The much more powerful synthetic ethinyloestradiol is prescribed in smaller doses as OCS. Mestranol is broken down in the body to form ethinyloestradiol. Up to a third of a given dose of ethinyloestradiol is excreted unchanged in women's urine. Oestrogen is rapidly and effectively absorbed through the skin and therefore HRT patches contain small amounts of oestradiol. Long-acting injections of 25,000, 50,000 or 75,000 micrograms oestradiol last for three to seven months. Blood concentrations of active extracted oestradiol can vary 30 fold (between 60 and 2900 umol/1 whichever route of HRT administration is used). Direct oestrogen assays give high readings due to the circulation of conjugated oestrogen. A dose of oestrogen too small to prevent osteoporosis can be powerful enough to change a recipient's copper/zinc balance whether or not side effects are noticed.

References

Chapter One

1 Grant E. *The Bitter Pill*. Hamish Hamilton 1985 and Corgi 1986, London.

2 Carlsen N E, Girwercman A, Keiding N, Skakkeback N E. 'Evidence for decreasing quality of semen during the past 50 years.' *BMJ* 1992; 305: 609–13.

3 Sharpe R M, Skakkeback N E. 'Are oestrogens involved in falling sperm counts and disorders of the male reproductive tract?' *Lancet* 1993; 341:1392–95.

4 Suominen J, Vierula M. 'Semen quality of Finnish men.' *BMJ* 1993; 306:1579.

5 Swyer G I M, Law R G. 'An evaluation of the prophylactic ante-natal use of stilboestrol. A preliminary report.' *J Endocrinol* 1954; 10, vi.

6 Diekmann W J et al. 'Does administration of diethylstilboestrol during pregnancy have any therapeutic value?' *Am J Obstet Gynecol* 1953; 66:1062–75.

7 Vessey M P, Fairweather D V I, Norman-Smith B, Buckly J. 'A randomised double-blind controlled trial of the value of stilboestrol therapy in pregnancy: long-term follow-up of mothers and offspring.' *Brit J Obstet Gynae* 1983; 90:1000–17.

8 Rock J A et al. 'Fetal malformations following progesterone

therapy during pregnancy: a preliminary report. *Fertility and Sterility* 1985; 44:17.

9 Seaman B, Seaman G. *Women and the Crises in Sex Hormones*. Bantam Books, New York 1977.
10 Greer G. *The Change* Hamish Hamilton 1991 and Corgi 1992, London.
11 Rhodes D, Klug A. 'Zinc fingers.' *Scientific American* 1993; 268:2, 32–39.
12 Davies S, Stewart A. *Nutritional Medicine*. Pan, London 1987.
13 Howard J M H. 'Serum, leucocyte, sweat and hair zinc levels – a correlation study.' *J Nutr Med* 1990; 1, 2:119–26.
14 Howard J H M. 'Muscle action, trace elements and related nutrients: the Myothermogram.' In: *Current Trends in Trace Element Research: Proceedings International Symposium on Trace Elements* Paris (1987). Ed Chazot, Abulla and Arnaud. Publ. Smith-Gordon and Co Ltd, London, 1998: 79–85.
15 Howard J H M. 'Magnesium deficiency in peripheral vascular disease.' *J Nutr Med* 1990; 1:39–49.
16 Vitale J J. 'Magnesium deficiency and cardiovascular disease.' *Lancet* 1991; 430:1224.

Chapter Two

1 Eichel E W, Muir J G. 'Homosexuality in the US.' *BMJ* 1993; 307:61.
2 Reisman J A, Eichel E W. *Kinsey, sex and fraud*. Lafayette Louisiana: Huntington House, 1990.
3 Hamer D H, Hu S, Magnuson, Hu N, Pattatucci A M L. 'A linkage between DNA markers on the X chromosome and male sexual orientation.' *Science* 1993; 26:321–27.
4 Moir A, Jessel D. *Brain Sex*. Mandarin, London 1989.
5 McCormick C M, Witelsan S F. 'A cognitive profile of homosexual men and women.' *Psychoneuroendorinology* 1991; 16:6, 459–73.
6 Rabin M, Wen X L, Hepburn M, Lubs H A. 'Suggestive

linkage of developmental dyslexia to chromosome. 1p34-p36.' *Lancet* 1993; 342:178.

7 Grant E C G, Howard J M H, Davies S, Chasty H, Hornsby B, Galbraith J. 'Zinc deficiency in children with dyslexia: concentrations of zinc and other minerals in sweat and hair.' *BMJ* 1988; 296:607–09.

8 Geschwind N, Galaburda A M. 'Cerebral lateralization: biological mechanisms, associations and pathology: part 1.' *Arch Neurol* 1985; 42;427–59.

9 Livingstone M S, Rosen G D, Drislane F W, Galaburda M A. 'Physiological and anatomical evidence for a magnocellular defect in developmental dyslexia.' Proc Nat Acad Sci USA 1991; 88:1943–47.

10 McManus I C, Byrden M P. 'Geschwind's theory of cerebral lateralization: developing a formal, causal model.' *Psychological Bulletin* 1991; 110:2, 237–53.

11 Ward N I, Soulsbury K A, et al. 'The influence of the chemical additive tartrazine on the zinc status of hyperactive children – a double-blind placebo-controlled study.' *J Nutr Med* 1990; 1:51–57.

12 Hales G. 'What does it mean to be dyslexic?' Paper presented at the British Dyslexia Association Conf, London, 1992.

13 Howard J M H. 'Serum, leucocyte, sweat and hair zinc levels – a correlation study.' *J Nutr Med* 1990; 1:2, 119–26.

14 Rimland B, Larson G E. 'The manpower quality decline.' *Armed Forces and Society* 1981; 8,1, 21–78.

15 Turner M. *Sponsored reading failure*. Pub. Education Unit, Wallingham Park School, Wallingham. 1990.

16 Burney P J, Chinn S, Rona R J. 'Has the prevalence of asthma increased in children? Evidence from the national study of health and growth 1973–86.' *BMJ* 1990; 300:1306–10.

17 Robertson C F, Heycock, E, et al. 'Prevalence of asthma in Melbourne schoolchildren: changes in 26 years.' *BMJ* 1990; 300:1306–10.

18 Bone M. *Family Planning Services in England and Wales.*
   HMSO 1973.
19 UK National Case-Control Study Group. 'Oral
   contraceptive use and breast cancer risk in young women.'
   Lancet 1989; i:973–82.
20 Jofen J. 'Long-range effects of medical experiments in
   concentration camps (the effect of administration of
   oestrogen to the mother on the intelligence of the
   offspring).' In *The Fifth World Congress of Jewish Studies.*
   Jerusalem 2, 55, 1972.
21 Potts M, et al. 'The Puerto Rico oral contraceptive study:
   An evaluation of methodology and results of a feasibility
   study.' *The British Journal of Family Planning* 1982; 7:99.
22 Saenz de Rodriguez C A, Toro-Sola M A. 'Anabolic Steroids
   in meat and premature telarche.' *Lancet* 1982; i:1300.
23 'Precocious development in Puerto Rican children.' *Lancet*
   1986; i:721–22.
24 Shoental R. 'Precocious sexual development in Puerto Rico
   and oestrogenic mycotoxins (zearalenone).' *Lancet* 1983;
   i:537.
25 Sumpter J P, Jobling, S. 'Male sexual development in "a
   sea of oestrogen".' *Lancet* 1993; 342:124–25.
26 Cooper A P. *The principles and practice of surgery,* vol 1.
   London: E Cox, 1836:333–35.
27 Beatson G T. 'On the treatment of inoperable cases of
   carcinoma of the mamma. Suggestions for a new method
   of treatment with illustrative cases.' *Lancet* 1986;
   ii:104–07.
28 Lingeman C H. 'Hormones and hormonomimetic
   compounds in the etiology of cancer.' In *Rec. Results of
   Cancer Research.* 1979; 66:1–48.
29 Herbst A L, et al. 'Adenocarcinoma of the vagina:
   association of maternal stilboestrol therapy with tumour
   appearance in young women.' *New Eng J of Med* 1971;
   284:878–83.
30 Mears E, Grant E C G. 'Anovlar as an oral contraceptive.'
   BMJ 1962; 2:75–79.
31 Grant E C G. 'The effects of oral contraceptives on the

endometrium.' *J Reproduction & Fertility* 1964;
8:275–78.

32 Grant E C G. 'Hormone balance of oral contraceptives.' *J
Obs & Gynae of Brit Commonwealth* 1967; 74:6,
908–18.

33 Kirkwood K, et al. 'Oral contraceptive use and the
occurrence of pituitary prolactinoma.' *JAMA* 1983;
249:16, 2204.

34 Vessey M P, et al. 'A long-term follow-up study of women
using different methods of contraception: an interim report.'
J Biosocial Science 1976; 8:373–424.

35 Mears E, et al. 'Preliminary evaluation of four oral
contraceptives containing only progestogens.' *BMJ* 1969;
2:730–34.

36 Diver M J. 'Monitoring of hormone replacement therapy.'
Lancet 1992; 340:1471.

37 Back D G, et al. 'Pharmacokinetics and potency of
contraceptive steroids.' *Lancet* 1984; 1:171.

38 Vessey M P, Villard-Mackintosh L, Painter R. 'Epidemiology
of endometriosis in women attending family planning
clinics.' *BMJ* 1993; 306:182–184.

39 Ramcharan S, et al. 'The Walnut Creek Contraceptive
Study. A prospective study of the side effects of oral
contraceptives, III.' *Center for Population Research
Monograph*, NIH, Bethesda 1981.

40 Ross R K, Pike M C, Vessey M P et al. 'Risk factors for
uterine fibroids: reduced risk associated with oral
contraceptives.' *BMJ* 1986 293:359–62.

41 The Centers for Disease Control Cancer and Steroid
Hormone Study. 'Oral contraceptives and endometrial
cancer.' *JAMA* 1983; 249:12, 1600-04.

42 'The Centers for Disease Control Cancer and Steroid
Hormone Study. Oral contraceptive use and the risk of
ovarian cancer.' *JAMA* 1983; 249:12, 1596–99.

43 Hunt K, Vessey M, McPherson K, Coleman M. 'Long-term
surveillance of mortality and cancer incidence in women
receiving hormone replacement therapy.' *Br J Obstet
Gynae* 1987; 97:620–35.

44 Willemsen W, Kruitwagen R, Bastiaans B, Hanselaar T, Rolland R. 'Ovarian stimulation and granulosa-cell tumour.' *Lancet* 1993; 1:986–88.

45 Harper P. Personal communication.

46 Beral V, Hannaford P, Kay C. 'Oral contraceptive use and malignancies of the genital tract. Results from the Royal College of General Practitioners Oral Contraceptive Study.' *Lancet* 1988; 2:1331–35.

Chapter Three

1 Jordan W M. 'Pulmonary embolism.' *Lancet* 1961; 2:1146.

2 Wright H P, in *Medical Physiology and Biophysics*. ed. Ruch and Fulton. W B Saunders, Philadelphia 1960.

3 Daniel D G, Turnbull A et al. 'Puerperal thromboembolism and suppression of lactation.' *Lancet* 1967; 2:287.

4 Little K. *Bone Behaviour*. Academic Press London 1973.

5 Walsh F B et al. 'Oral contraceptives and Neuro-ophthalmologic interest.' *Archives of Ophthalmology* 1965; 74:628–40.

6 Grant E C G. 'Relationship of arterioles in the endometrium to headaches from oral contraceptives.' *Lancet* 1965; 1:1143–44.

7 Grant E C G. 'Relation between headaches from oral contraceptives and development of endometrial arterioles.' *BMJ* 1968; 3:402–05.

8 Grant E C G. 'Changing oral contraceptives.' *BMJ* 1969; 4:789–91.

9 Grant E C G. 'Venous effects of oral contraceptives.' *BMJ* 1969; 4:73–77.

10 Inman W H, et al. 'Thromboembolic disease and the steroidal content of oral contraceptives: a report to the Committee on Safety of Drugs.' *BMJ* 1970; 2:203-.

11 Bottiger L E, et al. 'Oral contraceptives and thromboembolic disease. Effects of lowering oestrogen content.' *Lancet* 1980; 1:1097-.

12 Irey N S, Manion W C, Taylor H B. 'Vascular lesions in

women taking oral contraceptives.' *Archives of Pathology* 1970; 89:1-.

13 Osterholzer H O, et al. 'The effects of oral contraceptive steroids on branches of the uterine artery.' *Obstetrics and Gynaecology* 1977; 49:2, 227-.

14 Beral V. 'Reproductive Mortality.' *BMJ* 1979; 2:632–34.

15 Wynn V, et al. 'Effect of duration of low-dose oral contraceptive administration on carbohydrate metabolism.' *Am J of Obs and Gyn* 1982; 142:6, 739–45.

16 Gow S, MacGillvary I. 'Metabolic, hormonal and vascular changes after synthetic oestrogen therapy in oophorectomised women.' *BMJ* 1971; 2:73–77.

17 RCGP *Oral Contraceptives and Health*. Pitman Medical Books, London 1974.

18 Vessey M P, et al. 'A long-term follow-up study of women using different methods of contraception: an interim report.' *Journal of Biosocial Science* 1976; 8:373–424.

19 Ramcharan S, et al. 'The Walnut Creek Contraceptive Drug Study. A prospective study of the side effects of oral contraceptives, III.' *Center for Population Research Monograph*, NIH, Bethesda 1981.

20 Vessey M P, McPherson K, Yeates D. 'Mortality in oral contraceptive users.' *Lancet* 1981; i:549–50.

21 Vessey M P, Villard-Mackintosh, McPherson K, Yeates D. 'Mortality among oral contraceptive users; 20-year follow-up of women in a cohort study.' *BMJ* 1989; 299:1487–91.

22 Beral V. 'Oral contraceptives and health.' *Lancet* 1974; 1:1280.

23 RCGP. 'Mortality among oral contraceptive users.' *Lancet* 1977; 2:727–31.

24 Vessey M P. 'Female hormones and vascular disease – An epidemiological overview.' *British Journal of Family Planning* 1980; 6:3, 1–12.

25 'RCGP Oral Contraception Study. Further analyses of mortality in oral contraceptive users.' *Lancet* 1981; 1:541–46.

26 Thorogood M, Mann J, Murphy M, Vessey M P. 'Is oral

contraceptive use still associated with an increased risk of fatal myocardial infarction?' *Br J Obstet Gynae* 1991; 98: 1245–53.

27 Lidegaard O. 'Oral contraception and risk of thromboembolic attack. Results of a case-control study.' *BMJ* 1993; 306:956–63.

28 Stampfer M J, et al. 'A prospective study of postmenopausal estrogen therapy and coronary heart disease.' *New Eng J Med* 1985; 313:17, 1044–49.

29 Stampfer M J, Colditz G A. 'Estrogen replacement therapy and coronary heart disease: a quantitative assessment of the epidemiologic evidence.' *Prev Med* 1991; 20:47–63.

30 Wilson P W F, Garrison R J, Castelli W P. 'Postmenopausal estrogen use, cigarette smoking and cardiovascular morbidity in women over 50. The Framingham Study.' *New Eng J Med* 1985; 313:17, 1038–43.

31 Hunt K, Vessey M, McPherson K, Coleman M. 'Long-term surveillance of mortality and cancer incidence in women receiving hormone replacement therapy.' *Br J Obstet Gynae* 1987; 94:620–35.

32 Hunt K, Vessey M, McPherson K. 'Mortality in a cohort of long-term users of hormone replacement therapy: an updated analysis.' *Br J Obstet Gynae* 1990; 97:1080–86.

33 Grant E C G, Albuquerque M, Steiner T J, Rose F C. Oral contraceptives, smoking and ergotamine in migraine. In *Current Concepts in Migraine Research* Ed Greene R. Raven Press, New York 1979 pp 97–100.

34 Grant E C G. 'Oral contraceptives, smoking, migraine and food allergy.' *Lancet* 1979; i:581–82.

35 Grant E C G, Clifford Rose F. 'Smoking and migraine.' In *Smoking and Arterial Disease* Ed Greenhalgh R M. Pitman Medical 1981 pp 29–34.

36 Grant E C G. 'Food allergies and migraine.' *Lancet* 1979; i:966–68.

37 Mansfield J. *The Migraine Revolution*. Thorsons 1986.

38 Grant E C G. 'The causes of migraine.' In *L'Homme et sa douleur. Les Entretiens internationaux de Monaco* Ed. du Rocher. 1989 pp 141–47.

Chapter Four

1 Grant E C G, Mears E. 'Mental effects of oral contraceptives.' *Lancet* 1967; 2:945.

2 Grant E C G, Pryce-Davies J. 'Effect of oral contraceptives on depressive mood changes and on endometrial monoamine oxidase and phosphatases.' *BMJ* 1968; 3:777–80.

3 Stewart A. 'Clinical and biochemical effects of nutritional supplementation on the premenstrual syndrome.' *J Repr Med* 1987; 32:6:1–18.

4 Horrobin D F. 'Gamma linolenic acid; an intermediate in essential fatty acid metabolism with potential as an ethical pharmaceutical and as a food.' *Rev Contemp Pharmacother* 1990; 1:1–45.

5 Eaton K K, Hunnisett A. 'Abnormalities in essential amino acids in patients with chronic fatigue syndrome.' *J Nutr Med* 1991; 2:369–75.

6 Adams P W, Wynn V et al. 'Influence of oral contraceptives, pyridoxine (vit B6) and tryptophan on carbohydrate metabolism.' *Lancet* 1976; 1:759–64.

7 Greene R, Dalton K. 'The Premenstrual Syndrome.' *BMJ* 1953; 1:1007.

8 Dalton K. *The Premenstrual Syndrome and Progesterone Therapy.* Wm Heinemann Medical Books. London 1964.

9 Grant E C G. 'Creatures of the Moon.' *BMJ* 1978; 1:165.

10 Mears E, Grant E C G. 'Anovlar as a contraceptive.' *BMJ* 1962; 2:75–79.

11 Cohen S, et al. 'Histochemical studies on the human endometrium.' *Lancet* 1964; 2:56–58.

12 Southgate J, Grant E C G, et al. 'Cyclical variations in endometrial monoamineoxidase: Correlations of histochemical and quantitative biochemical assays.' *Biochemical Pharmacology* 1968; 17:21–26.

13 Michael R P. 'Hormones and sexual behaviour in the female.' *Hospital Practice* 1976; 10:69.

14 Grant E C G. 'The influence of hormones on headache and mood in women.' *Hemicrania* 1975; 6:4, 2–10.

15 Grant E C G, et al. 'Hormones and headaches in women.' In *Background to Migraine*, 6th Migraine Symposium, Migraine Trust, London 1974 p7.

16 Halsted J A, et al. 'Plasma-zinc and copper in pregnancy and after oral contraception.' *Lancet* 1968; 1:278.

17 Pfeiffer C C. In *Mental and Elemental Nutrients*. Keats, Conn 1975.

18 Kalsner S. 'Steroid potentiation of responses to sympathomimetic amines in aortic strips.' *Br J Pharm* 1969; 36:583–93.

19 Rose D P, Cramp D G. 'Reduction of plasma tyrosine by oral contraceptives and oestrogens: a possible consequence of tyrosine amino transferase induction.' *Clinica Chemico Acta* 1970; 29:49–53.

20 Truss C O. 'Tissue injury induced by candida albicans: mental and neurological manifestations.' *J Orthomol Psychiat* 1978; 7:1, 17–37.

21 Vessey M P, Fairweather D V I, Norman-Smith B, Buckly J. 'A randomised double-blind controlled trial of the value of stilboestrol therapy in pregnancy: long-term follow-up of mothers and offspring.' *Brit J Obstet Gynae* 1983; 90:1000–17.

22 Schoental R. 'Behavioural and other effects of secondary metabolites of certain fusarium species.' *Behavioral Models and the Analysis of Drug Action*. Proc. 27th OHOLO Conf. Israel 1982. Eds Speigelstein MY, Levy A. Elsevier Pub. Netherlands.

23 Bewley S, Bewley T H. 'Drug dependence with oestrogen replacement therapy.' *Lancet* 1992; 339:290–91 and 814–15.

24 Whitehead M, Stevenson J, et al. 'Dependence and oestrogen replacement.' *Lancet* 1992; 339:505–06.

25 Sheppard G. Paper presented at conference at Tycehurst Hospital, Kent 1993 and personal communication of data.

26 Glen A I M, Glen E M I, MacDonell L E F, Skinner F E. 'Essential fatty acids and alcoholism.' In *Omega–6 essential fatty acids: Pathophysiology and roles in clinical*

medicine. Ed. Horrobin D F. Alan Liss, New York 1990; 321:332-.

27 Grant E C G. 'Allergies, smoking and the contraceptive pill.' In *Biological Aspects of Schizophrenia and Addiction.* Ed. Hemmings G. John Wiley & Sons, Chichester 1982 pp 263–72.

Chapter Five

1 Schoental R. 'Xenobiotic contaminants and the deleterious effects of fats.' *Biochem Soc Transactions* 1989; 17:475–76.

2 Rees E L, Campbell J. 'Patterns of trace minerals in the hair and relationship to clinical states.' *J Ortho Psych* 1975; 3:53–56.

3 Grant E C G, Howard J M, et al. 'Zinc deficiency in children with dyslexia: concentrations of zinc and other minerals in sweat and hair.' *BMJ* 1988; 296:607–09.

4 Davies S. 'Effects of oral zinc supplementation on serum, hair and sweat zinc levels in 7 subjects.' *The Science of the total environment* 1985; 42:45–48. Elsevier Sci Pub. Amsterdam.

5 Solomons N. 'Biological availability of zinc in humans.' *Am J Clin Nutr* 1982; 35:1048–75.

6 Ward N I, Soulsbury K A, et al. 'The influence of the chemical additive tartrazine on the zinc status of hyperactive children – a double-blind placebo controlled study.' *J Nutr Med* 1990; 1:1, 51–58.

7 Rimland B, Larsen G E. 'Hair mineral analysis and behaviour: an analysis of 51 studies.' *J of Learning Disabilities* 1983; 16:5, 1–8.

8 Hambridge K M, Hambridge C, Jacobs M, Baum J D. 'Low levels of zinc in hair, anorexia, poor growth and hypogeusia in children.' *Ped Research* 1972; 6:868–74.

9 Davies S, Howard J M H. Personal communication of results of 16,766 hair mineral analyses.

10 Licastro F, et al. 'Zinc affects the metabolism of thyroid hormones in children with Down's syndrome; normalisation

of thyroid stimulating hormone and of reverse triiodothyronine plasmic levels by dietary zinc supplementation.' *Int J Neuroscience* 1992; 65:259–68.

11 Little K. *Bone Behaviour.* Academic Press, London 1973.

12 Ward N. 'Assessment of zinc status and oral supplementation of anorexia nervosa.' *J Nutr Med* 1990; 1:3, 171–78.

13 Capel I D, Grant E C G, et al. 'Disturbed liver function in migraine patients.' *Headache* 1979; 19:5, 270–72.

14 Grant E C G. 'The harmful effects of common social habits, especially smoking and using oral contraceptive steroids, on pregnancy.' *Intern J Environ Studies* 1981; 17:57–66.

15 Wynn V, Doar J W H. 'Some effects of oral contraceptives on carbohydrate metabolism.' *Lancet,* 1966; 1:715–19.

16 Wynn V, et al. 'Effects of duration of low-dose oral contraceptive administration on carbohydrate metabolism.' *Am J Obstet & Gynecol* 1982; 142:6, 739–43.

17 Spellacy W N, et al. 'Effects of norethindronone carbohydrate and lipid metabolism.' *Obstet & Gynaecol* 1975; 45:560–63.

18 Spellacy W N, et al. 'Carbohydrate and lipid metabolic studies after one year of treatment with ethynodiol diacetate in "normal" women.' *Fertility and Sterility* 1976; 27:900–04.

19 Spellacy W N, et al. 'Lipid and carbohydrate metabolic studies after one year of megestrol acetate treatment.' *Fertility and Sterility* 1976; 27:157–61.

20 Spellacy W N, et al. 'Prospective studies of carbohydrate metabolism in "normal" women using norgestrel for eighteen months.' *Fertility and Sterility* 1981; 35:167–71.

21 'Recent advances in oral contraception.' *Br J of Family Planning* suppl. 1984; 10:1, 1–48.

22 Back D G, et al. 'Pharmocokinetics and potency of contraceptive steroids.' *Lancet* 1984; 1:171.

23 Briggs M H. 'Megadose vitamin C and metabolic effects of the pill.' *BMJ* 1981; 283:1547.

24 Diver M J. 'Monitoring of hormone replacement therapy.' 1992; 340:1471.

25 Godsland I, Walton C, Felton C, Proudler A, Patel A, Wynn V. 'Insulin resistance, secretion and metabolism in users of oral contraceptives.' *J Clin Endocrinol Metab* 1992; 74:1, 64–70.

26 Thorogood M, Mann J, Murphy M, Vessey M P. 'Is oral contraceptive use still associated with an increased risk of fatal myocardial infarction?' *Br J Obstet Gynae* 1991; 98:1245–53.

27 Banks S, Marks I N. 'Case reports: hyperlipaemic pancreatitis and the pill.' *Postgrad Med J* 1970; 46:576–88.

28 Grant E C G. 'Food allergies and migraine.' *Lancet* 1979; i: 966–68.

29 Wynn V, et al. 'Some effects of oral contraceptives on serum lipid and lipoprotein levels.' *Lancet* 1966; 1:720–23.

30 Godsland I F, Crook D, et al. 'The effects of different formulations of oral contraceptive agents on lipid and carbohydrate metabolism.' *New Eng J Med* 1990; 323:1375–81.

31 Gow S, MacGillvary I. 'Metabolic, hormonal and vascular changes after synthetic oestrogen therapy in oophorectomised women.' *BMJ* 1971; 2:73–77.

32 Davies S, Howard J M H. Personal communication of results of toxic mineral analyses from 16,766 hair samples.

33 'RCGP Oral Contraception Study. Oral contraceptives and gallbladder disease.' *Lancet* 1982; 2:957–59.

34 Shaffer E A, et al. 'The effect of a progestin on gallbladder function.' *Am J Obst & Gynecol* 1984; 148, 504.

35 Erasmus V. *Fats and Oils*. Alive Books. Vancouver 1986.

36 Horrobin D F. 'The regulation of prostaglandin biosynthesis by the manipulation of essential fatty acid metabolism.' *Reviews in Pure and Applied Pharmacol Sci* 1983; 4:339–83.

Chapter Six

1 Darlington L G, Ramsey N W, Mansfield J. 'Placebo-controlled, blind study of dietary manipulation therapy in rheumatoid arthritis.' *Lancet* 1986; i:236–38.

2 'Osteoporosis Review Hormone replacement therapy. Why do so few women use it?' *J Nat Osteoporosis Soc* 1992; 1:2, 1–12.

3 Christiansen C, Riis B J, Rodbro P. 'Prediction of rapid bone loss in postmenopausal women.' *Lancet* 1987; i:1105–07.

4 Little K. 'Osteoporotic mechanisms.' *J Int Med Res* 1973; 1:509–29.

5 Gaby A R, Wright J V. 'Nutrients and Osteoporosis.' *J Nutr Med* 1990; 1:63–72.

6 Law M R, Wald N J, Meade T W. 'Preventing Osteoporosis.' *BMJ* 1991; 383:922.

7 Howard J M H, Hunnisett A, Davies S. 'Osteoporosis: alkaline phosphatase isoenzyme measurements and the effect of nutritional supplements.' In *Current Research in Osteoporosis and Bone Mineral measurement II* 1992 Ed. Ring E F R. British Institute of Radiology, London pp. 111–12.

8 Abraham G E. 'The Importance of Magnesium in the Management of Primary Post Menopausal Osteoporosis.' *J Nutr Med* 1991; 2, 165–78.

9 Bryce-Smith D, Deshpande R R, Hughes J, Waldron H A. 'Lead and cadmium levels in stillbirths.' *Lancet* 1977; 1:353–56.

10 Gibson S L M. 'Effects of fluoride on immune system function.' *Complementary Medical Research* 1992; 6, 3:111–13.

Chapter Seven

1 Grant E C G. 'Food allergies and migraine.' *Lancet* 1979; i:966–69.

2 North K, Davies L. 'Postexercise headache in menopausal women.' *Lancet* 1993; 341:972.

3 Maddox P R, Mansel R E. 'Management of breast pain and nodularity.' *World Surgery* 1989; 13:699–05.

4 Grant E C G. 'Why women should not be given hormone replacement therapy.' *Br J Hosp Med* 1989; 41:590 and 42:159.

5 Bagenal F S, Easton D F, Harris E, Chilvers C E D, McElwain T J. 'Survival of patients attending Bristol Cancer Help Centre.' *Lancet* 1990; ii:606–10.

6 Maddox P, Wilson N. *GP* 1992; 8 May:51–54.

7 Horrobin D F. 'Gamma linolenic acid: an intermediate in essential fatty acid metabolism with potential as an ethical pharmaceutical and as a food.' *Rev Contemp Pharmacother* 1990; 1:1–45.

8 Vessey M P, Doll R, Sutton P M. 'Investigation of the possible relationship between oral contraceptives and benign and malignant breast disease.' *Cancer* 1971; 28:1395–99.

9 Burn I. *In Hormone Replacement Therapy and Breast Cancer Risk* Ed. R D Mann. Parthenon 1992.

10 *RCGP Oral Contraceptives and Health*. Pitman Medical Books 1974 pp 25–26. and Kay C R. 'RCGP's oral contraceptive study: some recent observations.' *Clinics in Obstet & Gynae* 1984; 11:769–86.

11 UK National Case-Control Study Group. 'Oral contraceptive use and breast cancer risk in young women.' *Lancet* 1989; i:973–82.

12 Howard J H M. Personal communication. And Imura N, Naganuma A, Satah M, Chen J T. 'Trace elements as useful tools for cancer chemotherapy'. *Proc 1st Meeting of Int Soc Trace Element Research in Humans.* 1986; Annenberg Center, Rancho Mirage, CA, USA p77.

13 Cooper A P. *The principles and practice of Surgery*, Vol 1. Ed. Cox, London. 1836:333–35.

14 Beatson G T. 'On the treatment of inoperable cases of carcinoma of the mamma. Suggestions for a new method

of treatment with illustrative cases.' *Lancet* 1896;
ii:104–07.

15 Lingeman C H. 'Hormones and hormonomimetic
compounds in the etiology of cancer.' *Recent Results in
Cancer Research* 1979; 66:1–48.

16 Shoental R. 'Carcinogenic metabolites of fusarium.'
Advances in Cancer Research 1985; 45:244–89.

17 Drife J O. 'Breast cancer, pregnancy and the pill.' *BMJ*
1981; 283:778–79.

18 Anderson T J, Battersby S, King R J B, McPherson K.
'Breast epithelial responses and steroid receptors during
oral contraceptive use.' *Hum Pathol* 1989; 12:1137–143.

19 Greenberg E R, Barnes A B, et al. 'Breast cancer in mothers
given diethylstilboestrol in pregnancy.' *N Eng J Med*
1984; 311:1393–97.

20 Tokunga M, et al. 'Malignant breast tumours among
atomic bomb survivors, Hiroshima and Nagasaki.' *J Nat
Cancer Inst* 1979; 62:1347–59.

21 McPherson K, Doll H. 'Oestrogens and breast cancer:
exogenous hormones.' *Br Med Bulletin* 1990; 47:2,
484–92.

22 Pike M C, Henderson B E, et al. 'Breast cancer in young
women and use of oral contraceptives: possible modifying
effect of formulation and age at use.' *Lancet* 1983;
11:359–29.

23 Vessey M P, Lawless M, McPherson K, Yeates D.
'Neoplasia of the cervix uteri and contraception: a
possible adverse effect of the pill.' *Lancet* 1983; ii:930–33.

24 Peto J. 'Oral contraceptives and breast cancer: is the CASH
study really negative?' *Lancet* 1989; 1, 552.

25 'RCGP Breast cancer and oral contraceptives: Findings in
Royal College of General Practitioners' study.' *BMJ* 1981;
282:2089–93. And Kay C R, Hannaford P C. 'Breast cancer
and the pill – A further report from the Royal College of
General Practitioners' oral contraceptive study.' *Br J
Cancer* 1988; 58:675–80.

26 Bourke I, Goodare. 'Free for all: "Cancer positive" ' *BMJ*

1992; 304:1445. And Massam A. ' Cancer patients are talking back.' *GP* 1992, 22 May: 59.

27 Hunt K, Vessey M, McPherson K, Coleman M. 'Long-term surveillance of mortality and cancer incidence in women receiving hormone replacement therapy.' *Br J Obst Gynae* 1987; 94:620–35.

28 Hunt K, Vessey M, McPherson K. 'Mortality in a cohort of long-term users of hormone replacement therapy: an updated analysis.' *Br J Obst Gynae* 1990; 97:1080–86.

29 Grant E C G, Vessey M P. General discussion. In *Hormone Replacement Therapy and Breast Cancer Risk* Ed. R D Mann, Parthenon 1992.

30 Person I, Yuen J, Bergkvisk L, Adami H, et al. 'Combined oestrogen-progestogen replacement and breast cancer risk.' *Lancet* 1992; 340; 1044.

31 Barber R J, Studd J W W. 'Hormone replacement therapy and cancer.' *Br J Hosp Med* 1989; 41:142–49.

32 McPherson K. 'Latent effects in the interpretation of any association between oral contraceptives and breast cancer.' In *Recent developments in the study of Benign Breast Disease* Ed. R E Mansel, Parthenon 1991 pp 165–75.

33 Easton D F, Bishop D T, Ford D, Crockford G P. 'The Breast Cancer Genetic Linkage Consortium. Genetic Linkage analysis in familiar breast and ovarian cancer – results from 214 families.' *Am K Hum Genet* 1993; 52:678–701.

34 Hall J M, Lee M K, Newman B, et al. 'Linkage analysis of early onset familial breast cancer to chromosome 17q12–23.' *Science* 1990; 250:1684–89.

35 Steinberg K K, Thacker S B, et al. 'A meta-analysis of the effect of estrogen replacement therapy on the risk of breast cancer.' *JAMA*, 1991; 265:15, 985–90.

36 Schoetal R. 'Pathogenesis of AIDS.' *The Biochemist* 1991; 13:44.

37 Burger M P H, Hollema H, et al. 'Cigarette smoking and human papillomvirus in patients with reported cervical cytological abnormality.' *BMJ* 1993; 306:749–52.

38 Mears E, et al. 'Preliminary evaluation of four oral

contraceptives containing only progestogens.' *BMJ* 1969; 2:730–34.

39 Grant E C G. 'Oral contraceptive steroids and malignancy.' *Clinical Oncology* 1982; 8:2, 97–102.

40 Copplestone M. 'Epidemiology and aetiology of carcinoma of the cervix.' *Br J Hosp Med* 1962; 2:96.

41 (1) Melamid M R. 'Prevalence rates of uterine cervical carcinoma-in-situ for women using the diaphragm or oral contraceptives.' *BMJ* 1969; 3:195.
(2)'Cervical carcinoma and the pill: a possible link?' *World Medicine* 1968; 4:6, 1a.

42 Beral V, Hannaford P, Kay C. 'Oral contraceptive use and malignancies of the genital tract.' *Lancet* 1988; ii:1331–35.

43 Vessey M, Grice D. 'Carcinoma of the cervix and oral contraceptives: epidemiological studies.' *Biochem & Pharmacother* 1989; 43:157–60.

44 Stern E, Forsythe A B, Youlkeles L, et al. 'Steroid contraceptive use and cervical dysplasia: increased risk of progression.' *Science* 1977; 196:1460–62.

45 Grant E C G. 'Cervical cancer and oral contraceptives.' *Lancet* 1983; 1:528.

46 Snell R S, Bischitz P G. 'The effect of large doses of oestrogen and oestrogen and progestogen on melanin pigment.' *J Invest Derm* 1960; 35:73.

47 Ellerbrook J M, Lee J A H. 'Oral contraceptives and malignant melanoma.' *J Am Med Assoc* 1968; 206:649.

48 *The Walnut Creek Contraceptive Drug Study* Vol III, NIH Pub 1986 and including Beral V, Ramcharan S, Faris R. 'Malignant melanoma and oral contraceptive use among women in California.' P247–52.

49 Hannaford P C, Villard-Mackintosh L, Vessey M P, Kay C R. 'Oral contraceptives and malignant melanoma.' *Br J Cancer* 1991; 63:430–33.

50 Beral V, Evans S, Shaw H, Milton G. 'Oral contraceptive use and malignant melanoma in Australia.' *Br J Cancer* 1984; 50:681–85.

51 Makie R, Hunter J A A, et al. 'Cutaneous malignant

melanoma, Scotland, 1979–89.' *Lancet* 1992;
339:971–75.

52 Leahy M. 'Cancer of the testes.' *Lancet* 1992;
340:1281–82.

53 Barrat A. 'Testicular tumours.' *Hospital Update* 1984;
4:344–69.

54 Rosenberg L, et al; and Mettlin C, et al. 'Vasectomy and
the risk of prostate cancer.' *Am J Epidemiology* 1990;
132:1051–61.

55 Schroder F H. 'Prostate cancer: to screen or not to screen?'
BMJ 1993; 306:407–08.

56 Peeling B, Kirby R. cited in 'Prostate tests revive the debate
over screening.' *Doctor* 1991; 28, 11:44.

57 Johnson F L, Feogler J R, Lerner K G, et al. 'Association
of androgenic-anabolic steroid therapy with
development of hepatocellular carcinoma.' *Lancet* 1972;
iv:1273–76.

58 Neuberger J, Forman D, Doll R, Williams R. 'Oral
contraceptives and hepatocellular carcinoma.' *BMJ* 1986;
292:1355–57.

59 Edmondson H A, Henderson B, Benton B. 'Liver cell
adenomas associated with the use of oral contraceptives.'
N Eng J Med 1976; 294:470–72.

60 Forman D, Vincent T J, Doll R. 'Cancer of the liver and
the use of oral contraceptives.' *BMJ* 1986; 292:1357–61.

61 'Tamoxifen trial controversy.' *Lancet* 1992; 339:753.

62 'Early Breast Cancer Trialists' Collaborative Group.'
Lancet 1992; 339:1–15 and 71–82.

63 Bluming A Z. Also Fugh-Berman A, Epstein S S.
'Tamoxifen and prevention.' *Lancet* 1993; 341:693–95.

64 Fugh-Berman A, Epstein S. 'Tamoxifen: disease prevention
or disease substitution?' *Lancet* 1992; 340:1143–45.

65 Powles T. 'The case for clinical trials of tamoxifen for the
prevention of breast cancer.' *Lancet* 1992; 340:1145–47.

66 Katzenellenbogen B S. 'Antiestrogen resistance:
mechanisms by which breast cancer cells undermine the
effectiveness of endocrine therapy.' *J Natl Cancer Inst*
1991; 83.

Chapter Eight

1 Catterall R D. 'Biological effects of sexual freedom.' *Lancet* 1981; 1:315–19.
2 Grant E C G. Nutritional deficiencies and hidden infections in preconception couples. Paper presented at Buxton Clinical Ecology Conference 1990.
3 Adler M W. 'Complications of common genital infections and infections in other sites, ABC of Sexually Transmitted Diseases.' *BMJ* 1983; 287:1709.
4 Conway D, Glazener C M A, Caul E O et al. 'Chlamydial serology in fertile and infertile women.' *Lancet* 1984; i:191–93.
5 Cassel G (ed). 'Ureaplasmas of humans: with emphasis on maternal and neonatal infections.' *Ped Inf Dis* 1986; 5:6, Suppl.
6 Waites K B, et al. 'Chronic ureaplasma urealyticum and mycoplasma hominis infections of central nervous system in preterm infants.' *Lancet* 1988; 2:17–19.
7 RCGP *Oral Contraceptives and Health*. Pitman Medical 1974.
8 Vessey M P, Meisler L, Flavel R, Yeates D. 'Outcome of pregnancy in women using different methods of contraception.' *Br J Obstet Gynae* 1979; 86:548–56.
9 Buchan H, Villard-Mackintosh L, Vessey M, Yeates D, MacPherson K. 'Epidemiology of pelvic inflammatory disease in parous women with special reference to intrauterine device use.' *Br J Obstet Gynae* 1990; 97:780–88.
10 Singer A, et al. 'Genital wart virus infections: nuisance or potentially lethal?' *BMJ* 1984; 288:735.
11 Ho-Yen Do, Chatterton J M W, Joss A W L. 'Screening for infections in pregnancy.' *Lancet* 1988; 2:1031.
12 Hardy P H, et al. 'Prevalence of six sexually transmitted disease agents among pregnant inner-city adolescents and pregnancy outcome.' *Lancet* 1984; 2:333.
13 Fromell G T, et al. 'Chlamydial infections of mothers and their infants.' *J Ped* 1979; 95:28–32.

14 Schoental R, Bensted J P M. 'Immunotoxicity of N-nitrosamides: acute lesions and neoplasias of the lungs, the lymphoid system and the gastro-intestinal tract.' *Int J Envir Studies* 1989; 33:213–19.

15 Banatvala, et al. 'HIV screening in pregnancy.' *Lancet* 1991; 337:1218–19.

16 'Anonymised screening for HIV: first results.' *BMJ* 1991; 302:1229.

17 Maiman F, Fruchter R G, Serur E, Boyce J G. 'Prevalence of human immunodeficiency virus in a colposcopy clinic.' *JAMA* 1988; 15:2214–15.

18 Biggar R J. 'Preventing AIDS now. Treating other sexually transmitted diseases could help.' *BMJ* 1991; 303:1150–51.

19 Gardner G T. 'Promoting sexual health.' *BMJ* 1992; 305:586.

20 Aldous J, Hickman M, et al. 'Impact of HIV infection on mortality in young men in a London health authority.' *BMJ* 1992; 305:219–21.

21 Beral V, Bull D, et al. 'Risk of Kaposi's sarcoma and sexual practices associated with faecal contact in homosexual or bisexual men with AIDS.' *Lancet* 1992; 339:632–35.

22 Sherr L, Strong C. 'Safe sex and women.' *Genitourin Med* 1992; 68:32–35.

23 Renton A, Whitaker L. 'Preventing the spread of HIV infection.' *BMJ* 1991; 302:1207–08.

24 Editorial. 'Oral contraceptives and immune responses.' *JAMA* 1969; 209:3, 410.

25 Joshi U M et al. 'Effect of steroidal contraceptives on antibody formation in the human female.' *Contraception* 1971; 3:327.

26 Hagen C, Froland A. 'Depressed lymphocyte response to PHA in women taking contraceptives.' *Lancet* 1972; 1:1185.

27 Beaumont J L, et al. 'Anti-ethinyloestradiol antibody activity in oral contraceptive users.' *Clinical and Experimental Immunology* 1979; 38:445.

28 Casare H, Doull. 'Toxic responses of the immune system.' *Toxicology* 3rd ed 1986 p279.

29 Schoental R. 'Trichotheenes, zearalenone and other carcinogenic metabolites of Fusarium and related microfungi.' *Adv Cancer Res* 1985; 45:218–90.

30 Poel W E. 'Progesterone and mammary carcinogenisis.' *Potential Carcinogenic Hazards from Drugs* 1967; 7:162–71. Springer Verlag, Berlin NY.

31 Dawson J. 'Brainstorming the postviral fatigue syndrome.' *BMJ* 1988; 297:1151–52.

32 Chandra R K. 'Effect of vitamin and trace-element supplementation on immune responses and infection in elderly subjects.' *Lancet* 1992; 340:1124–27.

33 Grant E C G. 'The contraceptive pill: its relation to allergies and illness.' *Nutrition and Health* 1983; 2:33–40.

34 Goode H F, Kellcher J, Walker B E. 'Zinc concentrations in pure populations of peripheral blood neutrophils, lymphocytes and monocytes.' *Ann Clin Biochem* 1989; 26:89–95.

Chapter Nine

1 Barnes B, Bradley G. *Planning for a Healthy Baby*. Ebury Press, London 1990.

2 Barnes B, Grant E C G et al. 'Nutrition and pre-conception care.' *Lancet* 1985; ii:1297.

3 Rowland R. *Living Laboratories*. Lime Tree, London 1992.

4 Barber R J, Abdulla H I. 'Ovum donation.' *Brit J Hosp Med* 1989; 42:442–50.

5 Adams J, et al. 'Multifollicular ovaries: Clinical and endocrine features and response to pulsatile gonadotrophin releasing hormone.' *Lancet* 1985; 2:1404.

6 Homburg R, Armar N A, Eshel A, Adams J, Jacobs H S. 'Influence of serum luteinising hormone concentrations on ovulation, conception, and early pregnancy loss in polycystic ovary syndrome.' *BMJ* 1988; 297:1024–26.

7 Barnes A B, Colton T, et al. 'Fertility and outcome of pregnancy in women exposed in utero to diethylstilboestrol.' *New Eng J Med* 1980; 302:609–13.

8 Stillman R J. 'In utero exposure to diethylstilboestrol:

adverse effect on the reproductive tract and reproductive performance in male and female offspring.' *Am J Obstet Gynecol* 1982; 142:905–21.

9 Newlands E S, Fisher R A, Searle F. 'Gestational trophoblastic tumours.' In *Immune System in Disease, Clin Obstet Gynae.* Eds Stirrat & Scott, Baillière Tindall, London 1992 p519–39.

10 Barnes B. *Foresight Newsletter.* October 1991 Godalming, Surrey.

11 Foresight. *Recommendations for Preconception Counselling on a Shoe-string.* 1989 Foresight Godalming, Surrey.

12 Salversen K A, Vatten L J, Eik-Nes S H, Hugdahl K, Bakketeig L S. 'Routine ultrasound in utero and subsequent handedness and neurological development.' *BMJ* 1993; 307:159–64.

13 OPCS Monitor *Congenital Abnormalities.* 1991 HMSO London.

14 Gal I. 'Variations in the incidence of congenital malformations in spontaneous abortions, stillbirths and artificially interrupted pregnancies.' *Human Genetics* 1973; 20:367.

15 Gal I, et al. 'Hormonal pregnancy tests and congenital malformations.' *Nature* 1973; 216:83.

16 Gal I, Parkinson C E. 'Changes in serum vitamin A levels during and after oral contraceptive therapy.' *Contraception* 1973; 8, 1:13–23.

17 Ward N I, Durrant S, Sankey R J, Bound J P, Bryce-Smith D. 'Elemental factors in human fetal development.' *J Nutr Med* 1990; 1, 1:19–26.

18 'The MRC Vitamin Study Group. Prevention of neural tube defects: Results of the Medical Research Council Vitamin Study.' *Lancet* 1991; 238:131–37.

19 McPartlin J, Halligan A, Scott J M, Darling D G. 'Accelerated folate breakdown in pregnancy.' *Lancet* 1993; 431:148–49.

20 Vines G. 'Unmanned by a "sea of oestrogen".' *New Scientist* 1993; 138:5.

21 Goh K G. Chromosomal breakages in women taking birth control pills. *SSAFC* (Report) 1967 Oak Ridge Ass. Universities, 106, 97.

22 Bala Krishna Murthy P, Prema K. 'Sister-chromatid exchanges in oral contraceptive users.' *Mutation Research* 1979; 68:149.

23 Lejeune J, Prieur M. 'Oral Contraceptives and Trisomy 21. A retrospective study of 730 cases.' *Annals of Genetics* 1979; 22:2, 61.

24 Vessey M P, et al. 'A long-term follow-up study of women using different methods of contraception: an interim report.' *J Biosocial Science* 1976; 8:373–424.

25 Vessey M P, et al. 'Outcome of pregnancy in women using different methods of contraception.' *Br J Obst Gynae* 1979; 86:548-.

26 Harlap S, Davies M. *The Pill and Births: The Jerusalem Study.* National Institute of Child Health and Development, Bethesda USA 1978.

27 Grant E C G. 'The harmful effects of common social habits, especially smoking and using oral contraceptive steroids on pregnancy.' *International Journal of Environmental Studies* 1981; 17:57–66.

28 Grant E C G. 'Environmental and pollutional effects upon the learning skills of young children.' *Dyslexia Review* 1982; 5:1, 29–32.

29 Grant E C G. 'Recent advances in understanding toxic and teratogenic effects of hormones.' In *The Next Generation: Avoiding damage before birth in the 1980s.* Foresight 1983.

30 McCredie J, et al. 'Congenital limb defects and the pill.' *Lancet* 1983; 2:623.

31 Nora J J, et al. 'Exogenous progestogen and estrogen implicated in birth defects.' *JAMA* 1978; 240: 9, 837.

32 OPCS Monitor. *Sudden Infant Death Syndrome.* HMSO, London 1992.

33 Rimland B, Larsen G E. 'Hair mineral analysis and behaviour: an analysis of 51 studies.' *J Learning Disabilities* 1983; 16, 5:1–7.

34 Capel I D, Grant E C G, et al. 'Comparison of

concentrations of some trace, bulk and toxic metals in the hair of normal and dyslexic children.' *Clinical Chemistry* 1981; 27:879–81.

35 Oberleas D, et al. 'Trace elements and behaviour.' *International Review of Neurobiology* 1972 Suppl. 1, 83.

36 Grant E C G, Howard J M H, et al. 'Zinc deficiency in children with dyslexia: concentrations of zinc and other minerals in sweat and hair.' *BMJ* 1988; 296:607–09.

37 Goode H F, Kelleher J, Walker B E. 'Zinc concentrations in pure populations of peripheral blood neutrophils, lymphocytes and monocytes.' *Ann Clin Biochem* 1989; 26:89–95.

38 Ward N I, Soulsbury K A, Zettel V H, Colquhoun I D, Bundy S, Barnes B. 'The influence of the chemical additive tartrazine on the zinc status of hyperactive children – a double-blind placebo-controlled study.' *J Nutr Med* 1990; 1, 1:51–58.

39 Bray G W. 'The hypochlorhydria of asthma in children.' *Quarterly J of Med* 1931; xxiv:181–197.

40 (i) Crawford M A, Hassan A G, Stevens P A. 'Essential fatty acid requirements in pregnancy and lactation with special reference to brain development.' *Prog Lipid Res* 1981, 20:31–40.

40 (ii) Farquharson J, Cockburn F, et al. 'Infant cerebral cortex phospholipid fatty-acid composition and diet.' *Lancet* 1992; 430:810–13.

41 Lucas A, Morley R, Cole T J, Lister G, Leeson-Payne C. 'Breast milk and subsequent intelligence quotient in children born preterm.' *Lancet* 1992; 339:261–264.

42 Benton D. 'Vitamin-mineral supplements and intelligence. Nutrition and cognitive efficiency.' *Proc Nutr Soc* 1992; 52:295–302.

43 Lou H C, Henriksen L, Bruhn P. 'Focal cerebral dysfunction in developmental learning disabilities.' *Lancet* 1990; i:8–11.

44 Schoenthaler S S, Eysenick H J, et al. 'Controlled trials of vitamin-mineral supplementation on intelligence and brain function. In-Improvement of IQ and Behavior as a

Function of dietary Supplementation – a Symposium.'
Person individ Diff 1991; 12, 4:329–365.

45 Slauss A. Diet, *Crime and Delinquency* Parker House;
Berkley California 1981.

46 Miller J B. 'A double-blind study of food extract injection
therapy: a preliminary report.' *Ann Allergy* 1977;
38:185-.

47 Egger J, Stolla A, McEwan L M. 'Controlled trial of
hyposensitisation in children with food-induced
hyperkinetic syndrome.' *Lancet* 1992; 339:1150–53.

48 Arshad S H, Mathews S, Gant C, Hide D W. 'Effect or
allergen avoidance on development of allergic disorders
in infancy.' *Lancet* 1992; 339:1493–97.

49 Truss C O. 'Tissue injury induced by candida albicans:
mental and neurological manifestations.' *J Orthomol
Psychiat* 1978; 7:1, 17–37.

50 Truss C O. 'Restoration of immunologic competence to
candida albicans.' *J Orthomol Psychiat* 1980; 9:4,
287–301.

51 Korkia P, Stimson G V. 'Anabolic steroid use in Great
Britain.' *Lancet* 1993; 431:1407.

Chapter Ten

1 Adami H-O, Bergstrom R, Sparen P, Baron J. 'Increasing
cancer risk in younger birth cohorts in Sweden.' *Lancet*
1993; 341:773–77.

2 Griffen G C. 'Condoms and contraceptives in Junior High
and High School Clinics.' *Postgraduate Medicine* 1993;
93:5, 21–38.

3 Evans B, et al. 'Sexually transmitted diseases and HIV
infection among homosexual men.' *BMJ* 1993; 306:792.

4 Platt S. 'Fewer women in death attempts.' *Doctor* 1993; 4,
8:12.

5 Flynn A M. 'Natural family planning in developing
countries.' *Lancet* 1992; 340:309.

Glossary

Acid and alkaline phosphatases	Zinc-containing enzymes which break phosphate bonds and are concerned with secretory processes and cell division. Found in the womb and elsewhere. Their widespread actions are altered by the pill hormones.
ACTH	Adreno cortico trophic hormone secreted by the pituitary which regulates adrenal steroids.
Adenomyosis	Disease condition when the womb's glandular living tissues spread into the muscles of the womb wall.
Adrenal glands	Two small glands lying above each kidney which secrete body-regulating hormones, e.g. adrenaline and cortico steroids.
Adrenaline	A hormone controlling 'fight and flight' reactions.
AIDS	Acquired immune deficiency syndrome.
Aldosterone	Adrenal cortex hormone controlling salt and water metabolism.
Allergy	Exaggerated response.
Amenorrhoea	The absence of monthly bleeding.
Amine	Organic compounds derived from

	ammonia and containing a hydrocarbon radical.
Amino acids	Essential components of proteins which contain both an amino group and a carboxyl group. They are used as the body's building blocks.
Amnesia	Loss of memory.
Anabolic	Hormones which build up protein and muscle.
Androgen	Masculinising hormone, also found in small amounts in females.
Aneurysm	Distended sac at a weak point in an artery.
Anti-thrombin III	Blood factor which prevents clotting.
Arachidonic acid	N–3 series essential fatty acid.
Arterioles	Very small arteries.
Atheroma	Fatty deposit in artery walls.
Ascorbic acid	Vitamin C.
Benign	Simple, not malignant.
Benign intracranial hypertension	Raised fluid pressure in the spaces in the brain.
Biochemistry	The chemistry of living organisms.
Cancer	Malignant growth of gland cells which may spread to other parts of the body.
Candida	Fungus causing thrush.
Carbohydrates	Substances made from carbon, hydrogen and oxygen such as starches, sugars and cereals.
Carcinogens	Substances which can cause cancer.
Catabolic	Stress hormones which temporarily stop cell metabolism.
Cerebral	Belonging to the brain.
Cerebro vascular	The brain's blood vessels.
Ceruloplasmin	Copper-carrying blood protein, raised by the pill hormones.
Cervix	Neck of the womb.

Cholesterol	Fatty substance made in the liver, adrenals, ovaries and testes from which steroid hormones are produced.
Choriocarcinoma	Highly invasive malignant change occurring in a hydatidiform mole which can develop if any products of conception remain after a miscarriage or abortion.
Chorioamnionitis	Infection of the foetal membranes.
Chromosomes	Thread-like structures in the cell nucleus that carry genetic information.
CIN–1,2,3	Cervical intra-epithelial neoplasia or cervical carcinoma-in-situ: graded one to three.
Climacteric	Menopause.
Coagulation	Blood clotting.
COC	Combined oral contraceptive.
Co-enzyme	Co-factor for an enzyme.
COMT	Catechol-o-methyl transferase. A copper-containing enzyme which breaks down adrenaline and is altered by the pill hormones.
Congenital	From birth.
Conjugated oestrogens	A mixture of oestrogens chemically altered to be easily excreted in the urine. *See* Premarin.
Corpus luteum	Yellow cyst which produces ovarian hormones at the end of the normal cycle and in early pregnancy.
Cortex	Outer part of the adrenal glands which secretes steroids.
Cortisol	Adrenal steroid hormone which alters cell metabolism.
Cortisone	A steroid medicine with a cortisol-like action.
Cytomegalovirus	A virus which causes illness and foetal abnormalities.
D and C	Dilatation and curettage.

DES	Diethylstilboestrol.
DGLA	D-gamma lenolenic acid – a 6-series essential fatty acid found in evening primrose oil.
Diaphragm	Vaginal cap used to cover the neck of womb for birth control.
DNA	Deoxyribonucleic acid.
Dopamine	Amine derived from protein breakdown.
Dyslexia	Learning difficulties usually involving reading, spelling, writing, arithmetic and short-term memory.
Dysmenorrhoea	Pelvic cramps at period times.
EFA	Essential fatty acid.
Endocrine	The body's hormone secretions.
Endogenous	Belonging to the body of the individual concerned.
Endometriosis	Disease condition when the glandular womb tissue has spread elsewhere in the womb or pelvis.
Endometrium	Inner lining of the womb containing secretion-bearing glands.
Enzyme	A catalyst which speeds up chemical reactions in the body.
EPA	Eicosapentanoic acid – a 3-series EFA found in fish oils.
EPO	Evening primrose oil.
Ergot	Fungus found in mouldy grain.
Ergotamine	Drug used in migraine attacks.
Erosion	Rough, infected area on the neck of the womb.
ET	Embryo transfer.
Exogenous	Not belonging to the body of the individual concerned, e.g. hormones manufactured artificially or 'natural' hormones obtained from animal or human sources.
Fallopian tubes	Two tubes attached at each corner of

	the womb which stretch out towards the ovaries.
Foetus	Baby before birth.
Fibroid	Benign tumour overgrowth in the womb.
Folic acid	A vitamin essential for preventing foetal abnormalities. Reduced by the pill and stress.
FSH	Egg follicle stimulating hormone.
Galactose	A simple sugar.
Gene	Hereditary unit located on a chromosome.
GIFT	Gammete intra fallopian transfer.
GLA	Gamma linolenic acid: an EFA abundant in evening primrose oil.
Glutathione peroxidase	The body's only selenium-containing enzyme, which is an essential part of the body's cleansing antioxidant mechanisms. It is altered by the pill hormones.
Gynaecologist	Doctor specialising in women's illnesses.
Haemorrhage	Bleeding.
hCG	Human chorionic gonadotrophic hormone produced by the developing foetus.
Histology	Study of body tissues using a microscope.
Hormone	Body's chemical messenger.
Hormone receptors	Special proteins to which hormones attach.
HRT	Hormone replacement therapy.
Hypertension	High blood pressure.
Hypospadias	Congenital deformity of the penis which opens on the under side.
Hypothalamus	Part of the base of the brain which controls the endocrine system including reproduction.

Hysterectomy	Surgical removal of the womb.
Immune	Having resistance.
Intromission	Vaginal penetration during sexual intercourse.
IVF	In vitro fertilisation.
Kaposis sarcoma	Rare vascular skin malignancy.
LA	Linoleic acid – essential fatty acid in linseed oil.
Lactation	Breast feeding.
Leucocyte	White blood cell.
LH	Luteinising hormone which stimulates the corpus luteum to produce progesterone after ovulation.
Libido	Interest in having sexual intercourse.
Linoleic acid	Essential fatty acid obtained in diet from vegetable oils.
Magnesium	Element essential co-factor for hundreds of enzymes: commonly deficient impairing nerve and muscle function.
MAO	Monoamine oxidase, copper-containing enzyme which breaks down amines and is altered by the pill.
Megakaryocyte	Large bone marrow cell which makes the blood platelets.
Menarche	Start of menstrual cycles.
Melanoma	Highly invasive black cancer which can develop in a pigmented mole on the skin.
Menopause	Age at which menstrual bleeding stops.
Menstrual	Monthly.
Metabolism	The body's chemical reactions.
Microgram	A millionth part of a gram.
Micturition	Urination.
Migraine	Severe headache usually accompanied by visual disturbances or sickness.
Milligram (mg)	A thousandth part of a gram.

Mycoplasma	Tiny organism which causes a sexually transmitted disease.
Mycotoxin	Toxic mould.
Narcotic	Highly addictive sedating or pain-killing drugs.
Neurotransmitter	A substance released from nerve endings which transmits impulses.
Nitroso compounds	Organic compound that contains NO – nitric oxide.
Nucleic acid	Either DNA or RNA found in all living cells.
Obstetrician	A doctor who specialises in pregnancy and childbirth.
OCS/OCs	Oral contraceptive steroids/oral contraceptives.
Oestradiol	A natural oestrogen.
Oestrogen	Feminising hormone.
Oral contraceptive	Female hormones altered to be effectively absorbed when given as pills.
Osteoporosis	Thinning of bone structure.
Ovaries	Two hormone and egg-producing glands lying in the pelvis.
Ovulation	Release of an egg from an ovary.
Oxytocin	Pituitary hormone which contracts the womb.
Pancreas	Gland lying behind the stomach which makes digestive juices.
Pathogens	Disease-causing organisms.
Pathology	The study of body tissues.
Pharmacology	The study of medicines.
PID	Pelvic inflammatory disease.
The 'pill'	Usually a mixture of a progestogen and an oestrogen.
Pituitary	Endocrine gland attached to the base of the brain.
Platelet	Tiny blood cells involved in clotting.

PMS/PMT	Premenstrual syndrome/premenstrual tension.
POP	Progestogen-only-pill.
Prednisone	A steroid medicine which acts like cortisol.
Premarin	Conjugated oestrogens obtained from the urine of pregnant mares.
Premenstrual	A few days before a period.
Progesterone	Female steroid sex hormone which prepares for pregnancy.
Progestogen	Manufactured hormone which acts like progesterone. Called 'progestin' in America.
Prolactin	Pituitary hormone which stimulates milk secretion.
Prostaglandin	Chemicals which help to control vascular reactions, mood and immunity.
Prostate	Male gland which secretes chemicals into semen.
Psychiatrist	Doctor specialising in mental illness.
Psychosis	Madness, loss of reality.
Pulmonary embolism	Large blood clot which has travelled from the legs or pelvic veins to the lungs.
Pyridoxine	Vitamin B_6.
Renin	Kidney chemical controlling blood pressure.
Riboflavin	Vitamin B_2, part of the body's antioxidant mechanism and altered by pill hormones.
RNA	Ribo nucleic acid.
Sarcoma	Malignant growth of muscle, bone or other non-glandular tissue.
Schizophrenia	Mental illness characterised by 'split personality' with episodes of loss of reality, and often high copper and low zinc levels.

Sequential	Oral contraceptive or hormone combination when different hormones are taken on different days – usually oestrogen is taken for the first part of the month before the combined pill is started.
Serotonin	Amine derived from protein breakdown.
Sinusoid	Small veins.
STD	Sexually transmitted disease.
Steroid	A chemical compound which has its atoms arranged in four rings and includes natural sex hormones and oral contraceptives.
Sterols	Steroids such as cholesterol occurring in the fatty tissues of plants and animals.
Stilboestrol	Synthetic non-steroid oestrogen, known as DES (diethyl stilbestrol) in America.
Stromal condensation	A thickening of womb living tissue round the small veins.
Subarchnoid haemorrhage	Bleeding from an aneurysm in the tissues surrounding the brain.
Superficial phlebitis	Inflammation and clotting in a surface vein.
Teratogenic	Capable of causing congenital abnormalities.
Testes	Two male glands which produce sperm and male hormones.
Testosterone	Main masculinising hormone produced in large amounts in male testes.
Thrombosis	Blood clot.
Toxoplasmosis	An infection which can cause congenital abnormalities.
Triglycerides	Blood fats.
Tryptophan	Essential amino acid.

Uterus	Womb.
Vitamins	Essential co-factors for many enzymes, necessary for health, immune function and normal foetal development.
Vitamin A	Exists in two forms. Vegetable carotene is found in chilli pepper and carrots which, if zinc status is adequate, is converted in the liver into a more active form called retinol. Deficiency during early pregnancy causes brain and eye defects, penile abnormalities like hypospadias or undescended testicles. Retinol is fat-soluble and excess is toxic.
Vitamin B complex	Taking too much of one B vitamin can cause shortages of the others.
Vitamin B_1	Thiamine. Deficiency can cause learning defects.
Vitamin B_2	Riboflavin. Deficiency can cause limb defects.
Vitamin B_3	Nicotinamide or niacin. Deficiency can cause hare-lip or cleft palate.
Vitamin B_6	Pyridoxine – most commonly deficient especially in pill, HRT or other sex hormone takers because of their abnormal amine metabolism. Deficiency can cause depression, urinary tract cancer or dermatitis.
Vitamin B_{12}	Cyanocobalamine. Often deficient in smokers or vegetarians.
Folic acid	Lowered by the pill, HRT and fertility stimulants. Extra required during pregnancy. Deficiency can cause anaemia and spina bifida. Pregnancy supplements from 400 micrograms to 4 grams but too high doses could lower other B vitamins. Blood assay ideal.

Vitamin C	Ascorbic acid high in rose hip powder and chilli peppers. Lowered by pill hormones, smoking and tetracyclines.
Vitamin D	The sunshine vitamin prevents rickets. Found in fish oils. Fat soluble and excess is toxic.
Vitamin E	Important in preventing sticky platelets and blood clots. Also fat-soluble.
Zinc	Metal co-factor necessary for the correct functioning of reproduction and the immune system. Required by ninety enzymes. Lowered by the pill. Available in oysters and red meat.

Index

334

Diaphragm, contraceptive 189
Diet
  antifungal 99
  and fatty acid pathways 286
  low allergy 79–80, 111, 145, 172,
    260
  natural 107
Diethylstilboestrol 38
Dihomogamma-linolenic acid (DGLA)
  139
Dilated veins 64–5
Dilation and curettage (D and C) 51,
  149
Diseases, prevalent 144
Diuretics 171
Divorce 40, 265
Djerassi, Dr Carl 20–1
DNA (Deoxyribonucleic acid) 263
  and chemical damage 16
  effect of hormones 4, 9, 14–15, 251–2
  testing 265
Docosahexaenoic acid (DHA) 133
Doctors' knowledge of hormones 6
Dodds, Sir Charles 38, 41
Doll, Sir Richard 173, 181
Dorner, Dr Gunter 29–30
Down's syndrome 113, 249, 252
Drug companies advertising 266
Drugs, for synchronised cycles 241–2
Drugs, addictive 99, 100
  and AIDS 222, 223
  and essential fatty acids 135
  and hyperactive children 258
  oestrogen 99
Dyslexia 30–3, 109, 158, 255, 256, 257
  case study 31–2
Dysmenorrhoea see Period pains

Eating disorders 115–18
  case study 117–18
Ectopic pregnancies 213, 215
Eczema and steroids 257
Egg, human 15–16, 17
Eggs in diet 146
Eicosapentanoic acid (EPA) 133, 146,
  172
Ellerbroek, J.M. 195
Embolism, and pills 70, 204
Embryo, cell division in 9
Embryo transfer 240
Emotions, and hormones 10
Enavid 21

Endometrial ablation 149
Endometrial hyperplasia 46, 51
Endrometriosis 48–9, 151–2, 170
  case studies 49–51
Endometrium, and the pill 45
Enkephalin 100
Enovid 39
Enzymes 12, 22, 81, 85, 86
  and brain chemicals 91
  copper enzyme 96
  and oestrogen/progestogen 91
  and the pancreas 124
  supplement 165
  treatment 128
Epidemiologists, and pill trials 68
Epilepsy 257
Epstein, Samuel 203–4
Epstein-Barr virus 230
Erasmus, Udo 286
Ergotamine 77, 78–9, 103
Erythromycin 220
Eskimos, and fish oils 133
Essential fatty acids (EFAs) 16, 20, 47,
  63, 85, 103, 126–7, 130–1, 281–3
  blocks 284–6
  and the brain 137
  and cancer 172
  and cell membranes 131
  deficiencies 138–9, 149, 166
  and osteoporosis 166
  Six-Series 132–3, 149, 282
  Three-Series 133–5, 282
Ethinyl oestradiol 21, 23, 120, 121, 251
  and immune systems 227
  see also Oestrogen, synthetic
Ethynodiol diacetate 121, 123
Evening primrose oil (EPO) 47, 85, 103,
  104, 132–3, 138, 149, 172
  and alcohol reduction 137
  and cancer 172
Eye problems 61, 204

Falliers Dr 227
Fallopian tubes 213, 215
Family planning methods, pre-pill 40
Family Planning Association 40, 41, 42
  see also Oxford/FPA trials
Famine, effect on pregnancy 15–16
Fat
  avoidance in diet 111, 286
  and cholesterol level 20
  and heart disease 126

336

Minerals, trace 12
deficiencies 88, 89, 128, 255, 285
case studies 76, 151, 165, 239
and central nervous system
abnormalities 250
and cervical cnacer 191
excesses 285
and old age 128
supplements 103
Miscarriages 243–4
avoidance 19
case study 246
and diet 110
moles and choriocarcinomas 244–5
post-scan 248
recurrent 245
Mitogens 225, 226
Moir, Anne, and David Jessel, *Brain
Sex* 29
Moles and miscarriage 244–5
Monoamine oxidase (MAO) enzymes
85–6, 90–1, 92
Monoamine oxidase inhibitors (MAOI)
86, 99
Mood changes
and menstruation 84–5
and the pill 64, 90–3, 95–6
Moulds and disease 108, 170, 267
Multiple births 242–3
Multiple infections 220–1
Multiple partners *see* Sexual
promiscuity
Multiple sclerosis (MS) 61–2, 226
Muscle contraction test 13
Myalgic encephalomyelitis (ME) 230–2
case study 230–2
and fluoride 166
Mycoplasmas 210, 212, 215–16, 220,
254
Mycotoxins 22, 108

Nafarelin 242
Neonatal deaths 253
Nerve cell metabolism 114
Neurasthenia 115
Neurotransmitters and migraine 80, 86
see also Brain hormones
Newfoundland study on nutrition 232
Newlands, Prof. E.S. 244
Next generation 235–62
Nipples, changing 194
Nitrates 16

Nitric oxide (NO) 10, 16, 222
Nitrites 16
Nitrosamines 190, 222
Nitroso compounds 16
Nitrous acid 16
Nolvadex 241
Nora, J.J. 253
Norethindrone 21
Norethisterone 45, 121, 123
doses 275
Norethynodrel 21, 62
Norgestrel 45, 121, 122, 123, 150
doses 275
Nortestosterones and blood vessels 63
Nutrients 232–3
deficiencies 79, 245
case study 228–9
and embryo 9
and pregnancy 9, 20
supplements 76
Nutrition 210
and behavioural change 259–60
and osteoporosis 154–68
see also Diet
Nystatin 51

Oberleas, D. 255
Oestradiol implants 100, 240, 275
Oestrogen 3, 18
addictiveness 99–100, 101
amine breakdown 98
and antibodies 225–6
and cancer 24, 38, 54, 178, 229, 264
catechol 93
and cholesterol 71, 127
and depression 87, 96, 98
effect on enzymes 91
effects of 9, 97
in food 36, 267
gall bladder disease 129–30
and genital disorders 151
glucose tolerance 121
and heart disease 67, 71, 140
and hepatitis 200
homosexual use 222
and menopause 144, 146
and mental illness 99
and migraine 170
and monoamine oxidase 86
post-menopausal use 72–3
production 11, 17
and prostatic cancer 198

341